Dear Reader:

The book you are ab the St. Martin's True Crime calls "the leader in true cri nating account of the latest, d the national attention. St. true crime author and crim explores the dark, deadly links between a prominent Manhattan surgeon and the disappearance of his wife fifteen years earlier in THE SURGEON'S WIFE. Suzy Spencer's BREAKING POINT guides readers through the tortuous twists and turns in the case of Andrea Yates, the Houston mother who drowned her five young children in the family's bathtub. In Edgar Award-nominated DARK DREAMS, legendary FBI profiler Roy Hazelwood and bestselling crime author Stephen G. Michaud shine light on the inner workings of America's most violent and depraved murderers. In the book you now hold, THE BTK MURDERS, acclaimed author Carlton Smith tells the shocking truth behind the notorious BTK murders in Wichita, and the remarkable sequence of events that led to the killer's capture.

St. Martin's True Crime Library gives you the stories behind the headlines. Our authors take you right to the scene of the crime and into the minds of the most notorious murderers to show you what really makes them tick. St. Martin's True Crime Library paperbacks are better than the most terrifying thriller, because it's all true! The next time you want a crackling good read, make sure it's got the St. Martin's True Crime Library logo on the spine—you'll be up all night!

Charles E. Spicer, Jr.
Executive Editor, St. Martin's True Crime Library

For more than thirty years, the city of Wichita, Kansas, lived in the shadow of a nightmare. An unknown serial killer stalked the entire community, periodically surfacing to terrify—"BTK," he called himself, for "Bind, Torture, Kill." Then came the arrest and guilty plea of 59-year-old Dennis Rader—church and Cub Scout leader, local civil servant, father of two. "I am BTK," Rader told police.

Now, veteran journalist and serial murder expert Carlton Smith, author of *The Search for the Green River Killer,* takes a look at the horrific BTK case, and provides answers to five critical questions:

- Who was the real Dennis Rader, and why did he do it?
- How was he able to get away with it for so long?
- What kept the police from solving the case far sooner?
- Why didn't Rader's family and friends realize something was wrong?
- What role did the news media play in the crimes, and in their solution?

From the tricks he used to enter his victims' homes to the puzzles he sent to the newspaper, and the many chances missed to catch him, this is the story of a man one victim's family member called "a black hole inside the shell of a human being"—and the worst American monster since Ted Bundy.

St. Martin's True Crime Library Titles by Carlton Smith

Reckless

Death of a Doctor

Shadows of Evil

Hunting Evil

Bitter Medicine

Murder at Yosemite

Death in Texas

Dying for Daddy

Death of a Little Princess

Seeds of Evil

Vanished

THE BTK MURDERS

Inside the "Bind, Torture, Kill" Case That Terrified America's Heartland

CARLTON SMITH

St. Martin's Paperbacks

THE BTK MURDERS

Cover photo courtesy AP/Wide World Photos.

ISBN: 0-312-93905-1
EAN: 9780312-93905-2

Printed in the United States of America

St. Martin's Paperbacks edition / March 2006

St. Martin's Paperbacks are published by St. Martin's Press, 175 Fifth Avenue, New York, NY 10010.

10 9 8 7 6 5 4 3 2 1

BEATTIE AND THE BEAST

1:

BTK and Beattie

It was on one of those days that unfolds in every newsroom all across the country. Hurst Laviana, a long-time, experienced police reporter for *The Wichita Eagle*, was trying to think of a story, something that would engage his editors' attention, and hopefully, the newspaper's readers'.

It wasn't that Wichita, Kansas, didn't have news. A city of 350,000 always had something to write about, and Wichita, once a giant of the plains, then shrunken, now revitalizing around its edges, was certainly no exception. With that many people, and another 150,000 or so in its metropolitan area, somebody was bound to be doing something bad to somebody, somewhere, and that was the nature of Laviana's beast: to tell the good, the bad, and the ugly—but usually just the last two.

On this day in the second week of January 2004, Laviana opened his email, and noticed a query from his one-time reporting partner, Bill Hirschman, who had previously moved on to another newsroom in Florida. Laviana had spent some intense times with Hirschman, and now Hirschman wanted to know: was the *Eagle* going to write and publish a thirtieth anniversary story on the horrible murder case that he and Laviana had worked so hard on, for so long?

There's nothing so hoary and so detested by newspaper reporters as the "anniversary story," usually a grab-bag of factoids left over from something that was never really resolved, almost always couched in terms of jogging the readers' memory: "Mr. So-and-so still remembers the day, twenty years ago, when . . ." In the absence of anything harder in the way of news, the "anniversary story" was nothing more than a space filler—handled right, it could be a nice reader, but the chances were, before four or five paragraphs had elapsed, the reader's eyes had flipped on to some other subject, or worse, he'd have put down the newspaper altogether.

Laviana had no trouble knowing exactly which murder case Hirschman was referring to. For any newspaper reporter, murder cases come and go, a regular staple; and in a place like Wichita, there were probably twenty or thirty a year to choose from. But Laviana knew there were none like the one Hirschman meant: the so-called "BTK" murder case.

Which, in early 2004, in Wichita, Kansas, was really ancient history.

Somehow, over the last two decades, people had forgotten about "BTK"—the horrific initials claimed as a signature by an unknown killer who had once bound, tortured and killed his victims: "B" for the binding, "T" for the torture, "K" for the killing.

The murders had first come to light in early 1974, when four family members were found strangled in their house in a lower-middle-class section of east Wichita. The dead included Joseph Otero, his wife, Julie, and their children, Joey and Josie. For some reason, all had been tied up and strangled or suffocated. The children's deaths were especially shocking, and Josie Otero's death was particularly gruesome. Over the next three years, there had been—at least according to police officials—three other possible victims: Shirley Vian, a mother of three small children; a popular single woman, 25-year-old Nancy Fox; and one other victim whom the killer had anonymously boasted of but refused to reveal. Altogether there were seven dead. Maybe. That was part of the problem: no one except the killer, whoever he was, knew the precise number of victims, or how many times he'd broken into someone's house to kill, so many years before.

But the most bizarre aspect of the case was that the killer—or at least someone who *claimed* to be the killer—had had a penchant for writing letters to the public asserting responsibility for the crimes, almost as if he was taunting Wichita for the city's failure to identify him, signing them "BTK." And then, for some reason, in the late 1970s the letters stopped coming. Some police remained convinced that all of the letters were a hoax, someone's idea of a very sick joke, and that there was in fact no such person as "BTK." Still others were convinced that the killer was all too real, that he knew too much about the crimes to be some sort of diseased prankster. And when the communications stopped abruptly, the debate could not be resolved.

The silence had persisted for more than twenty years. And bit by bit, people put the murderer out of their minds and resumed their normal lives. By 2004, a good portion of the city's population had never heard of BTK or his supposed letters—they were simply too young to remember.

Which made the case ideal for one of those "anniversary" stories.

Well, why not? Laviana thought. He approached Tim Rogers, the *Eagle*'s assistant managing editor. What did Rogers think of a story reprising the old murder case?

Not much, Rogers told Laviana. Was there anything new to report? At just about that moment, *Eagle* reporter Roy Wenzl happened to walk by. Overhearing the discussion, he reminded Laviana of the Wichita law professor who claimed to be writing a book about the BTK case. Oh yeah, Laviana recalled: Bob Beattie, the former telephone pal of Charlie Manson.

In early 2004, Bob Beattie was 47 years old, and only occasionally practicing law. In fact, at least in an occupational sense, it would be fair to say that Beattie was semi-retired. Over the years, his interests had widened almost as much as his girth. The one-time fireman's hard body had spread into a Humpty-Dumptyesque arrangement, even as his intellect had sharpened.

In addition to taking on an occasional legal matter, Beattie taught two law courses at two different Wichita universities as an adjunct professor. One was "Psychology and the Law," and the other was on the American jury system.

Beattie had grown up in Wichita. He was, by almost anyone's account, an extremely bright person with many talents. After testing out at the top end of the intelligence scale as a child, Beattie had been encouraged to join Mensa, the society of people who have high IQ scores. At 17, he wrote a novel, and thought he'd become a writer. But after high school, Beattie enrolled in college, majoring in physics. When he realized that physics bored him, Beattie decided to become a doctor instead. An advisor suggested that before he embarked on a lifetime in medicine, he might want to see what it was all about—why didn't he take a summer job as a hospital orderly?

"I loved it," Beattie recalled later. He especially liked the ambulance. He remembered that some famous writers had worked with ambulances—Walt Whitman, John Dos Passos, Ernest Hemingway. So Beattie got a job driving the ambulance. Next he joined the Sedgwick County Fire Department, and after that became a paramedic. He married and then divorced. He later worked for Boeing as a fireman, on the flightline emergency team at McConnell Air Force Base, was trained in nuclear weapon safety procedures for B-1 bombers, and held a security clearance. He also consulted with NASA on emergency resuscitation procedures for shuttle astronauts.

He returned to college at night and obtained degrees in natural science and mathematics. He worked for a year on two Wichita in-patient psychology wards, where the violently disturbed people were kept under lock and key. He married a pediatrician he'd met while taking his training as a paramedic. He took a degree in human resource management. He decided to go to medical school after all, but his wife, the doctor, talked him out of it, suggesting he try law school instead.

After getting his law degree, Beattie worked as an associate at a Wichita law firm, but lasted for less than a year as an employee before opening his own law office. Within a few months of that he was arguing a major antitrust case before the U.S. Court of Appeals for the 10th Circuit. He won.

Later, Beattie ran for the state legislature as a Democrat, sharing a campaign manager with Nola Foulston, who would later become Wichita's district attorney after changing her party affiliation. He lost. He tended to be slightly left of center as a political candidate, which was probably to be expected from someone who had a legal caseload consisting primarily of people's immigration problems, employment discrimination, or fair housing cases. "At one point," he recalled, "all of my clients were black women."

But as the years went by, Beattie, the peripatetic paramedic/fireman/lawyer, found himself increasingly drawn back to academia, the place where his wide-ranging intelligence and curiosity found its most natural expression.

He most enjoyed teaching his two classes at the two Wichita universities, Friends and Newman. It helped that the two schools happened to be almost across the street from one another.

In late 1998, Beattie had decided to use the 1969 Sharon Tate murders in Los Angeles—attributed to the Charlie Manson gang—as the basis for his forthcoming fall 1999 class on the American jury system at Newman University. He wrote to Manson, the convicted Svengali who'd led the gang, and asked if the cult leader was willing to give a statement in his own defense for the jury class. The idea was to stage a mock trial for the famous criminal as a class exercise. The next thing Beattie knew, Manson was calling him—collect, of course. California prisons don't issue telephone credit cards.

Between late January of 1999 and early March, Beattie conducted three telephone conversations with the imprisoned Manson, and received several letters from him. The word soon leaked out that Beattie was talking to Manson, and almost before he understood what was happening, he was deluged with requests for interviews from the national news media, including a number of tabloid television shows, who played up the "new trial" angle for all it was worth, even though it was just an exercise to demonstrate how the jury system worked. Soon Beattie was getting hate mail from crackpots, some of whom seemed to think that Beattie was in fact defending Manson.

In the wake of all this notoriety, Beattie gave a guest lecture that touched in part on the Manson murders to a social psychology class at Friends University. He began with an opener he thought everyone in the class would immediately pick up on.

"The murder of Sharon Tate and the others by the Manson family panicked Los Angeles in the same way the murder of the Otero family by BTK panicked Wichita," Beattie told his class. He knew at once that his analogy had utterly flopped. The students all had blank expressions on their faces.

"You guys know what I'm talking about, don't you?" Beattie persisted. "Otero, BTK, serial killer here in Wichita?"

Beattie realized that the students didn't have the foggiest idea of what he was referring to. They were just too young.

"So I tell them the story," Beattie recalled, "and one student later told me, 'I thought you made up that story as some kind of test for us. Because it was too unbelievable. Then I went home and talked to my parents. And they said, "We didn't realize that you didn't know about this."' "

So that was when Beattie first made up his mind—someone had to get the BTK story down on paper before it was lost to history forever.

And also because Beattie knew that his student had been right about one thing—it *was* too unbelievable. Even if it was all true.

2:

A "Grand Jury"

Rising abruptly from the flat plains of the mid-southern portion of the state, Wichita was probably the model for Frank Baum's Emerald City, the one reached by Dorothy and Toto when they followed the Yellow Brick Road. A 19th Century rail center, a crossroads of wheat and cattle and oil, the city grew so fast in the early 20th Century as to take on some of the echoes of Chicago or even New York, and seemed to the rustic residents a nearly magical place.

Calling itself "the Peerless Princess of the Plains"—alliteration was very big back at the turn of the last century—skyscrapers soon sprang up, some of them elegant buildings of taste and distinction, the more notable for the fact that the surrounding countryside of Sedgwick County is so . . . well, flat.

Today, however, its downtown core is dwindling, sort of like an old man in a suit that now seems slightly too large for his frame, and a bit threadbare. Old commercial blocks downtown have the vacant look, like gaps in the teeth of the old man, while all around the area, dwellings cast up by the heyday of the early years of the last century have begun to sag and peel. Yet on the pastures of the outskirts of town, new shopping centers have been springing up, green shoots off the old core.

Partly because its relative isolation as a large city surrounded by a vast sea of agricultural endeavors, Wichitans tend to see themselves as a bit different from the rest of the country. As a metropolis athwart the national midsection, the city has a look that seems at first glance to be some sort of amalgam of the North and the South—part Chicago, part Dallas, half bricks, half clapboards. In the winter the cold wind roars down across the plains from the arctic, freezing bones to their marrow; in the summer the heat rises from the Gulf of Mexico and suffuses the city with the steam of the tropics. Every house in Wichita comes with a basement—protection from tornados, Toto. A river, the Arkansas—"Ar-KAN-sas," as the Wichitans pronounce it, not to be confused with the state of the same spelling farther downstream—serpentines through the middle of town, bound for the far-off Mississippi.

But what really sets Wichita apart from other places is the sense that many residents have—or at least had, until BTK—that the sort of unpleasant problems afflicting other parts of the country simply didn't happen there. The people who ran Wichita—sons and daughters of pioneers who'd built the place up from the days when it had just been a muddy buffalo wallow—liked it the way it was: a nice, quiet, decorous middle-American city, where extremes were frowned upon, and the cops kept everyone and everything in line, and did it quietly, too. And to Wichitans, it was the last place in the country where one might expect to find a serial murderer.

Following the experience with his students—and realizing that some would prefer to simply forget the past—Beattie began accumulating bits and pieces about the old BTK mystery. At first, this was a bit desultory on Beattie's part. As a native Wichitan, and one who had worked as a fireman, paramedic and ambulance driver before becoming a lawyer, he had come to know many Wichita police officers, a number of them now retired. Like everyone else, police officers, retired and otherwise, come in all types. Some were garrulous in talking about the old unsolved case with Beattie, while others were tight-lipped. Beattie found a number of references to the BTK case in various journals and other publications, but it was a bit like trying to piece together where the old Spanish galleon had sunk four hundred years earlier—finding documents was difficult, and even then they had to be translated from copspeak to plain English, which often meant reading between the lines. Much of the information was simply anecdotal—interesting, but not necessarily true.

Along the way, Beattie learned that in the late 1970s, the Federal Bureau of Investigation had come to Wichita to consult with the Wichita Police Department about the murders, and that when the killer stopped communicating shortly after that, the FBI's John Douglas, then in the early stages of his career as a profiler, had concluded that the police must have scared the killer away by having interviewed him without realizing he was the killer. This, of course, reinforced the Wichita Police Department's belief that they had the name of the killer somewhere in their records, it was just that they hadn't been able to figure out who he was.

Then, in 2002, Beattie learned that a local television station planned to broadcast an "investigative series" on the mysterious murders in February—just in time for the ratings sweeps period. Beattie bunkered himself in at home and switched on his VCR, thinking this might be a good way to accumulate some worthwhile background information on the old murder case. By now he had pretty much decided to devote a good chunk of his next "Psychology and the Law" class to the BTK case.

Watching the broadcast, Beattie was flabbergasted to learn that the television station had been in contact with a man in California who claimed to have proof that the BTK murders were connected to the notorious "Son of Sam" murders in New York City and—wait for it—the Zodiac murders of the late sixties in San Francisco.

What? What?! Beattie sat up in rapt attention. And the next factoid to emerge was—all of these murders had been organized by . . . Ted Kaczynski, the convicted Unabomber, as part of a Satanic cult calling itself, of all things, "4 Pi," meaning four times the Greek letter and mathematical symbol. *Are they kidding?* Beattie thought. No, it soon became apparent—they weren't.

Beattie called the television reporter who'd presented the first installment of the story. "Have you talked to any cops or anybody who actually *worked* on this?" he asked the reporter.

"Yeah, they said the BTK murders were committed by one man, and they don't think this is what happened," the reporter told Beattie, who already knew that. It turned out that the California man's "proof" was a thick stack of papers, replete with arcane symbols and algebraic formulas, that he claimed demonstrated "with mathematical precision" the existence of the Satanic cult behind the murders.

"And they took it to a math professor at Wichita State. And he looked it over and said, 'Hmm, I don't see anything in here . . .' " Beattie laughed, remembering. "The cops would not go on camera." Beattie couldn't blame them—no official with any sense of respectability wanted anything to do with this.

So Beattie volunteered to refute the wild if mathematically precise theory by going on camera himself. He told the television reporter that the killer was surely only one man acting alone, someone not connected to any Satanic cult, let alone Son of Sam or the Zodiac, and certainly not to Ted Kaczynski. In fact, Beattie said, no less than the eminent John Douglas of the FBI had told the Wichita police more than twenty years earlier that they had probably actually interviewed the unknown killer, who had then been scared off. But the way the tape was edited made it seem like it was Beattie—the now-rotund, peripatetic paramedic/lawyer—who was making this claim, not the more famous Douglas. The reporter introduced him as "Richard Beattie," which gave all of Beattie's long-time friends in Wichita a good laugh, especially since they'd always known him as "Robert" or even "Bob."

Arghh! Beattie was disgusted. He was especially disgusted when the bizarre television "investigation" won the Kansas Association of Broadcasters' award for the best in-depth news reporting in a series for 2002.

This experience made Beattie more determined than ever to get the facts straight about BTK. He was pretty sure that someone, somewhere, had to have already written a book about the notorious case, but was surprised to discover that none existed. "As I started asking questions," Beattie recalled, "I realized, these guys [the police] are too close-mouthed, that's why no one's written a book about this."

Beattie was scheduled to teach his jury class at Newman University in the fall of 2003. One of the quirks of Kansas law permits citizens, by means of a petition signed by a small number of voters, to compel the convening of an investigative grand jury. Beattie decided to use the jury class to explore just how this citizen-demanded grand jury functioned, and to use the by-now nearly mythological BTK murders as the subject to be "investigated" by the student "grand jurors."

"In old Kansas law, you know, the local sheriff and the district attorneys, sometimes were corrupt. And they wouldn't do things, and the citizens would say, 'We're gonna make you' . . . at one time, Kansas was really on the forefront of a lot of things. We weren't always going backwards, like not teaching evolution," Beattie later observed, in wry reference to recent political attempts in Kansas to get Darwin out of the public schools.

"So I really start working on it," Beattie recalled. He began digging up more old, retired cops, peppering them with questions, trying to find survivors of the victims, scouring for old records and scraps of paper that might shed light on what had actually happened. He had the idea that if someone didn't do this, the whole story was likely to wind up one of those modern myths, like alligators in the sewers, or alien crop circles.

Beattie prepared his course materials, dumping his original academic title for " 'The Naked Jury,' so the students would open the book!" he joked later. Part of the course book was a 31-page section on the BTK murders, which Beattie titled "Justice Delayed Is Justice Denied."

"So I'm writing this course material," Beattie recalled, "and one of the old detectives told me, 'You have to write a book. The story's going down, these old guys are dying off, and if somebody doesn't write it down, the story's going to be lost. And people don't know how huge of an investigation this was.' "

A book? The thought of writing a book himself hadn't occurred to Beattie until that moment, even though he knew no one had ever written down the whole story from start to finish. By the time he turned in the course materials to the university for printing in July 2003, Beattie had made up his mind—the BTK story needed to be dragged from the shadows so everyone would know what actually happened. It was history—it was part of Wichita, Toto. He would write his own book.

Beattie's class on the American jury began in late August. At the first class session, Beattie turned out all the lights and sat in the back of the room, telling the story. Afterward, when the lights came back on, Beattie noticed that a number of students seemed very upset—frightened, in fact. He worried that he had scared people so bad that they might drop the course. However, all but two students continued with the class.

"Well, first, I want to teach them how this works," Beattie said later. "The history, the political theory, why we have a grand jury, and the reason why we have this specific provision about a citizen petition." Beattie discussed several other cases in which grand juries had played roles, such as the JonBenét Ramsey case, and then came back to the BTK situation.

As he had done in his previous jury classes, Beattie provided the students with the basic information about the case, the who, what, when and where.

"I say, 'Here are the basics,'" Beattie recalled. "Now, typically, the people taking my class are interested in going to law school. Or they're in law enforcement. Or they're majoring in journalism . . . every semester, the editor of the school paper takes this class. So they can do some investigative journalism, they can exercise their skills in talking to strangers, which is what I have them do."

Relying on Beattie's basic findings, over the next month, students interviewed Ken Landwehr, who had formerly worked on the old BTK case back in the 1980s, and was now the lieutenant in charge of the Wichita Police Department's homicide squad; and Richard LaMunyon, who had been the Wichita police chief back in the 1980s, when the last strenuous, if fruitless, attempt had been made to solve the case, once again with the assistance of the FBI. Another student looked into advances in DNA typing techniques, and another scrutinized 1970s-era class yearbooks from Wichita State University with the idea of trying to match old composite drawings of the killer with students and faculty. Yet another student looked into the letters that "BTK" had supposedly generated in the 1970s, and found out that the originals of those communications had all been confiscated by the police.

By early October, the "grand jurors" were ready to sit and consider the "evidence." Beattie, who had developed good working relationships with the judges of the Sedgwick County District Court, convened his class in the courtroom of Judge Richard Ballinger. As it happened, Judge Ballinger was a very close friend of the family of one of the BTK victims, Nancy Fox, and had also been the legal advisor to the police on the BTK case back in the 1970s, when he served as a deputy district attorney. So the judge was particularly interested in the mock proceedings.

The week before the "grand jury" was to meet, Beattie learned that former chief LaMunyon would be unable to attend. He needed to find a "witness" who would replace LaMunyon. He broached the subject with Judge Ballinger.

"You know," Beattie told the judge, "I wish that Nancy Fox's mother was still alive. And if she was, that she could come and talk."

"She's dead?" Ballinger asked Beattie, shock all over his face. "Gosh, I just talked to her two weeks ago."

Beattie now expressed his own astonishment. He'd been under the impression that Nancy Fox's mother, Georgia Mason, had died years earlier. To that point, Beattie had only had contact with Nancy Fox's father, Dale; he'd been aware that a bitter divorce had taken place between Nancy's parents before her murder but had erroneously concluded that Nancy's mother had died in the twenty-six years since her daughter's own death.

"No, no," Ballinger corrected him. "I go to church with her. With the whole Fox family." In fact, he'd known the Fox family since he was a teenager, Ballinger explained.

Beattie asked the judge if he'd be willing to call Nancy Fox's mother to see if she'd agree to come to the mock grand jury class as a "witness," now that former chief LaMunyon couldn't attend. Ballinger said he'd be happy to do this.

Ballinger's close relationship to the Fox family gave Beattie's educational project an imprimatur of legitimacy, at least to the Fox family, and eventually, fourteen relatives and friends of Nancy Fox, murdered twenty-six years earlier, agreed to appear as "witnesses" before Beattie's "grand jury." The event was to prove a watershed in the history of the BTK murder case.

Early in the evening of October 8, 2003, as Beattie and his students made their way into the Sedgwick County Courthouse to assemble in Judge Ballinger's courtroom, a huge thunderstorm rolled in across the plains and settled in over Wichita. The rain began and didn't let up—a deluge that soon had the streets under several feet of water.

Inside Ballinger's courtroom, the students and their "witnesses" were largely oblivious to the raging weather outside. Instead of rain, what Beattie's "grand jurors" saw were tears. As members of Nancy Fox's family came forward to tell their stories—it was, Beattie later learned, the first time since Nancy's funeral that her father and mother were in the same room with each other—Nancy Fox ceased being a name on a piece of paper and became once again a real human being, as those who had known her best lovingly reassembled her from their memories. Her humor, her openness, her optimism, her hopes for the future, her love for her family and friends, all took her out of the bland public category of "victim" and made her live once again, if only for a few hours.

Judge Ballinger was the first of the "witnesses" to speak. He wasn't there, he said, because he was a judge who'd lent the use of the courtroom, but because he'd been a very close friend of Nancy Fox.

"We grew up together," Ballinger told the students. "We went to church together." They'd known each other since grade school, he added. And then he introduced Georgia Mason, Nancy's mother.

"The dear lady sitting next to me was just about half my mom, too." As he was growing up, Ballinger said, Georgia Mason had always been there for him, as she had been for her own children.

When he'd worked as a deputy district attorney, Ballinger continued, he'd been called out by police to go to the scene of a murder. Only the fact that he was giving his opening statement in a trial prevented him from having to learn that his good friend Nancy Fox was the victim his assistance was being requested for.

Georgia Mason now began to speak, but after managing to say that she was Nancy's mother, she couldn't continue, breaking into tears. Nancy's sister, Beverly, took over. She'd been living in Kansas City with her husband when Georgia Mason had called to tell them that Nancy had been murdered.

"It was a horrible time for my family," Beverly said. "I don't remember a lot of things. I remember I took a leave of absence [from her job] . . . being in Kansas City felt wrong. I needed to be here in Wichita." Beverly returned to Wichita, still trying to cope with the enormity of what had happened.

Others spoke as well.

"There is one image of Nancy that I wish I could get out of my head," said her best friend. "I keep thinking of her as a butterfly. I guess we were all butterflies." They were young women, she said, fun-loving and a little naïve. But all that had gone away on the day she heard that Nancy had been murdered.

The "testimony" was intense, and took several hours. At the end, Dale Fox, Nancy's father, approached each of the student "jurors" to shake hands with them.

"I sure hope you can find out something about what happened to my Nancy," he said. With that, the Fox family departed into the storm that was by now swirling around the courthouse.

"Everybody leaves," Beattie recalled, "and I'm sitting there, and the students were in the jury box. And we're sitting there and we're just emotionally wrung out, because of all these tears. It was just like the murder had just happened. They wanted to find out what happened, why this happened, who was this?"

Beattie and his students were awed by the experience. They wanted to do more, but knew that once the class was over, there would be little they *could* do, despite Dale Fox's entreaties. *Hey,* they told themselves, *it's just a class, right?*

Not so with Beattie. Something inside of him had changed—he knew it. He could feel it. He was going to write a book about what had happened to Nancy Fox, and the Otero family, and the others who had been murdered and never avenged. But not just a book, and certainly not just any book. He was going to use his book to tell people what had really happened.

But even more than that, Beattie decided, he'd use his book to help catch the damn killer.

3:

CAVEing Out

By the time the class was over, the storm was at its height. Altogether, a little over four inches of rain had fallen, most of it in less than an hour. All over the city, motorists' cars flooded, stranding people. Police and firemen were busy rescuing the distressed, and some parts of the city were under two to three feet of water.

The Sedgwick County Courthouse was similarly inundated.

"We could not cross north from the courthouse to the parking lot without getting water up to our knees," Beattie recalled. "One of the students—a tall basketball player who owned a truck with big wheels—waded over to the parking garage and then ferried us in his truck in two or three loads over to the parking garage."

Once the students had left the garage, Beattie stood for a while, watching the rain, thinking about what had just happened.

"I was changed," Beattie said. "It was like a metamorphosis." What had begun as a class project at first had turned into what Beattie thought of as "an armchair detective story," his proposed book. But after hearing from the Fox family, after feeling the intense emotion, Beattie felt suffused with a zeal to do something more.

After a few minutes to himself, Beattie got into his car and tried to drive home. Usually it took only fifteen minutes, but because of the flooding, this time it took nearly three-quarters of an hour. Like everyone else, Beattie drove in the middle part of the street, where the road crown was highest. He passed more than a dozen vehicles that had conked out.

This guy thinks he's some kind of quasi-cop or James Bond or something, Beattie reasoned, based on what others had told him over the years. *This guy thinks he's a secret agent in enemy territory. And the only reason he hasn't been caught before now is that he's hidden this side of his personality and seems perfectly ordinary to everyone who knows him. He thinks of himself as some sort of spy, so it stands to reason he will have a cover. How can I get him to blow his cover?*

Beattie by now knew enough about the BTK case and applied psychology to believe that he could provoke the killer into revealing himself—that would be the real purpose of his book, he decided. To jab at the killer—if, that is, he was still around and still alive. To get under his skin, to make him resume communications, and thereby to betray his cover. Beattie had already reached the conclusion, after conducting a number of interviews with former police officials familiar with the case, and by reading various psychological treatises on serial killers, that BTK was consumed with narcissism—that whoever he was, he saw himself as the star of the show, even if he was concealing himself in plain sight.

I'm going to tell this story . . . and he's not going to be able to take it. Because I'm not a cop, I'm a lawyer. Beattie thought that the killer, whoever he was, would be consumed with jealousy once he discovered that Beattie was going to write "his" book. That was just in the nature of being a narcissist, Beattie knew.

Beattie also knew that this could be a very dangerous game. Who could predict what might happen? What if the killer killed someone else just to spite Beattie? What if, in fact, the killer decided to kill Beattie himself, or his wife, Mary Ann?

Beattie realized that he couldn't make such a decision alone. When he finally made it home, Mary Ann was asleep. Watching her slumber, Beattie realized that she would understand why it was important to do something about BTK after all these years. If she'd been there when Georgia Mason had been too overcome to speak, he thought, Mary Ann would understand perfectly.

This has been affecting my life, and the people of Wichita, basically my whole adult life, Beattie thought. *Since I was 17 years old, when the Oteros were murdered. I want to know—I'm supposed to be this bright guy, who's been president of the Mensa chapter twice, I've got degrees in math and science, and people always expect things of me, and usually I come through. You know, I've led men through burning buildings on the fire department and always ended up team captain and president of the club and all that, and the school, and I've done some good things in my life, but . . .*

But he'd never before set out to trap a serial killer.

The next morning, Mary Ann told her husband that she knew exactly what he meant, and why he had to go forward.

Beattie's idea of using a book to flush the killer out of hiding was not just an idle conceit. For some years he'd been familiar with some fundamental principles of applied psychology used in human resource management and marketing. After all, he had a degree in human resources management, as well as science and mathematics. And he had practical psychological experience, too—he'd spent a year wrestling mentally disturbed people when he'd worked as a psychiatric orderly. So Beattie was familiar with two broad approaches he thought he might apply to the BTK problem, one of them calculated to predict the unknown killer's future behavior, and the other intended to provoke him into resuming contact. It was Beattie's idea that the more the killer communicated, the greater the prospect might be that he'd make some sort of mistake, inadvertently revealing his identity.

Of course, Beattie was well aware that this could all go horribly wrong. But then, he thought, *This is a thirty-year-old case. The police haven't been able to solve it. They've been working on it but not getting anywhere. Justice Delayed Is Justice Denied. If this guy is still living, he's lived his life. And as far as I can see, there's absolutely no reason* not *to tell this story.*

Besides, he thought: what if "the guy," as the police were wont to call him—if he really existed—were dead, as so many of experts had insisted in recent years? Putting out many of the details about the crimes might jog someone's memory; it might even lead a son or a daughter to look at some supposed "keepsake" in a new light.

Only a year or so earlier, in fact, Beattie had handled a legal matter in which the son of a World War II U.S. Army intelligence officer, who had died some years before, came in with a shoebox filled with dogtags that had once belonged to Japanese soldiers, along with photographs from what appeared to be a prisoner-of-war camp. The son had asked Beattie: should his father have had this stuff, even innocently? Should *he*? And what should be done to give it back? So Beattie knew it was possible that the killer's family, previously oblivious to everything, might stumble across something incriminating, something they had never before dreamed existed in the life of their loved one, and, with a jab from Beattie's book, might end up turning in something that might tie back to the murders.

For one of his two broad approaches to the problem of

BTK, Beattie had familiarity and practical experience with the work of three researchers at the University of Pennsylvania, Peter Schulman, Camilo Castellon, and Dr. Martin E. P. Seligman. Called Content Analysis of Verbatim Explanations, or CAVE, this system provided a scoring mechanism to assess optimism or pessimism on the part of a speaker or writer, which in turn had meaning in the treatment of depression, among other uses.

Studies have shown that optimism and pessimism correlate to success or failure, happiness and unhappiness, and even physical health. An athlete, for example, might remark that there was no way he could beat his previous best time in a sprint; chances are then quite good that he wouldn't. Alternatively, another runner might say she knew she was going to get better times in each succeeding race, and the chances are, she would.

The beauty of the CAVE approach, Seligman and his colleagues contended, was that it could be used when there was no other way to gauge a test subject's internal attitude, since it could be applied retroactively to both oral and written statements. At the same time, it cut two ways—it could also be applied to statements intended to stimulate future actions by others.

Life insurance companies, for instance, used it to determine whether to hire salesmen—they wanted people who didn't get discouraged by "no."

"It's widely used in personnel evaluations," Beattie said later. "It is used now in evaluating written statements for application to graduate school, to the military academies. Professional sports teams use it for draft picks." The CAVE scoring system for words and contexts used by a writer or speaker could be employed to determine the level of inner confidence of a communicator, and his or her persistence.

One of the most common fields where the CAVE technique has been used in recent years is in the field of politics. President Jimmy Carter's remarks about "a national malaise" in 1979 probably cost him his reelection in 1980; people began to see him as a pessimist, and voters don't like to vote for pessimists. Ronald Reagan, on the other hand, easily won reelection in 1984 with the slogan "morning in America," which stimulated a positive, upbeat reaction in voters. Since the 1980s, in fact, almost all political advertising has been CAVEd for its potential effect on voters.

Beattie thought he could apply the CAVE system to BTK's old communications, those that had come to public attention back in the 1970s, and thereby come to some sort of judgment about the prospect of being able to manipulate "the guy" into resuming his communications after almost two decades.

And as a second approach, Beattie recalled the research of a Nobel Prize–winning psychologist, Dr. Daniel Kahneman. Working with psychologist Amos Tversky, Kahneman had won the Nobel in 2002 for something they called "Prospect Theory Framing."

"Dr. Kahneman demonstrated the importance of how a subject *perceived* the risk of gain or loss in each stage of any process that led to a desired outcome," Beattie recalled. "In aggregate, human beings are loss averse. We are much more likely to act to avoid a loss than we are to seek a gain. Additionally, we create 'mental accounts' for each activity and struggle to keep these accounts 'in the black.' "

Beattie remembered that BTK's first communication had come in October of 1974, almost ten months after the Otero family had been murdered. The letter, he recalled, had been sent after police had arrested three people in connection with the murders. It appeared that the killer didn't want the three arrested men to get the "credit" for the murders, so he had sent the communication, in the form of a letter that provided a detailed account of what the crime scene had looked like to prove his validity.

From this, Beattie concluded two things: first, that the BTK killer craved public recognition—a conclusion that was buttressed by the killer's additional communications more than three years later, in 1978, demanding more publicity and threatening to kill more people if he didn't get it; and second, that if he thought someone else was now going to get credit for anything to do with "his" murders, he would soon communicate once more—if he were still alive.

Beattie later tried to explain this to skeptical police, and to several reporters. He made a simple analogy to illustrate Kahneman's theory: "You don't like to lose stuff you've already got," he said. "If you drop your five-dollar bill, you may step into the mud to get it back. But if you see a five-dollar bill flying by, you may not run into the mud to get it. But if it's your five-dollar bill, you may.

"I had absolutely no doubt, whoever BTK was, if he was still alive . . . he's going to see *me* as stealing from *him*. In his mind, this is *his* story. And me telling it, not him, would be a loss, and he might act by coming out of hiding."

That meant Beattie had to get publicity for his mock grand jury, and for his plan to write a book about the case. The more publicity, the greater the chance was that the BTK, if he was still alive, would see it. And if he saw it, as Beattie conceived it, he would be unable to resist resuming his communications. He wouldn't want Beattie to make off with his five-dollar bill.

A week or so after the mock grand jury, Beattie suggested that one of his students write an article on the BTK exercise for the student newspaper.

"I was trying to shake the tree with publicity," Beattie said. Something to engage the killer's attention. Unfortunately, the student newspaper wasn't interested in publishing a story on the mock grand jury, or in fact, anything about BTK. Beattie called the editors of the student paper himself, but no one ever returned his calls.

A day or so later, the same student—who worked in the Newman University library—emailed *Eagle* reporter Hurst Laviana, trying to interest him in writing a story about the grand jury exercise, while Beattie himself emailed another *Eagle* reporter, Roy Wenzl. Wenzl had written articles a few years earlier about Beattie's adventure with Charlie Manson.

The next day, Laviana responded to Beattie's attempt to drum up publicity by emailing back to him.

"I've written about BTK in the past and was surprised to hear that relatives of Nancy Fox are still around and talking about the case," Laviana wrote to Beattie. After briefly referring to the ill-fated television "investigation" of 2002—the so-called "4 Pi" theory—as the work of a crackpot, Laviana expressed mild curiosity about Beattie's mock grand jury.

"Anyhow, I am just curious about what you've been up to and what you have found," Laviana wrote. "I've been told that the handful of officers who reopened the BTK case in the 1980s each came away with a different conclusion as to who the killer was."

Beattie and Laviana next had a couple of brief telephone conversations; Laviana suggested that Beattie might want to review the newspaper's "scrapbook" on the BTK case, since it included copies of the supposed communications. This is exactly what Beattie wanted to do to assist his CAVE project, of course. Laviana said he didn't think there was anything new about the BTK case that was worth writing about.

A few days later, Beattie sent Laviana an email.

"If the police had one suspect, that would be interesting," Beattie told Laviana. "But, as far as I can tell, each officer that *has* any prime suspect has his *own* prime suspect, which is not the same as any *other* officer's prime suspect. And almost every officer seems quick to criticize other officers who have concluded that BTK is someone other than *their* favorite suspect."

Beattie was teasing Laviana with the possible germ of a story idea—police dissension—that Laviana might use as a hook for a story that would also say Beattie intended to write a book about the case. That, after all, was Beattie's objective—to use the newspaper to make the killer aware that someone else was going to "steal" his thunder.

"Different officers tell me different things," Beattie continued in this message to Laviana. "One insists that BTK is tall and one insists that BTK is short. Depending on whom I have spoken with, BTK is tall or short; thin or stocky; blonde or dark haired; works alone or has always worked with a partner, and that partner is either a man or a woman; and BTK has not been caught, not because he is smart, but because he is lucky, or because he is smart, uncannily smart.

"That narrows it down," Beattie concluded, wryly. "Who do I see at the *Eagle*'s library about the BTK scrapbook?"

Over the next week, Beattie spent several days at the library of *The Wichita Eagle*, perusing the "scrapbook," which included copies of the various communications thought to have been sent by the murderer over the years.

Reviewing the content of the old letters using the CAVE system convinced Beattie that the person who had written them was "realistically pessimistic" about his ability to continue killing without being caught. That was probably why, Beattie concluded, the murders appeared to have stopped years before. But, Beattie also determined, the killer was "unrealistically over-optimistic about his ability to continue to communicate" without being apprehended.

"They never got close to him from that," Beattie said. "He thought he could continue to communicate, and that's what I wanted him to do." The killer's egomania was his Achilles' heel, Beattie realized.

If the killer could somehow be convinced that he had less to lose by communicating than by remaining silent, the chances were that he would send more messages. The more messages the killer sent, the greater the likelihood that he would make a mistake, thereby leading to his identification. So Beattie had to find a way to suggest, as publicly as possible, that the killer was *safe* in making new communications, while at the same time goading him into claiming "credit" for the crimes by the threat to usurp his notoriety—in other words, to take his five-dollar bill.

But first Beattie had to get the publicity.

As it turned out, that took longer and was a bit harder than he had anticipated. And there was one thing Beattie could *not* tell anyone: that he had CAVEd BTK's letters, and that his plan was to goad the killer into surfacing once more. If BTK knew that, it would defeat the whole purpose, Beattie knew. It was a bit like telling the subject of a medical treatment experiment that he was getting a placebo—if the patient knew the medicine was fake, the experiment would be ruined.

As the fall of 2003 ended and winter arrived, Beattie was assailed by doubts. He interviewed two of the Wichita Police Department's top officials from the 1970s, retired former chief Floyd Hannon, and former deputy chief Jack Bruce. Both men insisted to him that there was no such person as BTK. In fact, Hannon said, the original "BTK" letter was so detailed in its description of the crime scene that the only reasonable conclusion was that it had to be some not-very-funny inside joke by some member of the Wichita Police Department. Bruce told Beattie that he'd always suspected that the original letter was the work of two pranksters assigned to the department's crime lab, although they had steadfastly denied it.

Maybe I'm a fool, Beattie mused. *Maybe Hannon and Bruce are right, there is no BTK. Maybe this is some sort of quixotic quest, battling a mere windmill I've mistaken for a monster . . .*

But the more Beattie studied the letters, the more he inquired of other retired cops, the more he was convinced that BTK *did* exist, or at least had at one time. If Beattie could only get a message out, he thought, they had a chance of getting one back in.

Then, on January 14, the day before the thirtieth anniversary of the Otero murders, *Eagle* reporter Hurst Laviana received the email from his old partner, Bill Hirschman, asking if the paper planned to write anything about the thirtieth anniversary of the old murder case. Laviana had his short, tepid conversation with Rogers. That was when reporter Wenzl happened by and asked, in effect: "What about Bob?"

That same afternoon, Laviana, now thinking that perhaps Beattie's proposed book on BTK *would* make a good peg for an anniversary story, emailed Beattie:

"Bob, is there a number where you can be reached this afternoon?" Laviana wrote. "I'm trying to put together something on the Otero 30-year anniversary and remembered that Roy said you were working on a book about BTK."

Beattie spoke with Laviana for about an hour that same

afternoon. By this point, Beattie had already conducted about sixty interviews for his book, including many with retired police officers who had worked on the case. After Beattie explained much of what he had done (although not the CAVEing or his concept of trying to filch the killer's symbolic five-dollar bill), Laviana was suitably impressed.

"You really *are* writing a book," he told Beattie.

Three days later, Laviana and the *Eagle* published a front-page story about Beattie and his proposed book. A large photograph of Beattie holding a scrapbook of newspaper clippings about the case illustrated the story.

In his article, Laviana established several facts that Beattie hoped would get under BTK's skin, although Laviana wasn't actually aware of this. The first was that Beattie was cutting down on his law practice to research "a book about the man considered by many police officers as the city's most notorious killer."

This, he hoped, would accomplish two purposes: to stimulate the sick ego of the killer by emphasizing his notoriety, and to convince him, along with everyone else, that Beattie was committed to actually writing the book.

"I did want people to know that I was serious enough about this book that I was cutting back my law practice," Beattie recalled. "If BTK was out there, then he would know this. I also wanted the cops to know that I was serious." That could only help him in future interviews, Beattie thought.

At another point in the story, Laviana quoted Beattie about the amount of money that had been spent on the case over the years, to no avail. This, Beattie hoped, would once again puff up BTK's sense of pride in his crimes. "If BTK was out there, I thought his ego would be stroked by knowing that a lot of money was spent to catch him, but that he was 'too clever to be caught,'" Beattie said later.

Then Beattie, through Laviana, dealt a sharp blow to the killer's ego, and simultaneously challenged him to resurface: "Although the killings remain firmly implanted in the minds of those who lived through them, Beattie said many Wichitans probably have never heard of BTK," Laviana wrote.

"Probably never heard of BTK"—that was a direct prick of the killer's balloon, essentially saying no one cared about him anymore. Beattie hoped this would motivate the killer to remind everyone of who he was.

Remembering his client with the shoebox full of Japanese dogtags, Beattie also told Laviana that he hoped some relative of BTK might read the book, or even hear about it, and think again about any odd mementos a deceased loved one might have left behind.

"I'm hoping someone will read the book and come forward with some information—a driver's license, a watch, some car keys," Laviana quoted Beattie. "If he has died, maybe some family members who have those items will realize their significance . . . But I do not think we'll be contacted by BTK."

Beattie hadn't meant this last line as a general statement, only that he did not believe either he or Mary Ann would be contacted directly by the killer. But the communal "we" could be read by the killer as another challenge—if Beattie was essentially saying the killer didn't have the nerve to communicate with the public again, wouldn't that goad him into doing exactly that?

If BTK did exist, if he was still alive, if he did still live in the community, Beattie was certain that reading that someone else was getting publicity for *his* crimes would stimulate him to come forward once again.

And on this point, as on so many others, Beattie would turn out to be exactly right. What he did not know, what he could never have imagined, was that the killer not only read about Beattie's book from this account, but had, years before, begun writing his own. Now all he had to do was get it "published," by relying upon the news media's ravenous appetite for sensation. He could mail his "chapters" anonymously to his "publisher," or use "dead drops," just like in the spy stories he was so fond of. His book would be better, much better than Beattie's, the killer thought.

And why not? Just as Beattie suspected he might, he had every detail of every case, and some that no one even suspected, completely documented and carefully indexed, right down to detailed crime-scene drawings, in a filing cabinet in his office, not ten miles from Beattie's own house. He called them "projects," "PJs" for short, as if they were elaborate covert operations, and he was "licensed to kill." In comparison to the killer, Beattie knew almost nothing, while he, *he* could go back to the scenes of the murders anytime he liked. And often did, at least in his mind.

The book race between Beattie and BTK was on.

“PJS”

4:

"PJ Little-Mex"

The killer waited by the rear fence, his "hit kit," as he called it, at the ready: two pistols, two knives, venetian blind cords pre-cut and knotted, rolls of duct and electrical tape and a supply of plastic bags, all of them stuffed in the pocket of his oversized parka. He wore gloves. There was still snow on the ground from a storm a few days before.

It was the morning of January 15, 1974, and the killer had had the house at the corner of North Edgemoor and East Murdock Streets in southeast Wichita under casual, intermittent surveillance for weeks. The Otero family, he knew, were recent arrivals in Wichita. He'd always had a letch for Hispanic women, and seeing Julie, 34, and her youngest daughter, Josie, 11, had particularly whetted his lust.

Despite his observations, the killer had only the vaguest information about the rest of the Otero family—the father, Joseph, 38, a retired U.S. Air Force sergeant; and sons Charlie, 15; Danny, 14; and Joey, 9. There was also another daughter, Carmen, 13, although the killer probably confused her, during his periodic observations, with her sister, Josie.

None of the Oteros were physically large people, although both Joe and Julie were trained in martial arts. Joe was five feet four inches in height, and weighed about 150 pounds. Julie was five-three and weighed about 120. The little children, of course, were even smaller. Still, with his military experience and his skill in martial arts, Joe could be a tough customer for someone not armed to the teeth. That was why the killer intended to get Julie and Josie alone that morning. From his vantage point, he could see the Oteros' garage. It contained a 1966 Pontiac Vista Cruiser station wagon, the same car that the killer had seen Julie drive in the past, so he knew she was home. The family's other car, usually driven by Joe Otero, wasn't around, so the killer concluded that Joe was gone.

The Oteros had come to Wichita in November 1973, after Joe had retired from the Air Force. A native of Puerto Rico, Joe and his wife had both grown up in New York City. His career in the Air Force had taken the family to various places around the world, most recently Panama. There Joe Otero was assigned to service Panamanian dictator Omar Torrijos' personal aircraft.

Since arriving in Wichita for their post-retirement life, Joe Otero had found work at a nearby airport as an aircraft maintenance mechanic, and as a flight instructor, while Julie had found a job at the Coleman plant in town. A lot of people in Wichita worked at Coleman, the maker of outdoor equipment such as lanterns, stoves and sleeping bags; the company was one of Wichita's largest employers.

The older Otero children, Charlie, Danny and Carmen, found themselves readily accepted in their new schools, although Carmen wasn't entirely sure that Wichita was all that great a place to live—it was too cold, she complained to her sister, Josie. But Josie, always the optimist, told her that she'd get used to it before long. "Give it a chance," Josie had told her sister.

"That was part of Josie's beauty," Carmen remembered later. "She always tried to see the bright side of everything."

Little Joey—9 years old—was the light of the family.

Carmen later remembered him as "the most loveable, fun, outgoing, friendly and adorable little brother anyone could ever imagine. He tried so hard to keep up with Charlie and Danny. Joey was a magnet. He attracted people of all ages."

The Otero family also had a dog, Lucky, who had come with them from Panama. The part German Shepherd was a bit wild, and as a matter of courtesy, the family usually put him outside when guests arrived.

Exactly what transpired that morning about 8:20 A.M. was never completely clear. But at just about that point, the killer suddenly jumped over the small white fence into the Otero back yard. He began cutting the telephone line at the rear of the house near the back door. Just as he severed the line, the back door opened, and Lucky ran outside—right past the killer, in fact, who, startled, dropped his knife. The next thing anyone knew, the killer was through the door, slamming it behind him to keep the dog out. He pulled one of his guns out, a .22-caliber semiautomatic Colt Woodsman—the preferred weapon of hitmen everywhere.

Astonished, the Oteros stared up at him. Julie and Josie had been making peanut butter sandwiches for Josie and Joey to take to school with them. The killer was surprised to find Joe Otero sitting at the kitchen table—he hadn't planned on a man being present. Still, he decided to go through with his "project."

"I'm a wanted man, I'm desperate," the killer told them, beginning his tale. "I need money, food, a car. Do what I tell you and you won't get hurt."

"Is this some kind of joke?" Joe Otero asked. "My brother-in-law put you up to this, didn't he?"

"No, no, this is no joke," the killer said. Brandishing his gun, the killer forced the four shocked Oteros into the living room and made them lie down on the floor. Quickly he produced the cords he'd pre-cut and knotted, then tied Joe Otero's hands behind his back and his ankles together. He moved on to Julie Otero and did the same to her, then to Josie and Joey. By now it was almost 8:40 A.M. He'd tied them too tight, they complained; the cords were cutting off their circulation. The killer said nothing.

Over the next few minutes, he forced the Oteros one after the other into the master bedroom. He put Julie and Josie on the bed, Joe and Joey on the floor.

Then he decided to kill them all.

He began with Joe Otero, reasoning that he was the most dangerous of the victims. He went back into the living room and returned with the plastic bags from his "hit kit." When they saw the plastic bags, the Oteros began to struggle against their bonds. The killer managed to get one of the bags over Joe Otero's head, cinching it around his neck with one of the cords. He got up on the bed with Julie and began to strangle her with another length of cord. Julie lost consciousness. The killer thought she was dead.

He got off the bed and realized that Joe Otero wasn't dead after all. He was still moving, trying to chew a hole in the plastic sack. The killer found a tee-shirt in the bedroom and tied it tight over the plastic sack, using a belt he found in the bedroom. Joe struggled vainly against his ropes; after several minutes he stopped moving.

The killer got back on the bed to turn his attention to little Josie. She was calling out to her mother.

"Mama, mama!" Josie cried. She stared up at the killer, who dwarfed her in size. "What did you do to my mama?" The killer began strangling Josie. She lost consciousness.

The killer got off the bed and put another plastic bag over little Joey's head.

"You killed my boy, you killed my boy," Julie yelled, struggling against the cords that still held her. The killer realized that Julie wasn't dead, either. He got back on the bed and put a gag in her mouth and a pillow over her face to suffocate her.

The killer got off the bed again. All of the Oteros seemed to be dead. Except Joey. The killer realized he was still moving. He picked Joey up and carried him into another bedroom. He put him on the bed, then placed a chair in the doorway. He tied a pillowcase over the plastic bag over Joey's head, then sat down in the chair to watch. Joey struggled to breathe, rolling frantically over the bed, then fell off to the floor. He shuddered and went limp.

The killer returned to the master bedroom. He discovered that Josie had regained consciousness. *Oh good,* he thought, *an encore.*

He pulled little Josie to her feet and maneuvered her toward the steps into the basement.

"Does your daddy have a camera?" he asked her. Josie shook her head no, no camera.

"What's going to happen to me?" she asked, once they were down in the basement.

"Well, honey," the killer said, "you're going to be in heaven tonight with the rest of your family."

About 10:30 that morning, two different people saw someone backing the Otero station wagon out of the small garage, then driving it down Murdock Street to the west. One witness described the solo driver as a man of "middle-eastern" appearance; the other said the driver had longish, dark hair, and a "swarthy" appearance. The car proceeded down the narrow, tree-lined lane, past older, lower-middle-class houses that lay behind small snow drifts on either side of the street. At Old Manor Road he turned left and drove south to East Central Avenue. A few blocks farther west, he turned into the small parking lot of a chain grocery market, Dillons.

The killer had a terrific headache. He realized he'd been sweating profusely. He got out of the car. A woman in the parking lot noticed him; she thought he was trembling with extreme nervousness. She averted her eyes from him, to avoid any contact. The man walked away, and got behind the wheel of his own car.

As he went through the pockets of his parka, checking on his "hit kit," he realized that he'd left his large knife in the Otero back yard. Chances were, his fingerprints were all over it. He knew he had to get it back—it was a risk he had to take, the killer decided. He drove back to the Otero house, putting his own car in the garage. Nothing seemed out of the ordinary. He found the knife where he'd dropped it by the back door, then got back into his own car. He drove home and took two over-the-counter pain relievers for his headache, then drove to a forest area north of the city. That afternoon, he burned everything that he thought might link him to the murders of four people. Then he drove home once more to his own wife and children.

What he did not know, what he did not learn until much later, was that one week before he initiated his "project," Joe Otero had been in an accident in the snow with the other Otero family car, which was being repaired in a shop across town. Because there was only one car in the garage, the one usually used by Julie Otero, the killer had thought Joe Otero wouldn't be home that morning. If not for the earlier accident on the ice, Joe Otero might not have been there, and so might have survived the assault that destroyed half his family. Or perhaps, instead, if the second car *had* been there, the killer might have realized that Joe *was* home, and so passed by the Otero house that morning. It was his erroneous assumption that had led him into the house, and so to murder four people he had never known.

Thus, human fate so often turns on the smallest of chance events.

Shortly after 3 P.M. that same afternoon, Danny and Carmen Otero walked home from school. When they reached their house at North Edgemoor and East Murdock, they tried to get in through the back door, but for some reason it wouldn't open. Lucky was in the back yard. Danny Otero decided to try the front door, and walked around the house. Carmen was able to open the back door. She called to Danny, but he apparently didn't hear her. She followed him around to the front.

As soon as Danny and Carmen entered the house, they knew something was wrong. They found the living room in disarray, their mother's purse open and contents strewn across the floor, and their father's looted wallet on the stove in the kitchen. They called out, but no one answered. Then they went into the master bedroom and found their mother tied up, face down on the bed, and their father also tied, face up on the floor, although his face was obscured with what seemed to be a shirt. Neither seemed to be breathing. Carmen removed a gag from her mother's mouth and searched for something to cut the rope around her neck, while Danny rushed to the kitchen to get a knife to cut the his father's bindings. Carmen found a pair of nail clippers and went to work on the cords around her mother's throat. Returning with a large knife, Danny tried to cut the belt and the cord, but was unable to do it. Joe still didn't move. Danny put the knife down and ran back into the kitchen for the telephone, but the line was dead. He ran downstairs into the basement, where there was another telephone, but that didn't work either. He ran back upstairs to his parents' bedroom and tried again to cut through the belt, but again couldn't do it.

At that point, Charlie Otero arrived home from school. He'd noticed that the garage door was open, and the Vista Cruiser was gone. He closed the garage door and went in through the back door. Carmen and Danny were in the bedroom, crying. They were in shock—the scene was too unreal to grasp. Charlie later remembered that Danny told him that their parents seemed to be playing a bad joke on them.

Charlie knew his father was dead. He cut through the belt around his father's neck, and pulled away the tee-shirt and plastic bag. He did the same with the cords around his mother's neck. He went out to the kitchen to try to use the telephone, but like Danny, found it didn't work.

Charlie now ran outside and encountered a neighbor, Dell Johnson, who was shoveling snow.

"Come quick, my father's dead, I think," Charlie told him. Johnson followed Charlie back to the Otero house and into the bedroom. He saw that the two Otero parents weren't moving. Charlie and Danny told him the telephones weren't working. Johnson told them he'd go back to his own house and call for help.

Just before 3:40 that afternoon, Johnson reached an emergency dispatcher for the city of Wichita and asked that an ambulance be sent to the Otero address on North Edgemoor. The dispatcher in turn contacted the police. In those days, the police routinely accompanied any ambulance dispatch in the city.

A few minutes later, Wichita Police Officers Robert

Bulla and Jim Lindeburg arrived at the Otero house. Charlie, Danny and Carmen met them outside. After telling the three teenagers to stay outside, the two officers went into the house. Looking into the bedroom, they saw Joe on the floor and Julie on the bed. A large knife was lying next to Joe. Julie's legs were hanging over the side of the bed. Both victims' hands were tied behind their backs. Bulla could find no pulse in either victim, and it appeared that rigor mortis had already begun. The ambulance crew, which now arrived, confirmed that Joe and Julie Otero had been dead for some hours.

While Lindeburg went outside to be with Charlie, Carmen and Danny, Bulla used his handheld radio to notify dispatch that there appeared to be two murder victims at the corner of North Edgemoor and East Murdock Streets. He looked around the death room. He noticed more pieces of white cord on the floor near Joe Otero's body, apparently fragments left over when Charlie had cut through the bindings with the knife that still lay on the floor next to him. Bulla noticed that all the drawers to the Oteros' dresser were pulled out, and the contents rummaged through as if the killer had been looking for something. After noting this, Bulla left the house to wait for his shift supervisor, Lieutenant Jack Watkins.

Shortly after 4 P.M., Watkins arrived at the house. He and Bulla reentered the dwelling, and this time a cursory search of all the rooms was undertaken. In a second bedroom, Watkins and Bulla found the body of 9-year-old Joey. Like his parents, Joey was also bound with venetian blind cord. Like his father, his head was encased in a plastic bag, covered tightly with a pillowcase.

Bulla and Watkins looked at the rest of the house. It appeared that Joe Otero's wallet had been emptied, as had Julie's purse. Apart from these personal items and the dresser, it did not appear that the house had been thoroughly tossed. To some, that later indicated that the killer or killers knew what they were looking for, and had found it. On the surface, that suggested a possible motive for the murders: drugs.

Then Bulla found his way into the gloomy basement. By now it was dark outside, so Bulla used his flashlight. He didn't want to touch any of the light switches in case there were fingerprints on them. When he got to the bottom of the steps, he saw a pair of "Beatle boots," one upright, the other lying on its side—footwear for a young girl, Bulla realized.

Bulla made his way through the basement. There was a bedroom, an area where someone had been putting together model planes, a television set, a rocking chair. At the end of the basement there was a little utility room that contained laundry appliances and a freezer, along with some storage shelves. As he made his way into this small enclosure with his flashlight, Bulla collided with something. It was the hanging body of Josie Otero.

"I've had nightmares about that moment," Bulla later told Beattie.

Casting the beam of his light over the body of the 11-year-old, Bulla realized that a rope around her neck ran up to a horizontal pipe above. It looked to Bulla like her toes were barely off the floor. She was wearing only a sweatshirt and dark blue socks. Her bra had been cut through and her panties were around her ankles. Bulla saw that cords had been tied around her hips, her knees and her ankles. Her hands had been tied behind her, just below her long dark hair, and in turn tied to the cord around her hips.

Bulla looked up at Josie's face. It looked as if she had been gagged with a fragment torn from a towel, but her swollen tongue had pushed that aside. Her eyes were closed. It must have been a horrible, agonizing death, one that took place over many minutes.

Staggered, sickened, Bulla stepped back, thinking, *What the hell happened here?*

By that evening, most of the command staff of the Wichita Police Department had been through the Otero home, including Police Chief Floyd Hannon. A cursory examination of the house by "the lab boys," as forensic technicians were called in those days, showed that a significant amount of semen had been found on the floor near Josie's body, as well as partially on her. It was clear that the killer had masturbated near her as she hung from the pipe.

Almost from the start, the Wichita detectives were in agreement: the Otero house presented probably the strangest crime scene they'd ever seen. There didn't seem to be anything about it that made sense. The disturbances to the family's possessions suggested that someone might have been searching for something. The bindings suggested to some that the victims had been repeatedly choked, then revived. Was there something that Joe Otero had that the killers had wanted? But why had the children as well as the parents been victims? And that was another thing—the consensus among the detectives was that there had to have been more than one killer for control over four people to be maintained that way; it only stood to reason. To some, the murders looked like some sort of torture for the purposes of extortion, then robbery, then execution.

But there was also Josie, hanging separately in the basement, with the semen on the floor. That was obviously a sex crime. A robbery that had turned into a sex crime? It seemed reasonable to assume that while one killer had tortured the family upstairs in an effort to force Joe Otero to tell whatever it was the killers wanted to know, another killer was downstairs with Josie. Or, some thought—maybe the killers had forced Joe to watch his 11-year-old daughter being hanged until dead in order to coerce him. Some noted that the way she was hung, the tips of Josie's toes barely touched the floor; she had probably stood on her toe tips for as long as she could before losing strength, then reviving, standing up again, then collapsing, over and over again, as the downstairs killer masturbated in front of her.

It was more than macabre, it was horrible.

The Wichita detectives had seen sex crimes before, and they had seen robberies that turned into executions. But none that involved half of an entire family, and certainly none in which the apparent motive for the murders was so mixed up.

Hannon was a veteran cop with nearly thirty years' experience in Wichita. An ex-Marine, Hannon's often salty tongue concealed the fact that he held a master's degree in police administration from Wichita State University. He'd taught police science courses in Kansas, and had also lectured at the FBI Academy in Quantico, Virginia.

To Hannon, a number of facts about the Otero murder jumped out for inference. First, there didn't seem to be any forced entry to the house. Second, the dog, Lucky, had been in the back yard—where Charlie and Danny had said the dog usually was when the family had guests. Third, the house had been partially tossed—at least the dresser had been searched, as had wallets and purses. Fourth, the chair in the doorway to the room where Joey's body had been found suggested that someone had watched him die—it was therefore possible that Joe Otero might have been tied to that chair as a form of torture.

These facts, taken together, made Hannon believe that there were at least two killers involved—maybe even more. If Julie and the children had been alone when they were confronted, Hannon would have been willing to believe that there was only one killer. In that case, he believed, the police were likely dealing with a sex crime—a strange one, but a sex crime nevertheless. But since Joe had been home, that suggested a different motive. A sex offender would have aborted his attack once he learned that a man was in the house, Hannon believed. So that meant that Joe Otero was the likely target of the murders, and that the others were killed, first, to coerce Joe Otero to give something up, and second, to eliminate witnesses. The difficulty of gaining control of four people made it most likely, Hannon thought, that there had been multiple killers—and most significantly, based on the absence of forced entry and the fact that the dog was in the back yard, the killers had probably been known to Joe Otero and/or his wife.

That didn't square with the discovery of Josie hanging in the basement, however. That was definitely a sex crime. How to explain this? Eventually Hannon came to believe that while one or more killers had stayed upstairs with Joe, Julie and little Joey, a second killer was downstairs with Josie. And Hannon did not believe that the initial impetus behind Josie's death was sex, but that in the course of hanging her, her killer had lost control.

"Chief Floyd Hannon told me that he thought the semen on the girl was not premeditated, but spontaneous," Beattie said later, after interviewing Hannon in early 2004. "Hannon thought that one of the killers got excited while Josie was being hung. Hannon thought that the killer himself may not have realized that he was going to become sexually aroused until it happened.

"Hannon was more interested in *why* the girl was tortured and hung," Beattie continued. "He thought that whoever committed these murders wanted something from Joseph Otero, and that Joseph Otero was probably forced to watch his daughter being hung. It was Joseph Otero who was being tortured, he thought, by seeing his daughter tortured. *That* interpretation of the evidence was consistent with killers entering when Joseph was home. It was the more reasonable conclusion to explain why the killing took place when two adults and two children were home. Those four were a manageable size to control in an attack, with the other three children at school."

The severed telephone wires in the rear only added to the general inference that the murders had been part of a planned attack, for some sort of understandable motive, if they could only figure out what it was. That meant looking intensely at the life of Joe Otero before he and his family had come to Wichita nine weeks earlier.

Whatever had happened, the place to start was with the three remaining kids. That evening, the surviving teenaged Oteros were interviewed by Wichita detectives at the police station. Was there anything they knew—or even did not realize they knew—that might explain what had happened?

Charlie Otero had some ideas about what was behind the deaths of his father, mother, sister and brother. He thought that something in his father's past career with the Air Force was to blame. He was under the impression that his father had been involved in covert missions for the Air Force in Central and South America. He thought it was possible that someone involved in clandestine activities, authorized or unauthorized, had shut his father's mouth forever.

Charlie told the detectives about a weird incident that had taken place only two nights before. That night, he said, the lights had gone off in the house. Joe had given his son a butcher knife and told him to get ready for when "they" attacked the house. The lights were out throughout the neighborhood, and soon came back on, though. Still, Charlie added, his father had lately been acting increasingly nervous about something.

Well, the Wichita detectives thought, this was consistent with the crime scene—a hit. Or at least most of it, if one didn't put too much emphasis on what had happened in the basement.

As January 15 rolled into January 16, and the "lab boys" continued their work at the Otero house into the early morning hours, Wichita's finest laid plans to find out what had been going on in Joe Otero's life. They all knew one thing, though—whatever Joe had been up to, nothing could possibly justify what had been done to little Joey and Josie Otero.

The surviving Oteros were soon parceled out among the family's relatives. As for the unfortunate Lucky, he was impounded and soon thereafter destroyed by the city as an unclaimed animal.

FOUR IN WICHITA FAMILY FOUND SLAIN AT HOME, the *Eagle* headlined the day after the murders. The paper quoted Chief Hannon: "I've worked homicides in this city for some twenty years, but this is the most bizarre case I've ever seen."

Hannon moved quickly to dispel the notion that the killer or killers were native Wichitans.

"Hannon said there might be an international incident involved with the murders," the newspaper reported, noting that the Oteros were "Puerto Rican."

"Something might have happened in the old country to bring on the incident," Hannon told the paper. That day and into the night, the city's television stations repeatedly broadcast footage of grim-faced detectives and ambulance attendants wheeling shrouded corpses out of the house and loading them into the coroner's van.

The following day brought a follow-up by the newspaper. POLICE BAFFLED ON MOTIVE IN MASS KILLING, read the new headline.

"The bizarre 'execution-type' slaying of four members of the Joseph Otero family Tuesday morning has Wichita officials baffled," the paper reported, adding that police were considering a number of theories about the murders. Hannon, for instance, suggested that the killer or killers had been known to the Oteros, and at the same time, that the person or persons might be suffering from some sort of mental disorder. Again there was the suggestion that if it was a crazy person who had committed the crime, it had to be someone from outside Wichita, someone connected to the Oteros' past. How could the Oteros have made the acquaintance of such a mentally disturbed person in Wichita if they had only lived there for two months? Because Julie and Joe were both trained in martial arts—certificates to that effect were hanging from walls in the house—Hannon guessed that the killer or killers had been armed with guns.

Hannon told the paper that he believed that if there were only one killer, he'd have come into the house while Joe Otero was taking the kids to school. In that case, Hannon said, the killer would have been able to surprise Joe when he returned. But if Joe had been in the house when the attack commenced, Hannon said, that seemed to indicate that there was more than one killer.

By this point, detectives had found the 1966 Vista Cruiser in the Dillons parking lot at East Central and North Oliver Streets. A search eventually turned up the car keys, which had been thrown onto the roof of the store. Canvassing detectives found a witness who recounted seeing a man in front of the Otero house about 8:45 A.M. on the morning of the murders. This man was described as about five feet ten to six feet in height, somewhat slender, with dark, shaggy hair below his ears. The man had been wearing a dark topcoat or possibly a trench coat.

Hannon said the man was not wearing a hat, and was "dark complexioned." The newspaper added: "He is believed to be of foreign extraction."

Meanwhile, other detectives had located the eyewitnesses who had seen the man who'd left the Otero house in the car about 10:30 A.M. Since autopsies of the four dead Oteros determined—probably erroneously—that all had died before 9 A.M., that created a puzzle: what had the killer or killers been doing in the house between 9 and 10:30 A.M.?

Hannon didn't want to talk about this. "There are other things that went on in the house that we cannot relate at this time," he said, apparently referring to the extended hanging of Josie Otero in the basement.

The *Eagle* that day disclosed another possibly relevant fact: two days before the attack on the Otero family, Julie Otero's supervisor at the Coleman factory had been the victim of a shooting. Two men had come to his front door and, in what appeared to be a robbery, had shot him in the abdomen. The supervisor, who did not know Julie Otero very well, survived. But apart from the Coleman coincidence, there didn't seem to be any real connection between the attacks; one seemed to be a robbery, and the other—well, no one was at all sure just what the Otero attack was intended to achieve.

At the time of the attacks, Beattie was a 17-year-old high school student. The family of one of his best friends in high school had known Joe Otero quite well; in fact, before the entire family had arrived in Wichita in November of 1973, Joe Otero had stayed some weeks with Beattie's friend's family. So the murder of the Oteros somehow seemed far more palpable to Beattie than something he'd merely read in the newspaper.

The night after the murders, several detectives secreted themselves in the now-empty Otero house on the hunch that the killer or killers might approach the place to see what was going on. But the publicity had made that a fruitless exercise. At the time, teenagers spent their evenings "dragging Douglas," that is, cruising one of the city's main streets; this was a way to meet other teens, much as portrayed in *American Graffiti*, and was (and is) a common practice throughout most of motorized America. But the night after the murders, the cruisers abandoned Douglas Avenue and decamped to North Edgemoor. All detectives could see from their vantage point inside the darkened Otero house was a cavalcade of cars, hour upon hour, as the teenaged drivers gawked at the scene of the horrible crimes.

Despite Hannon's, and the newspaper's, efforts to suggest that the killer or killers were outlanders, non-Wichitans, "dark-complexioned," possibly "of foreign extraction" and "from the old country," many Wichitans were taking no chances. Beattie recalled that the murders "sent a wave of panic through Wichita." Homeowners armed themselves with anything that came to hand—baseball bats, axes, and of course, guns. Strangers were viewed with suspicion, especially "dark-complexioned" strangers of possible "foreign extraction."

As public anxiety mounted, a new fact came into play. It turned out that the day before the murders, an airplane en route from Puerto Rico to Wichita had crashed in Florida. The plane had been carrying about 3,000 pounds of marijuana. So here it was again, a 1-2-3 deduction that pushed the motive far outside the boundaries of the

Princess of the Plains: Puerto Rico, airplane, Joe the aircraft mechanic from Puerto Rico, no robbery, torture to get information, or to send a message, possibly about drugs. For the facile among armchair detectives, it made for an easily jumped-to conclusion.

Hannon took steps to scotch this speculation, at least publicly. "There is nothing to show that the family was involved in illicit activity of any kind," he told the paper. But behind closed doors at the police station, Hannon and his detectives weren't so sure.

By late January 1974, the *Eagle* decided to adopt a more proactive role in resolving the bizarre murder case. It published a front-page story reporting the establishment of a "Secret Witness" telephone line for tips. People could call the line anonymously to report information about the Otero murders and other crimes. Each caller would be given a unique identification number in case the tip panned out, and they could collect the paper's reward of $5,000. Within a week or so, other contributions bumped the reward to $7,500. Soon the tip line was inundated with calls from cranks and the merely disturbed; it seemed that Wichita had its share of those, and in that respect was just like any other city. Beattie later learned that one woman had called in to report a suspicious man in a grocery store. The man was buying a large amount of broccoli. "Why did he need so much broccoli?" she wondered. "I thought it was suspicious."

Unbeknownst to anyone, however, the killer was one man, not two or more. He was not "dark complexioned," nor was he of "foreign extraction." He sat in the living room of his modest house, not eight miles away from the Otero home, quietly reveling in the massive publicity about the murders. A quiet man, then 28 years old, a former assembler in the heating and air conditioning division of the Coleman Company, he had just enrolled in Wichita State University's criminal justice program. Married, soon to be a father of two, he seemed absolutely ordinary to everyone who knew him, a quintessential Wichitan.

But the quiet man had a number of disturbing predilections which he kept well-hidden. For years, ever since he was a teenager, he'd had dark fantasies of bondage and torture, as well as a compulsive fondness for tying himself up, which usually led to auto-erotic self-hanging. He envisioned the dark basement of his parents' neatly maintained house nearby as a dungeon, a torture chamber; and so infested was his mind with these images that he began to draw them, repeatedly, if crudely, using himself as the model for what he desired to do to women and children. He clipped underwear ads out of newspapers and magazines, erasing the garments, sometimes with his tongue. He drew ropes and chains around the figures, then concocted a code to index his fantasies about each image. He kept all these things to himself, hidden away from everyone except the part of his brain that was suffused with them, and so well did he conceal them that not even his wife of two years ever suspected. He saw himself as a secret man, someone with powers no one could guess at, a trickster or even a hero of the dark side, someone who could move the world by his unguessed capacity to inspire fear.

Slowly the imagery that had been building in his mind for years began to harden; and the boundary line between imagination and action began to erode.

At some point in early January 1974, he said later, "the fantasy and the real world kicked over." He began carrying around his "hit kit," with the guns and knives and cords and plastic bags, in his car. He saw a bank teller at the Twin Lakes Mall, one of Wichita's oldest shopping centers, early that month and attempted to kidnap her, but "she fought me off, and I got scared and ran and hid, and I got out of there." Nevertheless, he continued to cruise the streets of Wichita, "trolling," as he put it, looking for someone real to put into his fantasies. It was while he was driving his wife to work at the Veterans' Administration offices on South Edgemoor, the killer later said, that he'd first seen Julie and Josie Otero. He'd begun his surveillance—he had time on his hands between his classes and his work at Coleman—and his ideas of getting Julie and Josie tied up and helpless under his control became the first of his "projects"—"Project Little-Mex," he referred to it privately, because he believed the Hispanic Oteros were in fact Mexican, not Puerto Rican by way of New York.

On the morning of January 15, 1974, he'd driven his wife to work, because she didn't like to drive on the snow and ice. On the way back he'd seen the Vista Cruiser parked in the open garage, which indicated to him that Julie was probably alone. He'd parked his own car some distance away, then walked to the Otero house, arriving around 8:30 A.M. or just a little after. He had stuffed the tools of his "hit kit" into his coat pockets, and had then jumped over the fence.

Now, in the aftermath of the murders—he hadn't expected to find Joe there, but had dealt with that unforeseen problem—he felt himself suffused with pride. He was the killer, the one everyone was talking about. He, and he alone—no one would ever suspect him.

A week after the murders, after his initial headache and panic, the killer ran the events of the killings back through his mind, savoring the pictures they formed there. He made a new series of notes, recalling the clothing each victim wore, and how he had tied them up. The notes were very detailed, almost photographic in their descriptiveness. He dated them: January 22, 1974. Then he began to refine them. He wanted to tell his story in his own way. He began to type:

DEATH ON A COLD JANUARY MORNING, he headed the document. Written in the third person, the killer was referred to as "Rex." It was larded with misspellings and typos.

> He knew the family left the house approximately 8:45, and they would walk out [to] the car and leave for school and in approximately seven mintue [sic] the lady, Julie, would return home . . . He had earily [sic] in the week, saw them leave for school one day; He thought to himself, say this maybe it [sic]. A perfect set up; a house on the corner, a garage set off from the house, a fenced yard, a large sapce [sic] from nearby neighbor [sic] house, especially the back door . . .

The killer went on to describe in graphic detail almost everything that had happened in the Otero house that morning. "Rex," it turned out, had an idea of what each of the dead Oteros would be doing in the hereafter. In what he called his "Afterlife Concept of Victim," "Rex" envisioned that Joe Otero would serve him as a bodyguard, Julie would bathe him and be his female servant, Joey would be a boy servant and "male sex toy," while Josie would be his main sexual object, whom he would use for bondage and sadistic sex.

"SBT," "Rex" noted—an abbreviation for "Sparky Big Time," meaning an erection.

At the end he dated it: February 3, 1974, the first chapter of what would eventually become his "book."

5:

Foreigners

Wichita's detectives of 1974 were all veterans of crime in the city. Holdovers from an era when detectives wore fedoras, white shirts and narrow ties, and packed snub-nosed .38s on their belts, rather than the heavier armament of today, they tended to see crime as it had been in the 1950s and 1960s. Murders almost always had a reason—a domestic dispute, a robbery gone bad, a sexual aberration—these they were used to. There was almost always a reason for deadly violence, they reasoned; the name of the detective game was to find it. If you could find a reason, you were more than halfway toward finding the culprit.

But the Otero murders didn't seem to have a reason. It was, as Hannon had put it, too bizarre to fit into any of the usual categories.

Confronted with what appeared to be mixed motives—violence targeting Joe Otero for some purpose, and sex—Hannon assigned ten teams of two detectives each to run down the possibilities. One group began digging into Joe Otero's history, and the other rounded up all the usual suspects—the sex offenders, that is.

Hannon himself undertook some of the work regarding Joe Otero. By February 1974, Hannon and his chief of homicide investigators, Bill Cornwell, went first to Puerto Rico, and then to Panama, looking for leads that might explain what had happened to the Oteros. On the way to Puerto Rico, according to Beattie, they were stopped by U.S. Customs officers, who had found a number of grisly crime-scene photographs in their briefcases. A delay ensued while the Customs people verified that Hannon and Cornwell really were police officers, not some hired killers bringing proof of their mainland success back to Puerto Rico.

Once they finally reached the island, the FBI escorted them everywhere. There they interviewed Joe Otero's mother and father, along with about two dozen others. But nothing seemed to shed any light on what had happened; Joe and Julie Otero seemed to have no sinister connections.

Hannon and Cornwell soon moved on to Panama. This time it was the Air Force escorting them. At first the Panamanian authorities were reluctant to cooperate, according to Beattie, but eventually Hannon and Cornwell were able to interview a number of people who had known the Oteros. The country was then under the control of Omar Torrijos, the leftist dictator. In fact, Hannon and Cornwell discovered that Joe Otero had actually performed maintenance on General Torrijos' personal aircraft. Was this pertinent? Maybe, maybe not. Seen from one perspective, it could only indicate that Torrijos didn't fully trust his own mechanics—with a U.S. Air Force mechanic, at least his survivors would know who to blame if the plane crashed with him aboard. (In a coincidence, General Torrijos did die in an airplane crash some seven years later.)

Hannon and Cornwell also interviewed a number of people who told of financial conflicts Joe Otero had had with others in Panama. These seemed to revolve around disputes over goods imported by air from South America. Again the drug theory surfaced, but there didn't seem to be any substance to it. Efforts were made to track the former Otero business associates down; all of them, it appeared, were now in the United States. But when these were interviewed by Wichita police, there seemed to be no reasonable connection between them and the murders.

The rational motive for the murders seemed to be fading fast. There just wasn't anything there. Usually, when an investigator pursues a theory of a crime, as additional information is developed, the indicator needle steadies on one suspect, one direction. That wasn't happening with the probe into Joe Otero's past. After six days in Panama, Hannon and Cornwell came back to Wichita, as mystified as they had been when they started out. Their needle was still spinning wildly.

Eventually, as February 1974 turned into March and then April, one Wichita detective came up with a novel theory of the murders. He thought that it was possible that Joe Otero had murdered his own family, then had tied himself up, intending to be discovered as a "victim," but had accidentally suffocated himself with the plastic bag.

Well, it was a neat theory—it disposed of the crime and the perpetrator as well as the victims. That way the case could be closed. But it was preposterous, and that anyone could put such a notion forward even semiseriously indicated just how bereft of ideas everyone was.

Hannon decided to go back to old-fashioned police work. He had an idea that an unidentified fingerprint found on the chair in the doorway to the room where Joey had died might belong to the killer. He ordered that every person arrested in Wichita from then on be fingerprinted; it's astonishing to us today that, in those days, not every arrestee was routinely fingerprinted in Wichita, but that's the way it was then. Sooner or later, Hannon hoped, the stray print would be matched to someone, and then they would find their killer.

But the killer wasn't worried. Although he didn't know about the print, he wouldn't have cared anyway. He'd worn gloves throughout, so no fingerprint could match

6:

"PJ Lights Out"

By early April of 1974, the murder of the Otero family had receded somewhat from the public consciousness. Whatever had happened, it seemed to be some sort of aberration. When people thought about the murders, there was sort of an unconscious dismissal—this was something that happened in places like Los Angeles or New York or San Francisco. It was straight out of *Helter Skelter* or the Zodiac murders. As Hannon kept insisting, it was too bizarre for Wichita.

The year 1974 was something of a cultural break point in the United States—a lot of institutions were on the move, in one way or another. The war in Viet Nam was over, the soldiers had come home; Richard Nixon was in dire trouble over Watergate and soon Gerald Ford would tell the country he was "a Ford, not a Lincoln"; recreational drugs, among them cocaine, were being fashionably consumed by ever larger numbers of young people. Musical styles had shifted significantly into the electronic spectrum. Men's hair was long, mustaches and sideburns were in, bellbottoms flared. Gas prices shot upward, the dollar was devalued, and on television, Archie Bunker and his family were acting out the new divide.

On April 4, 1974, the killer had some time off from his classes in the criminal justice program at Wichita State. He had previously noticed a 21-year-old blond woman named Kathryn Bright enter her small frame house on East 13th Street in east Wichita, not far from the university.

The killer knew virtually nothing about Kathy Bright—not her age, or the fact that she worked at Coleman, or that she was bright and funny and loved by her family, or what she wanted from her life.

"She fit the profile," the killer said later. In other words, she had fired his lust, triggered off his desire to tie a woman up and kill her. He began planning his attack—where he would park, what his approach would be. He envisioned getting the woman—he certainly didn't know her by name—alone in the small house. He selected a date, preparing his "hit kit" with only a few white cords, rather than the full complement he'd had at the Otero house. He practiced his story. He would pretend to be a student, and come to her door with books in his hands, and convince her to let him in. Once inside, he would pull out his gun and make her do what he wanted.

On the morning of April 4, the killer made his way to Kathy Bright's house. Standing on the small wooden porch, he knocked on the door. There was no one home.

Maybe this is better, the killer thought. *Maybe I can break in.* That way he could surprise the young woman, which would be something of a thrill in itself.

Casting a quick glance around to make sure he wasn't being observed, the killer went to the rear of the house. He tried the back door, but it was locked. He punched his way through a screen door, then a glass window in the rear door to let himself in. Then he thought, *That was dumb, because if she comes in the back door, she's going to run, she's not even going to come in the house, because a smart person wouldn't.* Once the victim noticed the glass, the killer thought, she'd run away.

"So I swept the glass up," he said later. Whatever had happened to the books—if indeed he'd really had any—was never made clear.

After he'd finished that, he searched the house, going through dressers, looking for scarves, nylon stockings, belts, anything he could use to tie someone up. Eventually, after accidentally firing his .22-caliber pistol while playing with it, he hid in a closet in one of the bedrooms, making a comfortable place to sit on a pile of clothing.

About half-past noon he heard the front door open and someone entering. He emerged from the closet and went out into the living room with his .22-caliber automatic out. He was dismayed to see that Kathy Bright was not alone. She was with a young man. This was not what he had fantasized. He did not know that the young man was Kathy Bright's younger brother, Kevin, 19 years old. Both brother and sister were much smaller than the killer, who towered over them and outweighed them both by about 70 pounds.

He pointed his gun at them.

"I'm wanted in California," he said. "They have posters out on me. I won't hurt you if you cooperate. I need a car, I need some food, I need some money. I need to get to New York." This is similar to what he'd also told the Oteros, and it seemed to work to calm his victims down, probably because they believed that as soon as he had money and a car, he'd leave. But he was lying.

He herded the couple into a bedroom with his pistol. He ordered Kevin to tie Kathy's hands behind her back and her feet together, using articles of clothing. Then he made Kevin Bright get on the floor, and using more articles of clothing, tied his hands and feet to the bedposts. He'd already decided not to use the same pre-cut venetian blind cord that he'd used for the Oteros—he didn't want the police to link this "hit" to the earlier one.

That done, he moved Kathy to another bedroom. He found a chair and tied her to it, again using some of the nylon stockings he'd found in the house. He went back to the first bedroom, turning on a stereo he saw in a corner of the living room to make enough noise to drown out what he meant to do to Kevin. He intended to strangle him first so he could have more time with Kathy.

As the killer began to strangle Kevin with a nylon stocking, Kevin began to violently resist. Somehow he was able to loosen his feet, which gave him leverage to throw the killer off him. The next thing the killer knew, Kevin had managed to free his hands, too. Both men stood up, glaring at each other. The killer pulled out his .22, and Kevin made a grab for it. With both men's hands on the weapon, Kevin thought he'd been able to pull the trigger twice, but it didn't go off. At that point, the killer pulled the gun away and shot Kevin once in the forehead. Kevin fell to the floor. The killer assumed he was dead.

In the other bedroom Kathy had heard the shot.

"What's going on, what have you done to my brother?" she called out.

The killer returned to Kathy and tried to calm her. "I had to shoot him," he said, "but I just wounded him, he'll be okay. As soon as I get out of here, I'll call the cops. He'll be okay."

Kathy didn't believe him and started to struggle hard against her bindings. The killer could see she wasn't going to be able to get loose, so he left her and went back to make sure that Kevin really was dead. But as soon as he came into the bedroom, Kevin jumped to his feet and began to wrestle with him. At one point Kevin got his finger on the trigger of a .357 magnum pistol the killer had in a shoulder holster, and the killer thought he was going to be killed himself. Backing away from Kevin, the killer pulled his .22 once more and shot him again, this time in the lip just below the nose. Kevin went down a second time.

By this point Kathy was screaming in the other room. The killer went back to her and tried to strangle her, but it was harder than he'd bargained for. Somehow, Kathy got loose from the chair and began to fight with him. The killer hit her several times, trying to knock her to the floor, but Kathy fought back, hard. He realized he wasn't going to be able to strangle her, or to do any of the things he'd fantasized about. At that moment he heard a side door slam and he realized that Kevin was still not dead, that he'd fled the house looking for help. He saw Kevin running down the street, trying to get someone's attention.

This is all going wrong, the killer thought. *The cops are going to be coming in here any minute. I've got to get out of here.*

He pulled both of his knives and began to slash and stab at Kathy, who fell to the floor, bleeding profusely. The blood splashed all over the killer's shoes and the lower part of his clothing.

He left the house through the back door; as he had before with the Oteros, he had made certain to find the keys to the victims' vehicle as soon as he had them tied up. He wanted "a backup plan" in case he had to make a quick getaway. He got behind the wheel of Kathy's car in the driveway, but couldn't get it to start. There was a pickup truck nearby, apparently belonging to Kevin. The killer tried that, but couldn't get it started either.

By now on the edge of panic, the killer began running up the street toward the university, where he'd left his own car. He wanted to get away from the scene as fast as he could.

Across the street, Kevin encountered William Williams and Edward Bell, who happened to be passing by.

"I've been shot," he told them, and it was obvious he had, with the blood streaming from his lip and his forehead. "There's a guy in the house doing a number on my sister, please help me."

Bell and Williams now drove Kevin to a hospital about a mile away, while the proprietors of a nearby business called the police. Because of a mix-up of the police emergency dispatcher, the first officer was sent to the business that had reported the alarm. By the time Patrolman Dennis Landon got things straightened out, an ambulance had been dispatched to the correct address, Kathy Bright's house on 13th Street.

Landon got there before the ambulance. He knocked on the screen door. No one answered. The front door behind the screen was open, so Landon peered inside. He saw a young woman lying on the floor deeper inside the house. It appeared to Landon that she was lying in a large pool of blood. He went in.

Kathy Bright was lying on her side outside one of the bedrooms, clutching a telephone in her hand. She was barely conscious. Landon turned her over to see where she had been hurt.

"What happened?" Landon asked, but Kathy wasn't able to say anything. She pulled up her blouse. Landon thought he could see at least three knife wounds to her stomach.

"Who did this?" Landon asked.

"Don't know," Kathy rasped. "Don't know him."

"What's your name?"

"Kathy . . . Bright?"

"How old are you?"

"Twenty-one . . ." she managed to say, and fainted.

Landon went to the kitchen and got a damp cloth to staunch her wounds. As he applied the cloth he noticed that a blue scarf was tied around her neck, along with a thin cord. She was holding a white rag in her right hand—probably something that had been used as a gag. A nylon had been tied around her ankles.

"Can't breathe," Kathy said, regaining consciousness for a moment. She wanted Landon to cut her legs free, so he used his pocket knife to cut the stocking. Landon realized that Kathy was in shock, so he elevated her legs. Another patrol officer, Ray Fletcher, now arrived. He and Landon tried to make Kathy comfortable, and assured her she'd be all right, that an ambulance was on its way. Both officers noticed that her face was severely bruised, as if she had been pistol-whipped. Blood was everywhere.

Landon noticed that Kathy's pupils did not react to stimuli—a sign of severe shock. She grabbed at Fletcher's arm.

"I can't breathe," she said. "Help me."

Both officers noticed that Kathy's body was cold and clammy, and that she was becoming blue, a sign that possibly one or both of her lungs had collapsed, either directly from wounds, or shock from the loss of blood pressure.

The ambulance finally arrived and took Kathy to the same hospital that was treating Kevin for his gunshot wounds.

After Kathy had been rushed away to the hospital, Landon and Fletcher looked through the house. They noticed that Kathy's purse had been upended, and its contents strewn across the floor, somewhat reminiscent of the Otero house. The dressers had been tossed, as in the Otero house. They looked at the telephone, the one that Kathy had been clutching when Landon arrived. The line, they saw, had been disconnected from the wall. Kathy had tried and tried to get help on the telephone, but no one had answered because the attacker had torn it out when he first entered the house.

At the hospital, Wichita Police Officer Ron Davenport interviewed Kevin. When he'd been brought into the hospital, a length of white cord was still around his neck. Davenport checked on Kathy—he learned that a length of white cord had been found around her neck, too. Her larynx had been broken.

Davenport watched as the emergency physicians tried to save Kathy's life. It appeared that she'd been stabbed not three times, but eleven—three times in the stomach, eight times in the back.

"Help me!" Davenport heard her gasp out in the emergency room. She died in surgery an hour later.

Davenport, two other police officers, and a hospital security official interviewed Kevin in the emergency room.

"Who did this?" one of the cops asked.

Kevin said he didn't know the man, but that just before he'd begun to strangle him, he had asked him if they hadn't seen each other before "at the university."

The assailant, Kevin now said, was a white man, about five-foot-ten, stocky in build, with dark brown hair and a mustache that curled around the corners of his mouth. He looked to be about 25 years old, and seemed to be wearing some sort of uniform. Kevin thought he'd been wearing a black stocking cap, an orange shirt and an orange jacket.

At one point, police showed Kevin a photo array of possible suspects. Kevin picked out one of the pictures—as it happened, a man with a violent psychiatric past who lived not too far from the Otero house. Like Julie and Kathy, the man also worked at Coleman.

Kevin spent two weeks in the hospital recovering from his wounds. A few days after his release from the hospital, detectives took him to one of the Coleman facilities in the city to observe employees coming and going at a shift change. Kevin picked out the same man he'd pinpointed from the photo array.

From that point forward, the Coleman worker became Wichita detectives' prime suspect. Interviewed, he denied committing the crimes. And there was not a shred of physical evidence capable of giving his story the lie—no blood, no hairs and no fibers, and his fingerprint did not match the stray found on the Otero chair. Nevertheless, the detectives were convinced that the circumstantial evidence was very solid. They asked the Sedgwick County District Attorney's Office to file murder charges against the Coleman worker. District Attorney Keith Sanborn declined. By this time, the police later said, Kevin had changed his mind about his description of the killer. They said he thought that the attacker had been possibly "Oriental" or "Mexican."

If so, here was another possible link to the Oteros: a swarthy or dark complexion, "foreign extraction," i.e., not a real Wichitan. Kevin's change in the description of the assailant from "white" to "Oriental" or "Mexican" caused the district attorney's office to doubt that it could get a conviction. Sanborn said a defense lawyer would destroy the credibility of Kevin's eyewitness testimony because of the variance in his description, and suggest that his identification had been tainted by police overzealousness.

Nevertheless, from the spring of 1974 forward, many Wichita police officers familiar with the murders considered the Coleman worker to be the most likely perpetrator. They persisted in that belief all the way up until the time, thirty-one years later, that they were proven wrong. If nothing else, this demonstrates one of the most persistent pitfalls of investigating serial murder—"tunnel vision," the experts call it, when something seems so right that it has to be true, even when it's not; blinding certainty, in other words.

Despite the real killer's effort to make the Bright crime scene look different from the Otero scene, there were some similarities that suggested they were linked. First, in both cases, the description of the suspect was fairly consistent—tall, dark-haired, dark-complexioned, possibly of "foreign extraction." Second, there were the attempted strangulations of both sexes—that in itself was unusual. There was the compelling fact that both adult women worked at Coleman. There were the white cords, found in both places. There was the use of a gun, inferred in the Otero case, proven in the Bright case. There was the disablement of the telephone line—cut in Otero, yanked out at Bright. There was the separation of victims into different rooms.

But there were also differences, some of them significant. First, Kathy Bright had been savagely, almost frantically stabbed, not a factor at the Otero scene. The outside telephone line had not been cut. The killer had not brought as many pre-cut cords with him, or plastic bags. He had broken in at Bright's, but seemed to have been willingly admitted at the Oteros'. Most important, there was no semen found at the Bright house. The differences and the similarities seemed to cancel each other out, leaving investigators—where?

7:

BTK Talks

Despite his initial panic, the killer had made his escape from the Bright house without attracting any undue attention. By the time he'd reached his car near the university, he was breathing almost normally. He'd driven back to his house, stripped off his bloody clothes and shoes, and cleaned up. He'd wadded the clothes up, then took them and the gun over to his parents' house, a short distance away. There he'd gone down into the basement, the place of his most intense fantasies, and hid the incriminating items. "Dad had an old saw box with sawdust," he said later. "I put my gun in there." Then he'd rushed home to greet his wife, who was just coming home from her job. He took great pleasure in being able to seem like nothing had happened—it was his ability to "compartmentalize," as he put it, one of the signal traits of psychopaths and spies, as John le Carré has so ably demonstrated in his fiction.

The killer was also at work on his own fiction: A few weeks after murdering Kathy Bright and attempting to murder her brother, he was back at his typewriter. This time the chapter was headed A DEATH IN APRIL. Once again "Rex" described his depredations in graphic detail—seven pages altogether, again splattered with misspellings, typos and ungrammatical language. Like his first chapter, he stashed it away in a place where no one could find it. He knew it wasn't ready for publication quite yet; he had to prepare the world for his debut first.

• • •

After the murder of Kathy Bright, and the correct decision of the district attorney's office not to prosecute the wrong man on the circumstantial evidence, the Otero and Bright murder cases settled into something of a holding pattern—the police holding the view that the Coleman worker was "the guy," and the district attorney holding out for more evidence. The worst thing that could happen would be to charge the Coleman worker with the crimes, then see him acquitted for lack of evidence. If he actually was "the guy," that would keep the authorities from ever charging him with the murders again, because of double jeopardy, or so the DA's office reasoned, and tried to explain to the frustrated police.

By this point, the police department itself was split—while some of the professional investigators believed in the Coleman worker, others among the higher-ups in the department were increasingly convinced that the two cases were unrelated, and more important, that they were not the deeds of any local residents, but committed by some criminal of "foreign extraction," who'd come to town, killed, and then left. After all, there was the story the "swarthy" killer had told Kevin Bright—that he was a wanted man, that he needed to get to New York. It seemed like that was just what it was—a desperate man looking for someone to rob. Of course, it didn't really explain why such a desperate out-of-towner would have targeted Kathryn Bright, of all people, who hardly lived on the beaten track; and it certainly didn't explain why he'd tried to strangle both Brights, rather than simply take their money and one of their cars and get out of town as fast as he could. Nor did it explain the "university" remark to Kevin.

And Hannon, for one, was still convinced that the solution to at least the Otero murders lay in learning whatever was hidden in Joe Otero's past. He still believed that there had to be a foreign connection. Why else would four members of a family, living in Wichita for only nine weeks, have been tortured and killed? It made far more sense to assume that the deaths were connected somehow with Joe's previous life in New York or Puerto Rico or, most likely, Panama. He had Charlie Otero's story about the night the lights went out and Joe's nervousness as evidence for this gut instinct.

Still, that didn't keep the Wichita police from continuing to work leads to the third leg of their stool—the usual suspects, the area's sex offenders. By the end of the summer, police had interviewed nearly 800 people in connection with the Otero murders, a great many of them because of records for sex offenses like peeping or flashing, as well as more violent crimes.

Then, in early October, the believers in the sex pervert theory of the Otero murder case had their hopes boosted by the arrest of a youth with a documented history of mental problems; an accusation had been made that he had molested a 5-year-old girl. According to Beattie—still a high schooler at the time—the story later circulated that the youth had been apprehended while trying to have intercourse with a duck in the front seat of a car. The duck's outrage at this unnatural act attracted the attention of the patrolling police. Checking, the patrol officer soon learned of the other allegation about the 5-year-old, and the youth was brought in for questioning.

Grilling this disturbed young man elicited some accurate information about the Otero killings. One thing led to another, and before the police knew it, they had a complete confession to the murders. But it was obvious that the suspect could hardly have committed the four crimes on his own—they were far too complicated for the young man's mental abilities. Under prodding, he gave up the names of two others who he said had assisted in the Otero killings—a brother and a cousin. As it happened, the young man's brother was in a psychiatric hospital after having attempted suicide. Detectives hustled over to the hospital, and sure enough, received a similar confession.

Police have long known that highly publicized crimes often stimulate the deranged to take the blame. Although police normally are overjoyed to get a confession, in such highly publicized situations, they do their best to treat the admissions with bored skepticism.

"Prove it," they should say. "Prove that you were the one who did it, because otherwise, I won't believe you." In that way, the eager confessor is forced to provide details of the crime that only the perpetrator would know—details never published, but known to the police. "How did you get into the house? What did you do in the basement? What was on the kitchen table?" Under this sort of skepticism, the false confessor is soon exposed; the real danger is that the investigator, so eager to solve the case, may inadvertently or even intentionally provide the answers to the false confessor in an effort to clear the case.

In the case of the duck lover, his brother and his cousin, the tales of the three men soon began to conflict in their details. Still, there was enough smoke in their respective stories to convince the police to book them, at least in mental health facilities, until things could get sorted out. The news of the arrests in the Otero case made its way to the *Eagle*, and was published in the edition of October 17, 1974. A police spokesman said if the stories stood up, the police would ask the DA to charge the batty trio for the Otero murders.

Reading this, or possibly seeing it on television, galvanized the real killer. This he could not allow—he could *not* permit three mental defectives to get the credit for *his* murders. He had to set the record straight.

On October 22, he made a telephone call to the *Eagle*'s Secret Witness tip line.

"Listen and listen good," he said, "because I'm not going to repeat it."

He told Don Granger, the *Eagle* columnist who managed the Secret Witness line, to go to the Wichita Public Library on Main Street, directly across from the police station. Granger should go to a section containing a particular engineering textbook to find an important message from the Oteros' killer.

Granger called Chief Hannon.

Hannon sent Detective Bernie Drowatsky to the library to check the story out. Finding the correct book, Drowatsky removed a typewritten letter addressed to the newspaper's Secret Witness Program.

Headed OTERO CASE, the letter began:

> I write this letter to you for the sake of the tax payer [sic] as well as your time. Those three dude [sic] you have in custody are just talking to get publicity for the Otero murders. They know nothing at all. I did it by myself and with no ones [sic] help. There has been no talk either. Let's put it straight . . .

And with that, the letter writer proceeded to describe exactly how each of the Oteros was murdered and where in the house they had died.

So specific was this information that some detectives believed that the person who wrote it had to have taken photographs of the scenes. It was simply too detailed. Some detectives pointed out that certain particulars about the master bedroom were a little off. But then, the crime scene had been slightly disarranged by the fruitless resuscitation efforts of Charlie, Carmen and Danny, so maybe the description represented how things were before the teenagers had discovered the appalling scene. Yet others argued that the writer had made mistakes in his description of some of the clothing worn by the victims—the colors or patterns were wrong in some cases, which suggested that the writer hadn't actually been at the scene, only that it had been described to him, with slight inaccuracies.

The letter writer noted that Joe's watch had been taken. That certainly had never been publicized. "I needed one, so I took it," the letter writer said. "Runsgood.[sic]"

The letter had two concluding paragraphs:

> I'm sorry this happen [sic] to society. They are the ones who suffer the most [sic]. It hard to control myself. You probably call me 'psychotic with sexual perversion hang-up.' When this monster enter [sic] my brain I will never know. But, it here to stay. How does one cure himself? If you ask for help, that you have killed four people they will laugh or hit the panic button and call the cops.
>
> I can't stop it so the monster goes on, and hurt [sic] me as well as society. Society can be thankful that there are ways for people like me to relieve myself at time by day dreams of some victims being torture [sic] and being mine. It [sic] a big complicated game my friend of the monster play [sic] putting victims number down, follow them, checking up on them, waiting in the dark, waiting, waiting . . . the pressure is great and sometimes he run [sic] the game to his liking. Maybe you can stop him. I can't. He has already chosen his next victim or victims. I don't know who they are yet. The next day after I read the paper, I will know, but it to [sic] late. Good luck hunting.
>
> YOURS, TRULY GUILTILY [sic]
>
> P.S. Since sex criminals do not change their M.O. or by nature cannot do so, I will not change

> mine. The code words for me will be . . . bind them, toture [sic] them, kill them, B.T.K., you see he [sic] at it again. They will be on the next victim.

From the moment Drowatsky brought this letter back across the street to the police station, there was ferocious controversy about it. Hannon, still clinging to his international intrigue angle, was convinced the communication was a hoax. So, too, was Deputy Chief Jack Bruce. Bruce, in fact, was convinced it had to be the work of two known pranksters serving with "the lab boys." He confronted them, telling them everyone enjoyed a good joke, but this was going too far. The pranksters indignantly denied concocting the letter.

Still others, particularly some in the department's homicide squad, took the letter quite seriously. The level of detail about how the victims had died, and where in the house, meant that it had to be someone who'd been there or who had seen pictures of it, and if it wasn't one of the "lab boys," who else could it be but the real killer? Some also noted something interesting: despite the possible links to the Bright murder, the killer didn't claim *that* one, which seemed to indicate that it was not connected. After all, if the killer was going to confess to the Otero murders, why wouldn't he also admit the Bright murder, if he'd committed that one as well? In a perverse way, this actually added to the letter's authenticity, in some minds. Wouldn't it make him look even more frightening—get him even more publicity?

That, it seemed clear to most, had to be the killer's purpose in leaving the letter for *Eagle* columnist Granger—to get publicity for himself and his crimes, and especially, to make sure that the three half-wits in custody didn't get it instead. That was why he'd sent the newspaper man to get the letter, rather than calling the police themselves.

Now another debate blew up about that very issue—publicity. Some thought the letter should be published, or otherwise released to the public, but the higher-ups among the police were adamant that it remain secret. If the letter *was* legitimate, it represented the first possible lead to the killer. And the killer seemed to be indicating that he was struggling against the impulse to commit more murders, referring to the killings as the work of a "monster," something outside himself which had invaded him. Maybe, just maybe, if contact could be made, the person who wrote the letter could be identified, and if he were in fact the killer, maybe he could be stopped before he killed anyone else.

What would happen if the letter were released to the public? No one knew. It might scare the killer back into hiding, if it really was from the killer. It might excite him so much he'd go right out and kill again, and as soon as possible. It would certainly crank up the crackpots, at least some of whom would use the facts in the letter to claim *they* were the killer; and it might even stimulate some crafty soul who wanted to kill, to kill in such a way as to make the police think it was BTK.

No, to the police, the downside of publicizing the letter was much greater than the slim upside that someone might recognize the writer's language, style or choice of words. This wasn't some sort of English composition class, for Pete's sake, the police told themselves. This was serious. This was *murder*.

The *Eagle* was willing to be compliant with the apprehensions of the police brain trust—if the top cops said to keep it quiet, the newspaper would play ball. Still, some effort had to be made to induce the letter writer to resume the contact. But a soft approach was in order.

Two days after the letter appeared, a personal ad appeared in the newspaper. It ran for four days:

BTK
HELP IS AVAILABLE.
CALL [a telephone number maintained by the police] BEFORE 10 P.M.

For four days, police waited by the telephone. No one called.

Finally, at the end of October, the police upped the ante slightly. They authorized Don Granger to try to contact the letter writer through his column. On Halloween of 1974, Granger told his readers that the Wichita police had been trying to make contact with "a man who has important information on the Otero murder case—a man who needs help badly."

Granger did not disclose that a detailed letter about the Otero murders had been placed in a book at the public library, or that the letter writer had essentially said he would kill again. But he published his home telephone number in the column, in an effort to convince the letter writer that he could communicate again with safety. "There really is a B.T.K.," Granger wrote, implying that the initials represented the killer's given names. But no one called, that is, no one who really knew anything about either the murders or the letter writer. Police staked out the library, thinking that maybe someone resembling the description of the man of "foreign extraction" might appear there to plant another communication, but this surveillance was unfruitful.

Then there was another murder.

8:
Sunlight

Three weeks after the letter appeared in the library book, 23-year-old Sherry Baker was found dead in her small house on New York Street in north central Wichita, a little less than three miles west of the Otero house and two miles southwest of the Bright house. Found face down on the living room floor and dressed only in a negligee and panties, her hands were bound behind her back with coiled telephone line. As Josie Otero had been, she was gagged with a portion of a torn towel. She had been stabbed at least seventy times, her throat had been cut, and a pair of scissors had been thrust into the rear of her head, breaking off one of the blades. It appeared that the house had been tossed, and a window jimmied to gain entrance. She was a student at WSU. And, as Beattie learned much later, her house was one block away from the Coleman human resources department—the firm's hiring facility.

Sherry's murder was heavily covered by the newspaper and the broadcast outlets in Wichita. The possible parallels to the Otero and Bright murders seemed obvious to the police: Coleman, hands tied behind the back, gagged with a strip torn from a towel, incapacitated telephone, frantic stabbing as in the case of Kathy Bright, possible sexual motive, forcible entry to the dwelling. Again, there was no semen. And there was a possible "New York" angle: Kevin Bright had said that Kathy's killer had told them he was on his way to "New York." Now there was a victim on New York Street. Was that just a coincidence?

Chief Hannon realized that plumbing the mental depths of someone capable of committing such crimes—if indeed they were all connected—was a little out of the police line of expertise, especially when the subject was someone they had never seen or talked to. He decided some expert help was called for. As it happened, the mayor of Wichita in 1974 was Dr. Garry Porter, a psychiatrist. Porter was well acquainted with a psychologist who also practiced in his building, Dr. Samuel Harrell. Harrell was not only a clinical psychologist, he had also been a professional homicide investigator in prior years when he worked for the U.S. Air Force's Office of Special Investigations while serving as a military policeman.

The police provided Harrell with copies of all their reports, including autopsy findings, as well as photographs of the crime scenes. They also gave him the letter from the library, and one more thing—a pen-and-ink drawing of a woman with a pair of scissors protruding from her skull. Just where this drawing came from was not made clear to Harrell. Years later, to Beattie, he recalled that it came with the other materials, but was contained in a separate envelope.

After sifting through the police reports and crime-scene photographs, Harrell formed some definite impressions of the person or persons who had killed the Oteros. Whoever did it, Harrell theorized, was someone who took erotic pleasure in tying people up; and if the person or persons followed the pattern he was thinking of, they would have enjoyed tying themselves up as well.

Harrell was particularly reminded of a notorious case that had taken place in Los Angeles in the late 1950s. There, a similar bondage-style killer named Harvey Glatman had killed three women in 1957 and 1958, after first hiring them as models to pose for him. A television repairman in real life, Glatman had convinced the women that he was a professional photographer on assignment for detective magazines. He convinced his victims to come to his house to pose. When they arrived, he pulled a gun, then tied them up. Once the victim was restrained, Glatman raped them, photographed them, then took them out to the desert, assaulted them again, and then capped off the nightmare by strangling them. He again took pictures of them after they were dead. He was caught when one of his victims managed to escape, even though Glatman shot her in the leg.

"I used the same five-foot length of sash cord for all three," Glatman said of his victims after his arrest. "I kept it in my car with the gun. I made them lie on their stomachs. Then I tied their ankles together, looped the end of the cord around their necks and pulled until they were dead."

Glatman had an overbearing, controlling mother who nevertheless doted on her son; he also had an addiction to auto-erotic hanging that had begun very early in his life. His murders made him very proud of himself, and after his apprehension, he relished describing the most horrific details. He was executed in the gas chamber at San Quentin on August 18, 1959—a little more than a year after his arrest.

From the Otero crime scene, Harrell deduced that the killer, like Glatman, was powerfully addicted to erotic bondage. That in turn suggested to Harrell that, like Glatman, the killer had a long history of auto-erotic self-bondage and hanging. Harrell agreed with Hannon that it was more likely there were two killers rather than one; and if that were the case, it was very likely that one person would be the dominant personality, telling the other what to do. The chances were very good, if there were two killers, that the pair had a long-term relationship that involved tying each other up before they had branched out to strangers. If it turned out that there was just one killer, the chances were very good that the Oteros were not his first victims—the scene was too organized, too practiced for it to be a first attempt.

Harrell also thought the library letter was a genuine communication from the killer, not some prank by someone in the know. The letter had some of the self-aggrandizement of the Glatman confession, although with not quite the same boastfulness. Given the eyewitness descriptions of the man seen around the Otero house—that is, someone 25 to 30 years old—it was possible that the Otero killer or killers may have been old enough to have had familiarity with Glatman's story, which was, ironically, prominently featured in detective magazines of the era after his apprehension. If the killer or killers were at the upper end of the age range, this would mean he or they would have been 15 or 16 years old at the time of Glatman's execution—a particularly susceptible age for such imagery.

As for the scissors drawing, Harrell concluded that it had *not* been made by the same person or persons involved in the Otero murders. Based on the number of stab wounds Sherry Baker had sustained, some of them clearly after death, it was most likely that her killer was someone who knew her very well. Such a stabbing frenzy, Harrell knew, usually came from some deep, interpersonal rage.

What to do? Harrell suggested to Hannon that the detectives try to follow up on the bondage fetish so obviously present in the Otero case. They might begin by offering a reward to prostitutes to tip the names of any clients who preferred bondage; they should also attempt to identify any publications circulated in the Wichita area that featured bondage imagery; and last, they should place ads in these publications in an attempt to lure the Otero killer or killers into making contact.

According to Harrell, Chief Hannon rejected these recommendations. He didn't agree with Harrell that the letter was a legitimate communication from the killer; he still thought it was a hoax. He could just envision himself trying to explain to the city council the reason that his police department had used tax dollars to pay for advertisements in bondage publications, and why it had subscribed to same.

Eventually, according to Beattie, roughly thirty Wichita-area psychologists and psychiatrists reviewed the library letter. It appeared that many also copied it. Some agreed with Hannon: the letter was a hoax. Others agreed with Harrell: the letter was the real deal. Some thought the letter should remain secret, while others thought it should be published. Some, in fact, warned that the letter should be made public to prevent the killer from killing again. But psychological analysis and profiling is like intelligence analysis in the foreign policy field: often the most accurate assessments are on the extremes of possibility, not in the consensus middle. In the center, there's usually too much qualification, too much hedging, to produce anything of real value.

But the letter, suppressed by the *Eagle* at the request of the police, and analyzed and overanalyzed by the shrinks, turned out to have a life of its own. With so many people having copies of it, it was only a matter of time before it leaked.

That happened in the first week of December 1974, when a copy of the library communication, with its dreadful detail of just what had happened at the Otero house, and its discussion of "monsters" and more murders, came to the attention of Cathy Henkel, a writer for the Wichita *Sun*. The *Sun* was an alternative news weekly, of the type that was then springing up all around the country, in the mold of *The Village Voice*, or the *Chicago Reader*. It was underwritten by the owners of KAKE-TV, the city's oldest television broadcasting company.

Henkel obtained a copy of the library letter, and was told by someone—just who remains a journalistic secret kept by Henkel ever since—that unless the writer of the letter got his due public notice, he would kill again. Henkel wrote a classic turn-the-tables-on-the-establishment-press story that publicly revealed much of the letter's content, and then proceeded to examine the murder of Kathy Bright, and the attempted murder of Kevin Bright and the Coleman supervisor who had been shot during the supposed robbery, and made the link: Coleman for Julie Otero, Coleman for Kathy Bright, Coleman for the wounded supervisor. It also mentioned the dope-loaded airplane that had crashed on its way to Wichita from Puerto Rico, and something of Joe Otero's financial conflicts with people in Panama.

Before writing the story, Henkel met with Chief Hannon, who was clearly upset that the letter was about to be made public.

"Chief Hannon was so angry, so red-faced, that the temple on the side of his forehead was visibly pounding," she later told Beattie.

"Hannon never told me not to publish the letter," she also recalled. "He was too much in shock; just wanted me out of his office as fast as he could so he could figure out their next step. I waited to talk to him until the day we went to press (we were a weekly, remember), so there wasn't much time . . ."

Henkel interviewed Wichita Police Major Bill Cornwell, who told her that the drug angle had been investigated and discounted, and that Joe Otero's financial conflicts were unavailing as an investigative lead. As for the possible Coleman connection, police said it was a coincidence.

On December 11, 1974, the *Sun* ran a large article about the Otero murders, and for the first time anywhere in print, linked them to the attack on Kathy and Kevin Bright, although Cornwell said the connection had been discounted by his detectives. More important, the paper revealed that someone who called himself "BTK" had sent a letter to the *Eagle* via the public library, claiming to have killed the Oteros. While it knew what "BTK" represented, the *Sun* chose not to spell the words out, but made it clear that the initials were *not* those of a person, but rather the killer's own self-description, related to his m.o. The *Sun* recounted the details of the recovery of the letter from the library, and Granger's circumscribed attempts to renew contact with the killer.

The same evening the *Sun* article appeared, KAKE-TV featured it on their nightly newscast. Watching the broadcast from off-camera, Henkel was approached by two Wichita detectives. They wanted to know if she was sure that the person who had provided her with the copy of the letter wasn't the killer. She was sure of that, she said.

Henkel did not appear on the KAKE newscast. "Back then," Henkel said, "newspaper reporters wrote and reported; they didn't go on TV . . . editors probably commented on the story for television, but I never did." Henkel was just as glad to remain behind the scenes. "I didn't want my face known," she said. "I was very careful, generally, after the story came out, as you can imagine." There was no point in tempting BTK.

When some asked why the *Sun* had published it when

the *Eagle* had not, the *Sun*'s editors pointed to the editorial explanation that had appeared with the story: "The responsibilities of a free press and those of the police sometimes clash, but the public good is the usual result . . . [the publication] feels that, after some two months under wraps, this letter should be made public for two separate but equally important reasons: the community's right to know, and the possibility that the *Sun*'s comprehensive circulation and the letter's contents could bring forth information on the case."

Besides, the paper's editors added, they hadn't included any of the details of the crime scene that the writer had cited, nor had they revealed what BTK meant. If the police ever did find a viable suspect, they would still have these secret facts to help them separate the false confessors from the real.

Henkel agreed with the editors. "I believe information is power, and that the public needed to know there was a serial killer out there stalking his next victim," she recalled. "They needed to know the Otero family weren't victims of some drug deal gone wrong; that there was a dangerous man on the streets, that the Otero killings weren't an isolated incident. With this knowledge, people could be more aware of their surroundings, take precautions, that sort of thing."

To Beattie, Henkel gave an even more pertinent reason for the publication of the letter.

"The advice I got was that the killer needed that kind of exposure or he would kill again," she said.

And if that was the advice given to Henkel, it seemed to have at least some validity: for a little over the next two years, no one heard from the letter writer who had called himself BTK. But there were no similar murders in Wichita, either.

9:

"PJ Waterfall"

By early 1977, more than three years after the Otero murders and two years after the letter found in the library, the BTK matter had largely faded away in the memories of most Wichitans—an aberration that could no more be explained than it could be solved. Hannon remained convinced that the letter was a hoax, and that there was no such person as BTK. The murders, of course, were real: Hannon was clear on that, as well as on the fact that whoever had killed the Oteros had to be a sick person, even if there was some sort of rational motive that had not yet been uncovered. Hannon was likewise convinced that Kathy Bright's murder had to be the work of a transient criminal, on his way through town, just as the killer had told Kevin Bright. But with the apparent cessation of the bondage murders, things were finally back to normal in the Peerless Princess of the Plains, and that's the way Hannon liked them.

Hannon retired in late 1976, to be replaced by Lieutenant Richard LaMunyon. LaMunyon was vaulted over a number of higher ranking Wichita officers to the chief's job, because of all the applicants, he was the only one who possessed a master's degree. Until his promotion, LaMunyon had been running the department's training division. Certainly, he was not intimately involved in any of the events surrounding the controversy over the murders, and the problematic existence of BTK.

All that, however, was soon to change.

• • •

On March 17, 1977, the killer wore his favorite tweed coat and carried his briefcase. He parked in the lot at the Dillons grocery at the corner of South Hydraulic and East Lincoln Streets in southeast Wichita, about three miles southwest of the Otero house, and a little over five miles southwest of the Bright house. He made his way around the corner and down South Greenwood Street, past the large trees that were still bare, toward a particular address. The killer felt he was "spiffy looking" that day, the way he imagined James Bond might look. *Shaken, not stirred.* He guessed he might come across as a debonair man-about-town, maybe even a detective. In his briefcase he had everything he needed—none of which was necessary to a real detective.

In the 1200 block of South Greenwood, a lower-economic enclave of the city, the killer stopped at the house he wanted and knocked on the door. No one answered. So much for "Project Green."

Shoot, he thought, *I can't break in, not wearing my good clothes.* But, he figured, he might as well try some other doors, as long as he was ready to go to work.

The killer walked a block east on East Bayley Street, then turned south on South Hydraulic Street. He had another project in mind—"Project Blackout," he called it. The target was a young woman he'd met briefly at a club near the university, the Blackout Tavern. He'd followed her home one night, and had discovered that she was the mother of a 6-year-old boy.

As he turned the corner, he watched a young boy walking down the street, carrying a paper bag. Six-year-old Steve Relford was coming back from the Dillons market.

The logic ran through the killer's mind like this: here's a young boy, who's not in school on a school day, which therefore must mean that his mother is home, and probably alone. *Opportunity*, the killer thought.

He approached the young boy, summoning up his most official manner. *You're a detective*, he told himself. He produced a photograph of a woman and a boy—his own wife, it was, and his own son, but any prop would do for this.

"Have you see this woman or this boy?" he asked young Steve.

No, Steve said, shaking his head. He'd never seen those two people before.

The killer grunted, dismissing him, and Steve continued on his way home. His mother, 26-year-old Shirley Vian, was sick that day, and had sent him to Dillons to get soup and to cash a money order. Looking over his shoulder on his way home, a block south, Steve saw the man "with the suitcase" go up the steps of another house and knock on the door. A few minutes later Steve reached his own house, and after giving his mother the soup and the cash from the money order, began to watch cartoons with his older brother Bud, 8, and his sister Stephanie, 4.

A few minutes later, just before noon, they heard a knock on the door. When Steve and his brother opened it, they saw the man who'd shown Steve the picture a few minutes earlier. The man put his foot through the door, showing them some sort of card, saying he was a detective. He pulled out a gun.

Shirley Vian got out of bed and came into the living room to demand an explanation. Wide-eyed, the three children listened as the man said that he was going to tie Shirley up and take some pictures of her. She certainly understood what the man meant to do, even if the kids didn't entirely.

"I'm sick," Shirley told him, as the killer bound her hands behind her back with electrical tape.

"I'm going to have to tie up the kids, too," the killer told her, ignoring her protest.

"Don't do that," she said.

"Have to," said the man. He began trying to tape Bud's hands, and Bud began to cry, resisting.

Steve and his sister began to get agitated too, so the killer decided to forget about taping them up. He herded the children toward the bathroom, then tied one end of a rope around the pipe under the sink, and the other end around the doorknob.

"You guys stay in here," the killer told them.

"I'm going to get out," Steve told him, defiant.

"If you do, I'll blow your head off," the killer told him.

A second door from the bathroom opened into that room, but the killer fixed that by moving the bed so it blocked the door. Now that the three children were imprisoned in the bathroom, he could go to work. He tied Shirley to the bed frame.

"Oh, I'm so sick," Shirley said, and vomited.

The killer went to the kitchen and got her a glass of water. He told her that it would all be over very soon, that he just wanted to take pictures of her tied to the bed. He removed Shirley's bathrobe, and tied her feet to the bed with nylon stockings and venetian blind cord. Then, straddling her from the rear, he looped the same kind of cord around her neck and began to strangle her.

"You leave my mom alone!" Steve Relford yelled from the bathroom. He'd managed to get the tied door open enough to he could see the killer trying to strangle his mother. He and Bud and Stephanie started banging on the door, trying to force it open. The killer stopped trying to strangle Shirley, and found some toys to put into the bathroom—a small airplane, a fire truck and a car. Incredibly enough, he had the idea that this would divert their attention.

"Somebody's coming over in just a minute or two," Steve told the killer. The killer ignored him.

He went back to the bedroom and resumed strangling Shirley. The children kept banging on the door, shouting at the killer to leave their mother alone. The killer wrapped his cord tighter around Shirley's neck, and then put a plastic bag over her head. Remembering Joe Otero's attempt to chew his way out of the bag, he covered it with Shirley's nightgown, and knotted it tight. He stood up and began to masturbate into Shirley's blue panties as she struggled for air.

The telephone began to ring.

"You better get out of here!" Steve Relford shouted from the bathroom.

The killer was torn between wanting to stay, strangling the boys and hanging little Stephanie, or getting out of the house. *Geez,* he thought, *there's always something you never know about.* It seemed like he was always being interrupted, or having to abort his plan.

But who knew? *Someone could be coming, just like the kid said*, the killer thought. The telephone kept ringing. If no one answered it, would someone decide to see what was wrong?

Time to book, the killer told himself. He grabbed two more pair of Shirley's panties, then let himself out the front door, leaving his semen on the other panties he'd dropped by her motionless head. Later he would call this cowardly attack on a sick woman and her three small children "Project Waterfall," because of the name of the street—Hydraulic.

In the bathroom, Steve and Bud continued to struggle trying to get the door open. They called out to their mother, but she didn't answer. Bud decided to break the window in the bathroom. Steve was worried that Bud would get in trouble for breaking it—that's how confused the kids were.

Bud cut his hand on the broken window and began to bleed, badly. He shouted through the window for help, trying to get a neighbor's attention. Steve broke through the lower wooden panel of the bathroom door and ran through the house, but the killer was gone. His mother wasn't moving. He ran outside the house to a neighbor's and pounded on the front door. Finally someone answered.

"Call the cops," the precocious Steve told them. "My mom is dead."

The neighbors followed him back to the Vian house, and found Bud and Stephanie in the bedroom with their mother, hysterical. It was obvious that Shirley had been strangled to death—her pink nightgown and the plastic bag were still over her head, and she wasn't moving.

That afternoon, after the children had been taken away for interviews, the Wichita homicide detectives tried to reconstruct the events. The electrical tape, the nylons and the white cord were ominous signs, as was the plastic bag with the nightgown sealer. The fact that Shirley's feet were tied to the bed frame, that she was on her stomach with her hands taped behind her, was very reminiscent of the scene at the Otero house. So was the apparent masturbation.

"This looks like BTK," said Wichita Detective Bob Cocking.

"Knock that shit off," one of the supervising detectives told him.

Years later, Beattie tracked down former detective Cocking, who swore that this exchange actually took place that afternoon at the Vian house. It was clear to him,

Cocking told Beattie, that none of the higher-ups in the department wanted to admit that they had a possible serial killer loose in Wichita.

Especially one who left letters in libraries and who wanted people to call him BTK.

10:

"PJ Foxhunt"

Efforts to identify the killer of Shirley Vian were unavailing. According to Beattie, who later interviewed many of those who investigated the case, Wichita detectives interviewed forty-eight people, looking for any information that might shed light on what had happened. Obviously, the three most critical interviewees were the eyewitnesses—Steve, Stephanie and Bud.

As best as they could describe the man who had come to the house, he was in his 30s or 40s, was somewhat heavyset, and had dark hair. Unfortunately, according to what Beattie was later told, that description also seemed to match the interviewing detective, so it wasn't clear that it was really a portrait of the killer. An offer from the famed Menninger psychiatric center in Topeka to interview the children in an attempt to flesh out their understandably traumatized memories was for some reason rejected, according to what Beattie later learned.

No one in the department ever publicly mentioned BTK in association with Shirley's murder, and after Cocking's experience, it seemed clear that the department's administrators preferred to consider BTK a phantasm, and certainly not one to stir up the public about.

By the late fall 1977, there had been two other murders that some dissenting detectives thought might be connected to the ephemeral, possibly imaginary killer; but neither—one a violent stabbing at a WSU dormitory, the other a drowning north of the city in which the victim, Denise Rathbun, a young mother, had apparently been abducted from a Laundromat not far from the Otero house—seemed to match the BTK m.o.; there was no evidence of the bondage fetish that seemed so prominent in the murders of the Oteros, Shirley Vian, or even Kathy Bright. Eventually, the dormitory murder was solved. It turned out the killer in that case had been in prison during the Otero and Bright murders, so he was excluded from those crimes. The drowning case remains unsolved, although the fact that Denise Rathbun's body and a coin purse belonging to her were found along different stretches of Hydraulic Street gave some investigators the idea that her murder might have been committed by BTK.

But generally, as the temperatures of the autumn plummeted, the BTK situation was not at the forefront of anyone's thinking.

Certainly Nancy Jo Fox, 25 years old, wasn't thinking about BTK when she arrived at her small duplex in southeast Wichita on the night of December 8, 1977.

But BTK was thinking about her.

For weeks, the killer had been following Nancy Fox. He knew that she had two part-time jobs, one at a law firm, and another at a jewelry store in a downtown shopping mall. Nancy was a regular churchgoer and sang in the Parkview Southern Baptist Church's choir. She had a very active social life, and was very popular with her many friends. She particularly enjoyed partying at a trendy nightspot called Scene Seventies. Although Nancy spent time at the club—she'd once dated the club's manager—she did not drink.

Nancy told friends she thought that someone had broken into her house to rifle through her underwear, but she did not call the police about this; certainly she didn't associate this unpleasant incident with the Otero murders of three years before. But other than this unexplained irritant, she was largely oblivious to the man who was watching her. She had no idea that he'd checked her mailbox, or that he had at one point even gone to the jewelry store to surreptitiously view her while she was behind the counter.

There was something about Nancy that fired the killer's lust. He made extensive notes about her movements and habits. He appreciated the fact that she kept her house neat and clean. He thought of her as a "family girl," meaning innocent.

"She really appealed to me as a potential victim," he said later. Once he'd begun obsessing about her, he tried to keep her in his sights. "Whenever I had time . . . I had other obligations, social obligations; married, I got kids, school, I had jobs." The killer knew he had to keep everything about his life as ordinary as possible so that no suspicion would ever fall on him. By now he and his wife had purchased a small house in the Wichita suburb of Park City, about eight miles north of downtown.

Just after 8:30 P.M. on the night of December 8, 1977—the date was important to the killer—he told his wife he was going to the WSU library to work on a term paper for his class at the university. "That was my alibi," he said later, " 'going to the library.' "

The killer instead drove to Nancy's house on South Pershing. She lived in one half of the duplex; the other portion of the building was unoccupied, a fact that had not passed unnoticed by the killer. Nancy's duplex was a little less than two miles south of the Otero house and a little over two miles east of the Vian house. In fact, when the Bright house was located on a map, all four houses were less than three miles from each other in east Wichita, and all were of similar type in age and construction.

Arriving near Nancy's house in his car, the killer parked a few blocks to the west. He walked back to the front door and knocked to make sure no one was home. The house was dark and empty, so he went to the rear. He cut the telephone wire, then pried off the screen in front of a window that opened into Nancy's bedroom and threw it into some nearby bushes. He jimmied the window open and climbed in, knocking over a potted plant inside the bedroom. He went to the thermostat and turned up the heat—he didn't want Nancy to notice that it was abnormally cold in the house from the pried-open window. Then, after checking out the rest of the house, he returned to the bedroom, made another "nest" of clothes in the closet, and sat down to wait.

Just after 9:30 P.M. he heard the front door open. Still he did not move; he wanted to make sure that Nancy was definitely in for the night. From his place in the closet, he could hear Nancy moving about. He could hear the tap in the kitchen run. A few minutes later, Nancy came into her bedroom. That was when the killer emerged from the closet with his gun.

Nancy wasn't quite the docile victim the killer had envisioned.

"Who are you?" she demanded. "What are you doing here? You'd better get out. I'm going to call the police." She picked up the nearby telephone.

"It won't do you any good," the killer told her. "I already cut the line."

Now Nancy threw the killer a curve.

"I've got to have a smoke," she said, and she turned to leave the room. She walked back into the living room area and sat down at the dining table. A cigarette she had already lit was burning in an ashtray.

"What are you here for?" she asked the killer after she'd taken a drag.

"I'm a bad guy," the killer told her. "I've got this problem, I like to tie people up, for sex. I want to take pictures of you."

"No, that's not going to happen," Nancy told him. "You have to leave."

The killer decided he needed to take charge. He hadn't expected this sort of calm resistance from "the family girl."

"No, it's going to happen like I said," he told her. "I'm going to tie you up and rape you, take some pictures."

"You're sick," Nancy told him.

"Yeah, I'm sick," the killer admitted. "But this is what's going to happen."

He took her purse and dumped its contents on the table top. He pawed through the contents until he found her driver's license. He put it in his pocket.

She put her cigarette down in the ashtray, where it still burned.

"All right," she said, "let's get this over with." She stood up. "I've got to go to the bathroom first," she said.

The killer followed her into the bathroom to make sure she couldn't get out through the small window, and to make sure there were no possible weapons in there. Then he let her go ahead, stuffing a sock in the door so the door wouldn't close all the way. When she came out, she was wearing her sweater, bra and panties. She neatly hung her skirt on a nearby clothes rack. She saw the killer had put on gloves and had arrayed his ropes and handcuffs.

"What're those for?" Nancy asked him.

"That's part of the deal," the killer said. "I've got to have them or it won't work."

"You're sick," Nancy told him again, and again he agreed.

The killer told her to lie face down on the bed. He began to take his own clothes off.

"This is ridiculous," Nancy said. "This is bullshit."

The killer fastened the handcuffs around her wrists in back. "You're sick," Nancy told him again.

But the killer wasn't listening to her any longer. He pulled off her underpants. He slid his belt under her and moved it up her body until it was at the level of her neck. He looped the belt around her neck and pulled on it until she passed out.

He eased the pressure off until she regained consciousness. The killer leaned over her and whispered into her ear.

"I'm BTK, I'm a bad guy," he told her. "And you're gonna die."

Nancy began fighting to throw him off. The killer pulled the belt tighter. Nancy managed to grab his testicles. She squeezed as hard as she could while the killer kept the pressure on his belt. After some minutes Nancy's grip loosened, and then stopped altogether. The killer knew she was dead.

He got up and removed his handcuffs, then tied Nancy's hands behind her back with a nylon, then tied the hands to the stocking around her hips. He tied her feet together with something else. He searched the bedroom and collected a number of underthings. He found her nightgown and masturbated into it.

At about 10:30 P.M., the killer climbed out the rear window and walked back to his car. He'd finished his "term paper" at the "library," and now his wife would be expecting him home.

The next morning, December 9, 1977, was just two days short of three years from Cathy Henkel's exposé about

BTK. The killer looked in his morning newspaper, but found no mention of BTK, or in fact, any murder. He turned on his radio, but there was no report there either.

This was very unsatisfactory, the killer thought. The police were certainly falling down on the job. He decided to be a good citizen and help them out.

He found a pay telephone at a market at 527 East Central. At 8:18 A.M., he called the telephone operator, and asked to be connected to the police. When the police dispatcher came on the line, the killer provided his assistance:

"You have a home-i-cide at 843 Pershing," he said, pronouncing the "hom" of *homicide* as "home."

The dispatcher's screen automatically noted the address of the telephone. She attempted to keep the caller on the line while simultaneously alerting a patrol car to get to the location ASAP.

"I'm sorry, sir," the dispatcher said. "I can't understand you. What is the address?"

The telephone operator helpfully broke in. "He said 843 South Pershing," the operator clarified.

"That is correct," the killer said, and he walked away from the pay phone without bothering to hang it up.

Just as he walked away, an off-duty Wichita fireman emerged from the store, intending to use the same telephone. Fifty-nine seconds after the call was logged by the automatic dispatch system, the fireman glanced up at the retreating figure of the previous caller—the killer. Of course, the fireman didn't know that, and he gave only the most cursory inspection to the man walking away. Later, when pressed by investigators, he said he thought the caller had been about six feet tall, and that he might have had blond hair. He seemed to be wearing some sort of industrial uniform, possibly blue-gray. But then, a lot of people in Wichita wore industrial uniforms. He also thought the man might have been wearing a cap with earflaps, but those were common, too, in early December in Wichita. The fireman had a vague impression that the man got into some sort of relatively new, windowless van, like something used at a shop, one that had some sort of lettering on the sides.

Even as the man was driving off in the none-too-well-described van, a dispatcher was signaling Wichita Officer Lowell Hollingshead to call in on a secure land line. At the time, most Wichita PD radio transmissions could be monitored by the public—as they also regularly were by the news media—and if the department wanted to keep something secret, the best way was to use the regular telephone. Hollingshead called in, and was told to check the residence at 843 South Pershing. The dispatcher said nothing about a possible homicide or even "home-i-cide"; there was every chance the caller at the pay phone had been another crank.

Hollingshead drove to the location, and was soon joined by Officer John DiPietra. They decided to walk around the outside of the building first. Who knew what might be inside? The best and the safest thing to do, the procedurally correct thing to do, was to evaluate the perimeter before deciding whether to go in.

At the rear of the house both officers saw the missing window screen, the jimmied window, and the cut telephone line. They both knew what this probably meant—BTK might have been a phantasm to the department's bigwigs, but that didn't mean the lower ranks didn't believe in him.

DiPietra told Hollingshead that they were going to find a body inside the house.

They went around to the front of the house and put their hands on the butts of their firearms, just in case. Hollingshead knocked on the front door. No one answered. He put his hand on the doorknob. The door was unlocked. He pushed it open. The two officers entered the house, calling out to anyone who might be inside. Again there was no answer.

Turning into the bedroom, they discovered the body of Nancy Fox, lying face down on the bed. It was a shocking, horrible sight. Her hands and legs were tied with nylons and scarves. Blood had flowed from her mouth as she had bitten her lips during the strangulation. Her face was flushed red from the hemorrhaging that had accompanied the choking. Near her head was the nightgown despoiled by the killer.

Nancy had been absolutely correct: the killer was sick—very, very sick.

But he was also still at large.

11:

BTK Stirs Things Up

Despite the bondage, despite the semen, despite the cut telephone wire, despite the forced entry, despite the strangulation, the command levels of the Wichita Police Department kept quiet about the striking similarities between Nancy Fox's murder and the earlier crimes claimed by the man who called himself BTK. The wisdom of this course of inaction is debatable.

Police as a rule tend to be conservative about most things—their politics, usually, as well as how they view the capacity of the public to cope with the unexpected. And why not? When police officers usually encounter members of the public in the midst of a crisis—a robbery, a shooting, even a car wreck—they often find that citizens' judgment under pressure is lacking. It's different for those who carry badges—not only are they trained to cope with crises, they have vastly more experience in dealing with them than the average person. Their reflexive reaction to a problem is: leave it to us, we're the professionals.

Of course, there are situations and events when this is just not sufficient. A recent example was the fiasco in the late summer of 2005 over Hurricane Katrina on the Gulf Coast. One of the major dysfunctions uncovered in the investigation of the response to the disaster was the fundamental unwillingness of the authorities to admit that they were overwhelmed, and to enlist immediate help to deal with the most pressing problems, by organizing and giving ordinary people instructions on how to do the things that need to be done, the way a sheriff might have organized a posse in the Old West. But the way many professionals saw things in New Orleans, handling the disaster was *their* job—grievously, it turned out to be a much bigger job than they were capable of handling, and the talents and energies of the public were not only shoved to the sidelines, but actively discouraged.

In the case of BTK in the winter of 1977–1978, it appears that the Wichita Police Department was simply unwilling to warn the public that a serial murderer, a bondage fetishist who called himself a monster, was loose in the Peerless Princess of the Plains. The police probably believed that this might forestall panic, and at the least would give them enough quietude to pursue their investigations effectively; but at the same time, it cut them off from much assistance that the broader public might have been able to render. Public discussion of the bondage fetish, for example, would certainly have resulted in tips to the police about people with such predilections, which couldn't hurt. Yes, there would have been a huge influx of valueless information, but this was the job of the police—to effectively sort through this mélange of fact and fancy, however fatiguing it was, to make sense of it. That was what they were being paid for.

The information about the cut telephone lines found in the Otero and Fox cases, as well as the disabled telephone in the Bright house, could have been disseminated to warn the public to check their telephone lines when they got home, and potentially save lives.

Most important, public discussion of a deadly serial predator could have formed the basis of neighbors watching out for each other—like pioneers circling the wagons. When people know they should be paying attention to what's going on around them, that they have a responsibility for their neighbors' safety, a lot less can go wrong, and in fact, a watchful public is really the first line of defense against all predators. Even the bison that once roamed over the ground that later became Wichita knew that.

But among the higher-ups in the police department, the doubts about the reality of BTK persisted. There had been no additional communications, no more letters in the library, after the fall 1974. Hannon, though now retired, still insisted that BTK did not exist, that the library letter was the work of some hoaxster. His replacement, LaMunyon, if he thought about it at all, was inclined to think that Hannon was right. Former deputy chief Jack Bruce still half-believed the "lab boys" had cooked up the letter; then, when they realized it wasn't at all funny, had clammed up about it.

The detectives actually assigned to investigate murders, however, were rather more split. Some believed in BTK, while others did not. No one much talked about it, though—insisting on the flesh-and-blood reality of something the top brass didn't take seriously was no way to climb the ladder of professional success. Or, as Cocking was told, "Knock that shit off."

Unknown to LaMunyon and his investigators, however, BTK *was* trying to communicate.

The three-by-five index card came inside a plain envelope to the *Eagle* in the mail of January 31, 1978. Printed on the card, by means of a child's printing set, was an inane poem that began with a line modeled on a traditional nursery rhyme:

SHIRLEYLOCKS SHIRLEYLOCKS WILT
THOU BE MINE

The poem was very short, only seven lines, and crudely constructed. It ended:

A POEM FOR FOX IS NEXT

The card was signed "BTK."

Because this card came in with other mail, it was interpreted by the *Eagle*'s mail-openers as a Valentine's Day personal ad, and sent on to the advertising department. The trouble was, there was no return address, and more important, no payment. The ad department shuffled it off to the paper's dead-letter file and promptly forgot about it.

This made the killer very unhappy—it seemed to him that everyone had forgotten about BTK in the three years since he'd left the letter in the library. He resolved to get the media's attention by being much more direct.

On February 9, 1978, he mailed an envelope to KAKE-TV. Since the *Eagle* hadn't reacted to his sly poem, perhaps the television station would—if he was much more blatant.

The next morning, a Friday, a woman assigned to open the mail at KAKE slit open the envelope and pulled out four photocopied pages. Two pages were in the form of a typed letter, a third page was a poem about Nancy Fox's murder, and the fourth page—this is what initially shocked the KAKE letter-opener—was a detailed drawing of how Nancy's body had been left, face down on her bed.

When she glanced at the badly typed letter, she got another shock:

> I find the newspaper not wirting [sic] about the poem on Vain [sic] unamusing. A little paragraph would have enough to I knom [sic] it [sic] not the news media fault. The Police Cheif [sic] he keep things quiet, and doesn't let the public know there a

psycho running lose strangling mostly women, there [sic] 7 in the ground; who will be next? How many do I have to Kill before I get a name in the paper or some national Attention. Do the cop think that all those deaths are not related? Golly-gee, yes the M.O. is different in each, but look a pattern is developing. The victims are tie up-most have been women-phone cut-bring some bondage mater [sic] Sadist tendencies-no struggle, outside the death spot-no witness [sic] except the Vain's [sic] Kids. They were very lucky; a phone call save them. I was going to /// tape the boys and put plastics bag over there head like I did Joseph, and Shirley. And then hang the girl. God-oh God what a beautiful sexual relief that would been. Josephine, when I hung her really turn me on; her pleading for mercy then the rope took whole, she helpless; staring at me with wide terror fill eyes the rope getting tighter-tighter. You don't understand these things because your not under the [sic] influence of factor)x). The same thing that made, Son of Sam, Jack The Ripper, Harvery Glatman [sic], Boston Strangler, Dr. H.H. Holmes Panty Hose Strangler of Florida, Hillside Strangler, Ted of The West Coast and Many more infamous character kill. Which seem a senseless, but we cannot help it. There is no help, no cure, except death or being caught and put away. It a terrible nightmarebut [sic], you see I don't lose any sleep over it. After a thing like Fox I ccome [sic] home and go about life like anyone else. And I will be / like that until the urge hit me again. It not continuous and I don't have a lot of time. It take time to set a kill, one mistake and it all over. Since I about blew it on the phone-handwritting [sic] is out-letter guide is to long and typewriter can be traced too, [sic] My short poem of death and maybe a drawing; later on real picture and maybe a tape of the sound will come your way. How will you know it me. Before a murder or murders / you will receive a copy of the initials B.T.K., you keep that copy the original will show up some day on guess who?

May you not be the unluck one!

P.S. How about some name for me, its time: 7 down and many moreto [sic] go. I like the following. How about you? "The B.T.K. STRANGLER", "WICHITA STRANGLER", "POETIC STRANGLER", "THE BONDAGE STRANGLER" OR "PSYHCO," "THE WICHITA HANGMAN," "THE WICHITA EXECUTIONER," "THE GAROTE PHATHOM [sic]," "THE ASPHYXIATER."

The next page of the typed letter continued:

#5 You guess motive and victim.

#6 You found one Shirley Vain [sic] lying belly down on a unmade bed in northeast bedroom-hand tied behind back with black tape and cord. Feet & ankles with black tape & legs. Ankles tied to west head of the bed with small off white cord, wrap around legs, hands, arm, finally the neck, many times. A off white pla stic [sic] bag over her head loop on with a pink nitie [sic]. Shirley was nude with small eye ring Had blue house coat on before and-house a total mess-kids took some toys with them to the bathroom-bedagainst [sic] east bathroom door. Chose at random with some preplanning. Motive Factor X.

#7 One Nancy Fox-lying belly down on made bed in southwest bedroom-hands tied behind back with red panty hose-feet together with yellow nitie [sic]-semi-nude with pink sweather [sic] and bra small neckless [sic]-glasses on west dresser-panties below butt-many different color panties hose around [sic] neck, one across the mouth-strangled with man belt first then the hosery [sic]. She had a/ smoke and went to the bathroom before the final act-very neat housekeeper& dresser-rifled pursein [sic] kiteken [sic]-empty paper bag-white coat in living-room-heat up to about 90 degree-Christmas tree lights on-cizrette [sic] / // mostly burn down pants in bathroom rifled east top dresser on top-nities[sic] and hose around the room-hose bag of orange color it and hosery [sic] on bed-driver licence [sic] gone-seminal stain on or in blue woman wear. Chose at random with little pre-planning, Motive Factor "X".

#8 Next victim maybe: You will find her hanging with a wire noose-Hands behind back with black tape or cord-feet with tape or cord-gaged [sic]-then cord around the body to the neck-hooded maybe-possible seminal stain in anus-or on body. Will be chosen at random. Some pre-planning- Motive Factor "X".

B.T.K.

The letter-opener at KAKE quickly summoned one of the station's reporters, Larry Hatteberg. Hatteberg glanced at the badly typed letter, poem and drawing and immediately recognized it as another communication from the phantom BTK. He called executive news producer Ron Loewen, who was at home, and asked him to come into the station at once. Loewen soon arrived, looked over the material, and consulted with station manager Martin Umansky. Both men decided to call Police Chief LaMunyon.

At a meeting in LaMunyon's office a short time later, Loewen and Umansky handed the envelope and its contents to the chief and his top aide, Deputy Chief Bill Cornwell. Umansky—who had been publisher of the *Sun* when the Cathy Henkel story was published three years earlier—told LaMunyon that the station intended to broadcast the story about the new letter unless LaMunyon told him the letter was a fake. LaMunyon and Cornwell asked for a few minutes to consult privately.

Fifteen minutes or so later, the chief and his deputy came back to Umansky and Loewen. The letter was legitimate, they told the newsmen. But, they asked—couldn't the station withhold the actual text of the letter? It might help the police identify the killer if they had something that only the killer and the police would know. A compromise of sorts was reached—the police would confirm that the letter had been received by KAKE, and permit the release of a summary of its contents, but the station would keep the actual text secret. This would prevent BTK from concluding that the police had ceded all control over the situation to him, and hopefully keep him at least somewhat off balance.

Years later this would be one of the communications from BTK CAVEd by Beattie. The strains of both of Beattie's conclusions, of a lack of confidence in being able to continue killing, but confidence in being able to continue communicating, are evident in the letter.

"How many do I have to [negative] Kill before I get a name in the paper or some national Attention," BTK had written. Although there was no question mark with this sentence, to Beattie it indicated that the killer had doubts about his ability to continue to kill without getting caught. A killer confident of killing would more likely have written, "I will kill again and again and again, and you can't stop me [positive]." And later: "Since I about blew it on the phone—" was another indication of nervousness about getting caught. His detailed account of what he had done with each victim showed a desire to reassure himself that he *was* capable of committing the murders, indicating doubt (negative).

But the fact that the killer wanted attention so badly also indicated that he was comfortable sending communications—for him, that was one of the objects of the murders. And there was the promise of more communications in the future: "will come your way [positive]," not, "might come your way [neutral]," or, "will if I can [negative]."

LaMunyon knew nothing of the principles of CAVE-ing in 1978; what he did know, what he immediately recognized, was that the killer was eager to communicate with *someone*. He explained to Loewen and Umansky that after the 1974 letter, the psychological experts had advised that if no publicity was given to the library letter, the killer was likely to stop murdering. In fact, the experts had been split on this issue at the time; the three-year gap between the Otero murders and the Vian murder actually suggested the opposite—after the Granger column and the Henkel story, it appeared that the killer *had* stopped, at least for a while. In any event, LaMunyon told the broadcasters, the first strategy hadn't worked, so they might as well try the second and give the killer the publicity he so obviously craved.

Because the killer had sent his latest communication to KAKE, the police thought the station would offer the best method of encouraging BTK to send more communications. The first thing to do, they agreed, was announce the fact that the killer was real, that he was still out there. This would serve two purposes: it would put the community on the alert, and at the same time it might serve to assuage the killer's desire for notoriety.

The other thing to do was track down the "poem on Vain [sic]" that had previously been sent to the newspaper. Police went to the *Eagle*, and found themselves in luck: the card containing the "SHIRLEYLOCKS" poem was still in the dead-letter file in the advertising department.

That afternoon, LaMunyon held a press conference. The so-called "BTK" murderer had communicated again, he told reporters, this time claiming responsibility for three other murders besides the Oteros. "BTK," he said, stood for "Bind, Torture, Kill." This was the first time the initials had been spelled out for the public.

"I know it is difficult to ask people to remain calm, but we are asking exactly this," LaMunyon told reporters. "When a person of this type is at large in our community it requires special precautions and special awareness by everyone."

LaMunyon was asked why his department had never publicly acknowledged BTK after picking up the letter in the library more than three years earlier. He said the experts who had examined the 1974 letter had advised against giving the killer publicity.

"We felt the lack of news coverage would forestall any more killings—that was what was hoped at the time," LaMunyon said. But now "It would appear that this individual is seeking recognition." Maybe, LaMunyon implied, this would induce the killer not to kill again.

LaMunyon refused to release copies of either of the letters, or the poems; and certainly not the ugly drawing, which wouldn't have been published or aired in any event. Somewhere along the line, some reporters came away with the impression that the police were completely at sea—that they did not know where to turn next.

"Police have said they have no concrete leads, suspect, or even a description of the killer," wrote *Eagle* reporter

Casey Scott the next day. But that wasn't true: they had descriptions of a man or men seen near the Otero house, apparently at the time of those murders; they had an original description of a bondage-type killer from Kevin Bright before someone convinced him that the man he'd seen had been "swarthy"; they had descriptions of a bondage killer from Steve, Bud and Stephanie Relford; they had the fireman's description of the man in the blue-gray uniform who had used the telephone to call in Nancy Fox's murder, as well as his van; they had a sample of a typewriter he used, as well as a sample of the letters made by the child's printing set. They even had a recording of his voice, albeit brief—"You have a home-i-cide . . ."

In other words, the police had a number of leads that, if they had been disseminated to the public, would have been likely to generate a number of useful tips. By saying that they had no leads and no description, it was almost the same as saying anyone could be the killer—rather than focusing the public's attention on the most likely fits, it virtually ensured that the tips they did get from the citizenry would cover the entire gamut of possibilities, discouraging anyone who might actually know something, and simultaneously reducing the value of the information that *was* received.

Keeping the images of the communications secret was also likely an error. While the police wanted to keep the complete texts confidential—particularly those portions that specifically described how each victim had been murdered—permitting the release of images of a *portion* of each communication could have been of assistance. That was certainly true of the child's printing set—the chances were that the set had been used for some innocuous project by someone's child; and it was likely that the rubber type used in the printing set had unique characteristics—cracks and chips, for instance—as in the sole of a sneaker. The number of such sets in the Wichita area was certainly finite. Publishing an image of one or two of the lines of the "SHIRLEYLOCKS" poem might have caused people to compare them to their own children's rubber printing sets. This was a potentially valuable avenue of investigation.

And even in describing the text of the letters, the police erred in permitting the impression by some reporters that there was a vast difference in the style and quality of the communications.

"The first letter, in contrast to the one received by KAKE, was poorly typed and contained many misspelled words and improper grammar," *Eagle* reporter Casey Scott noted. But that simply wasn't the case—*both* letters were riddled with typos, spelling errors and grammatical flaws, as release of the KAKE letter would have shown. This in turn would have demonstrated that the killer was certainly not a touch typist, and that his writing skills were very crude.

Police did not release the text of the "poem for Fox" that had been included in the material sent to KAKE, either. This read:

OH! DEATH TO NANCY
What is this taht [sic] I can see,
Cold icy hands taking hold of me,
For Death has come, you all can see.

Hell has open [sic] it,s [sic] gate to trick me.

Oh! Death, Oh! Death, can you spare
me, over for another year!

Then the tone, meter and even perspective of the poem abruptly altered:

I'll stuff your jaws till you can't talk
I'll blind [sic] your leg's [sic] till you can't walk
I'll tie your hands till you can't make a stand.

And finally, I'll close your eyes so you can't see
I'll bring sexual death unto you for me.

There were a number of other aspects of both letters as well as the poems that shed considerable light on the killer:

- The killer's reference to other serial killers, including the not-widely known "Harvery [sic] Glatman," showed that BTK was familiar with and admired other serial killers, not for the acts they had committed as much as for the notoriety they had achieved. This was a potentially useful piece of information to disseminate to the public—someone who had previously spoken of the little-known Glatman, for example, in casual conversation about serial killers would have been an obvious suspect.
- The two letters, taken together, indicated a personality that had a very weak ego—someone who had a crucial need to get attention. This in turn very likely indicated that the killer was something of a non-entity in the community, an ineffectual personality, someone with a dead-end job. The person didn't have to be at all clever to have committed the murders. A moron could have done them, as long as he had no sense of right and wrong, and a willingness to be brutal. But the killer had an obvious need to make others think he was clever.
- The killer had a peculiar penchant for superficial

precision. His description of the murders themselves showed he was someone who lived by following checklists, such as an auto mechanic or other occupation relying on rote manual dexterity, using by-the-numbers, step-by-step procedures.

- The killer was not well-educated, or certainly not a good student. He was a very bad speller—"Vain" for Vian could not have been an attempt at irony. This was, in fact, a suggestion that the killer may have been dyslexic, an affliction in which the brain consistently reverses certain letters. Someone in the public—a parent, a spouse, a co-worker—might have been able to recognize this tendency had the relevant, verbatim texts of the letters been published.
- Based on the choice of victims, the killer was almost certainly Caucasian; serial murderers almost always select victims of the same racial type as themselves. The selection of locations for the murders likewise indicated someone intimately familiar, and comfortable with, the city's geography, which indicated that the killer was someone who had lived most of his life in the city—in other words, a native, not someone of "foreign extraction."
- The killer had an obsession with abbreviations, starting with BTK. These were his "codes," he had indicated. Such an obsession again is often found with technical workers (Wichita had a lot of those, unfortunately), as well as security personnel, including police, who often rely on such abbreviations to streamline things as reports—"KSA," for Kansas Statutes Annotated, or DUI, or MPH, or numbers indicating various statutes and crimes. The fact that the killer seemed to in-

vent his own abbreviations indicated that he was unfamiliar with official terms, but wanted to seem as though he was.

- The details of each crime scene, categorized as they were by method and motive, in other words, m.o., had all the earmarks of a personality who identified with the police. The chances were very good that the killer had either studied to be a police officer, or had even applied to be one. It was likewise obvious from the letters that the killer was *not* a police officer, if for no other reason than the sheer sloppiness of his communications. No police department would ever have employed anyone as incompetent in his report-writing as BTK was.
- Finally, the "poem for Fox" that the killer had enclosed was markedly different from the two letters. Where the letters had been riddled with misspellings and ineffective grammar, the poem was for the most part spelled perfectly—it had clearly been copied, just as had the form of the "SHIRLEYLOCKS" poem sent two weeks earlier to the *Eagle*. The cribbing of the form of the two poems showed that the killer was an aper, not an author, and that he had to have access to books that contained the originals of the poems. The transmutation of both poems, especially in the second portion of the Fox poem, showed a clear lack of imagination, let alone poetic ability. Again, this was a sign that the killer craved recognition that was in reality beyond him to achieve. So was his rather ludicrous, even grandiose, suggestion that the news media refer to him as the "Poetic Strangler."

• • •

CITY'S 'BTK STRANGLER' CLAIMS HE'S KILLED 7, the *Eagle* headlined the next day.

"A killer claiming responsibility for seven Wichita murders—at least six of them strangulations—still is in the area and has threatened to strike again, Police Chief Richard LaMunyon warned in a terse, bombshell announcement Friday," the paper reported on February 11, 1978.

After recounting that the police believed that someone calling himself "BTK" had killed three other people besides the Oteros, the paper had LaMunyon ominously warning everyone that there was no way to prevent the killer from striking again. Now, for the first time, people were warned to check their telephone lines. But the paper seemed to meekly accept LaMunyon's rationale for withholding the text of the communications, both in 1974 and now.

"Police are withholding parts of the letter to try to prevent cranks from learning details that might entice them to convincingly claim they are the killer," the paper reported.

The failure of the police to inform the public about BTK after the murders of Shirley Vian and Nancy Fox did draw some questioning, however.

"Asked why police had [previously] refused . . . to acknowledge the killer may have been responsible in the Vian and Fox slayings, LaMunyon said, 'There . . . were definite similarities, but at the time there were very significant differences.' He refused to elaborate."

The *Eagle*'s Casey Scott noted that after the Otero murders, police had released an artist's sketch of a "dark-complected man thought to be the killer." But, Scott said,

Deputy Chief Cornwell had said at the press conference that other information later obtained by the police had led them to believe that the man in the drawing was not the killer. But once again, the police refused to say just what had led them to this conclusion. The obvious implication was that the description did not match the one provided by the Relford children, Kevin Bright or the fireman, none of whom said anything about a "dark-complected man" of apparent "foreign extraction."

On the other hand, this in turn suggested that the police had decided that the Vian and Fox murders, and possibly the Bright murder, were connected to the Otero case even before the killer had decided to communicate with KAKE, but had decided to keep the citizens of Wichita in the dark.

12:

Oh! Death!

The blast of publicity that wafted over Wichita in the wake of the KAKE letter was immensely satisfying to the killer. It even helped him in his job.

As Beattie later recalled the scene, almost immediately the entire city ran to their telephones to check the lines. Many continued this practice on a daily basis for years, even decades, afterward, every time they returned home.

"Thousands of back-yard windows and doors were nailed shut or boarded over," Beattie later recalled. Dwellings with bedrooms on a second floor or higher fetched a premium. People routinely kept their closet doors open—just to make sure that BTK couldn't spring out at them from the dark, like some sort of hellish bogeyman.

"Gun sales skyrocketed," Beattie remembered. By then a fireman for Sedgwick County, Beattie recalled that the police told him that they were getting a vast upsurge in calls from people who wanted to know if they could use a gun in self-defense, in case the killer broke into their house.

In the absence of more specific information about the killer, the volume of calls about suspicious people in neighborhoods almost tripled from the normal volume. Police began to worry that in the present state of anxiety, residents might begin shooting one another by mistake before they realized that the man they thought was BTK was really just the guy next door, who only wanted to borrow a cup of sugar.

The market for home-security systems took off. And as a result, the killer suddenly had more work than he could handle, because he'd been working as a burglar-alarm installer for the previous three years, while also taking classes in criminal justice at Wichita State University. And with the new letter from BTK, now that everyone was aware that someone out there was committing "home-i-cides," putting in an alarm system suddenly seemed like a sensible thing to do. The killer was happy—he had his publicity, and he also had some job security.

As Hannon had before him, Chief LaMunyon decided to bring in some expert consultants. This time, however, it was the Federal Bureau of Investigation, not local psychologists. Early in the year 1978, the bureau conducted a training session for local homicide investigators in Kansas. This was just about the time that the bureau was organizing its Behavioral Sciences Unit in Quantico, Virginia, and Special Agents John Douglas, Robert Ressler and Roy Hazelwood, three of the earliest members of the new unit, were detailed to explain to the locals just what the bureau proposed to do with the new program.

Later, Ressler recalled meeting with the Wichita detectives, and learning a bit about BTK. He remembered being shown the communications, and evaluating them for the Wichita authorities. All three FBI agents were struck by BTK's mad passion for publicity—in their experience evaluating serial crimes so far, this was pretty unusual. But the circumstances of the communications, and their contents, convinced both men that BTK had an unfulfilled desire to be a police officer. They were likewise convinced that the killer would try to insert himself into the investigation, both to find out what the police knew, and to "help" them solve the crimes. Indeed, the descriptions of the crime scenes sounded almost as if the killer were filling out a police report on himself, giving the detectives the data they needed to solve the crimes. They thought the killer would frequent places where detectives congregated, in order to eavesdrop, and eventually to include himself in their efforts. This would make him feel good about himself, they concluded, would make him feel as if he were on the team—and this in turn would give meaning and color to his otherwise unexceptional life.

Ressler also recalled that he and Douglas advised that the Wichita police encourage this joining as a way of ferreting out the identity of the killer. Community meetings should be held, they suggested, to discuss the murders. Undercover officers should monitor the audience, looking for someone who had over-avid interest, while taking the license plates of cars. Whatever they did, the two agents suggested, the detectives should make it clear to the killer that he could not get away with murder—that his arrest was simply inevitable. The chances were, when they finally had a suspect in custody, the man would spill his guts, so eager would he be to have their approval.

The two agents also had some specific suggestions—like others, they had noticed the possible Coleman connection. That in itself wasn't much—sometimes it seemed like half the people in town worked at Coleman. But Ressler and Douglas also had an idea that BTK, the wannabe cop, was a student at Wichita State University's criminal justice program. That fit the tone and style of the letters. They suggested that the police obtain lists of students in the criminal justice program, and compare them to lists of Coleman employees. While there would be many names on the two lists, the overlap might be far smaller. But for some reason, the list comparison was never made—possibly because of legal considerations. After all, the authorities did not have the specificity required for a search warrant to obtain the lists from Coleman and the university—a general request for the names and addresses of all employees and all students would be a sort of fishing expedition, one likely to be resisted by the university as well as Coleman.

In the meantime, one Wichita detective, John Garrison, took the "Oh! Death to Nancy" poem to a WSU folklore professor, P. J. Wyatt. There was something about the poem that triggered Garrison's instinct—it seemed to him like it was probably cribbed from some sort of folklore—the words and cadence seemed archaic. Not the second half, of course, but the first.

Wyatt glanced at the poem, and almost instantly gave her verdict:

"He's a plagiarist," she declared. In fact, the first part of the poem was adapted from an old Appalachian folk song, pretty much as Garrison had sensed, especially from the colloquial phrase "spare me over," which had the sound and rhythm of the hill country. Of course, the previous semester Garrison had taken Professor Wyatt's folklore course, which only goes to show that a liberal arts education is good for everyone, even cops.

In fact, Professor Wyatt had even used the folk song in her class in previous years.

Garrison was excited—what were the odds that any killer would select this folk song, this very one used by Professor Wyatt in her class, by sheer coincidence? Probably a billion to one. That meant that the killer might have actually taken Wyatt's class. In turn, that meant the universe of possible suspects would be vastly narrowed. This *was* a form of specificity. Soon other detectives developed even more information that tended to support Garrison's notion—the basement of the building where Professor Wyatt had taught her class from 1964 to 1973 had a photocopy machine. After extensive lists, experts employed at the Xerox Corporation determined that the copies of the Fox letter and poem had been produced on that same machine, which meant that the killer had spent time in that building.

At length the police obtained the cooperation of the university, and obtained lists of people who had taken Professor Wyatt's class, as well as university employees and vendors—in short, people with access to the photocopy machine, and who might have encountered materials from Professor Wyatt's folklore class. In the end, according to what Beattie was later told by the retired cops, more than a year was spent trying to run down the elusive "Oh! Death!" connection, to no avail.

As it happened, the killer had never taken Professor Wyatt's course. But that didn't mean that someone he knew hadn't.

As for the cops, they consoled themselves with wry, bitter humor. Recalling the "home-i-cide" tip, they reminded themselves, as Dorothy had told Auntie Em. "There's no place like home."

The only question was, whose home would be next?

13:

"Now Call the Chief"

No one, of course, can remain in a state of panic for very long. Sooner or later, the waiting, the watchfulness, the anxiety wears off; the adrenaline is depleted, shapes that seemed weird and darkly ominous resume their normal proportions. People who have looked under the bed for alligators for too many nights eventually realize that there are no alligators, and so they fall into bed without the habitual second glance.

By March 1978, the public ado over BTK was beginning to abate. The volume of calls to the special tip line receded like the aftersplash of a spent wave. From the tips that had been phoned in, and from other sources, the detectives had culled a list of about fifty possible perpetrators. Now, as each was eliminated, one by one, the police were getting as frustrated as they were fatigued. This wasn't like some ordinary crime, one where you had witnesses, a motive, a clear shot at the bad guy. It wasn't like a hold-up at the Wichita First National. The bad guy could be anyone in this case; and while it was true there were witnesses, the descriptions hadn't gotten them anywhere. Even the Coleman worker identified by Kevin Bright seemed immune from any hard evidence linking him to any of the murders. Almost on cue, the duck aficionado of the fall of 1974 popped back up, confessed again, and was investigated once more, at least until someone remembered what had happened a few years earlier.

LaMunyon reached down into his department's narcotics squad to put out a screen of undercover, plainclothes cops. These were assigned to keep a number of uneliminated suspects under covert surveillance. Most of the undercovers looked like hippies, and so they stuck out like painted clowns to the uneliminated suspects, who were anything *but* hippies. The suspects were mostly the kind of guys who wore their cigarettes rolled up in the sleeves of their tee-shirts, and had tattoos on their hands, arms and other portions of their anatomy. Both the surveillors and the surveillees had a variety of adventures in the spring and summer of 1978, as Beattie would later recount in his book, many of them humorous, appalling or both. But nothing came of the surveillance—except that once more the murders seemed to have stopped. Although it griped him, LaMunyon was wondering if the antidote to the killer was in the news media's alarm bell.

"All this guy has to do is write a letter and he becomes headline news," he complained to the *Eagle* one day. Still, he added, people should err on the side of caution—if they saw something that was out of place, they should call it in.

The newspaper did what newspapers usually do in these situations—it cobbled together a "survey story" that listed the number and some of the details of Wichita's unsolved homicides. There were eighteen of them, the paper reported. It ran the usual retrospective on the Otero murders, and proffered "how to" advice about locks and strangers and checking the telephone lines—"news you can use," it would later be called.

On another front, the paper tried to figure out the identity of the unnamed BTK victim—"#5 You guess motive and victim." The *Eagle* soon focused on Kathy Bright as one of the strongest possibilities. After recounting the details of the attack on Kathy and Kevin, the paper noted that the assailant had tied both up, and that he'd been hiding in one of the bedrooms when they entered the house. This report was one reason why every Wichitan made it a habit to keep their closet doors open—if they came home and found them closed, it was a sign to get out.

As the spring of 1978 turned into summer, LaMunyon and his investigators hoped to find some way to reestablish the contact with BTK. Some thought that since the killer had expressed his disdain for the newspaper—it hadn't published his "SHIRLEYLOCKS" poem—the thing to do was to work with the television station KAKE. It was pretty obvious that he watched that channel—why else would he have sent the February package to the station? That was one reason why LaMunyon had made a special appearance, with executive news producer Loewen, on the station's newscast the evening of the big press conference in February. It was one reason the police were a bit more cooperative with KAKE in sharing information. Both LaMunyon and Loewen hoped that BTK would watch the coverage, and be moved to send another letter.

But nothing happened.

Months went by, while LaMunyon's detectives consulted with the FBI, ran down various suspects, put people under surveillance, and checked out students in Professor Wyatt's old classes. Eventually someone took a hard look at the drawing of Nancy Fox that had accompanied the February 10 letter.

Hey! one of the detectives said, *Do you know what? I think this drawing is actually a tracing. I think he must've taken a photograph, a Polaroid, of the scene. And then I think he must've traced this drawing from the picture. Because you know what? It's* too *detailed—it's too exact.*

When the other detectives looked at the drawing more closely, they had to agree. There were way too many fine details in the drawing. In fact, there was one detail in the drawing that hadn't actually been there—at least, it wasn't in the crime-scene photographs.

This was a pair of eyeglasses that the drawing showed were on the dresser. But the same eyeglasses were not on the dresser in the crime-scene photographs. They were gone.

These were the killer's own eyeglasses, someone realized.

So now they'd learned something new—the killer wore eyeglasses. And that explained the strange little insignia that had been on the letters—it was the initials BTK, stylized to look like a pair of eyeglasses split by a long, sharp nose.

Maybe.

Still, by the summer of 1978, LaMunyon was ready to try just about anything. Someone had the idea of hypnotizing the killer. Well, not exactly hypnotizing him, but planting a message in his brain. The killer watched television, that was evident. Why not use a subliminal insert to induce the killer into revealing himself?

Beattie, who heard this tale much later, thought that somebody had watched one too many *Columbo* episodes.

The idea was to have the KAKE television people interview LaMunyon—a progress report on the hunt for the killer. Of course, the program would be exclusive, and hyped on the air beforehand, in order to get the killer's attention. Then, in the middle of the taped interview, accompanied by a drawing of a pair of distinctive eyeglasses, technicians would splice in a brief written message that would go by so fast that most viewers would only see a brief flash of white:

NOW CALL THE CHIEF

" 'Now Call the Chief,' " Beattie later shook his head, marveling. "They thought the killer would be . . ." here Beattie mimicked someone in a trance, " 'Oh yeah, okay, now I've got to pick up the phone and call the chief.' Because they thought he would be watching it." Beattie said he was told the station had to get special permission from the FCC to insert this message. If anyone actually called the chief after this, Beattie never heard about it.

But when this call to confession aired in the summer of 1978, the killer was busy with other things.

"Social obligations," he called them, meaning his marriage and his two small children, a boy and a girl, the girl newborn that same June. If the killer had one talent, it was his capacity to keep things compartmentalized. It was as if he were two different people—his cover, his "legend," as the spies called it, and the secret man inside him. He never let the two sides contaminate each other—that was the whole trick. Once, when he was trying to compose the "SHIRLEYLOCKS" poem, his wife came home unexpectedly. Quickly he stuffed the notes down between the cushion and the side of his chair. Then he forgot about them. A few days later, his wife had found them.

"What's this?" she'd asked, puzzled and not a little alarmed at the crude verse.

"Oh, that's just something for school," he'd told her. "We're working on the BTK thing." She accepted this explanation, never dreaming that it could be anything other than what he'd said it was.

By day he went to work, installing alarm systems in homes and businesses. It was a logical job—there were certain parameters that each system called for, and they never varied. There were just so many places where the perimeter could be breached, and just so many places where the system could detect the intruder. Volts and amps, connections and transistors, leads going in, leads going out—they were all closed circuits with clear, immutable logic. He'd been doing this so long it was automatic for him. He could do it by the numbers, and he had, ever since he'd been trained to do it in the U.S. Air Force. He could do it with his eyes shut. He could look over a house and know exactly how to break in.

By night he came home and enjoyed his wife's excellent cooking. He sat in his chair and watched television, particularly his favorite station, KAKE-TV. KAKE had been *his* station since he was a little boy in Wichita—one of the first television broadcasters in town. In those days, in the early 1950s, it had broadcast live kids' shows, with real kids on camera, playing games or with toys, while their adult hosts beamed. He could still remember the times when his mother had taken him to the station studio to be on these shows; for a while, he was a star. Ah, those were the days.

He loved his mother and his father. They still lived in their neat little house, no more than a mile or two away. He still visited them, and of course, the basement.

The basement—that's where it was at. That's where it had all started. There was a pipe, he remembered, that ran horizontally across the ceiling of the basement. A thick pipe that ran out to the sewer line under the street. It was dark and a bit dank in the basement, a place where he could be where no one watched, and he could do what he wanted, think the things he liked to think about, imagine the sorts of things that made him feel odd—but pleasurably odd. There was a musty, earthy smell that reminded him of decay. It was a place in the earth, the imaginary dungeon, where he could pretend he was someone's victim, and the place where he could pretend he had his own victims. The place where he'd learned to loop a cord around the sewer pipe and choke himself while he had his hand in his pants, the place where the only really important question was—who would finish first? "Rex," or the thing inside him that wanted to kill him—or maybe, kill someone else? Himself, or himself? Who would live and who would die?

On Saturday he worked around his small house in Park City, working with his hands, keeping things in shape. Soon his boy would be old enough for the Scouts—he'd loved being a Scout, when he was growing up. Once, in fact, he'd even saved another boy's life. The other boy had fallen into a river, and was going to drown. But he'd saved him. He was a hero. Everyone had said so.

And on Sundays, he would go to church. He was a member of Christ Lutheran in Wichita Heights, the church across the street from his old high school. He'd been going to church all his life. He couldn't imagine *not* going to church. If it wasn't for the church, he didn't know what he would do. Because the church was what told him how to be—how to maintain, how to perfect his cover, his legend. The church was perfect, and he was perfect. Perfect on the outside, perfect on the inside.

Life was perfect.

14:

"PJ Pinecone"

Fifteen months went by after the KAKE letter. And if the police seemed no closer to identifying BTK than they had been on January 15, 1974, at least there had been no new murders. So maybe the answer *was* publicity—giving the killer his ink might have mollified him.

But that wasn't exactly the case. The killer had his wife, his kids, his job, his church, but it was all for show. The real person inside continued to ferment, bubbling all the time, emitting toxic vapors aloft into the killer's consciousness. By now he had an extensive collection of homemade pornography—most of it cut-outs from magazines and newspapers, many of them pictures of children, and he embroidered them with drawings of ropes, hoods, chains . . . all manner of bondage. The photocopy machine was a wonderful invention, he thought. He was able to reduce the size of his pasted-up images to index cards—on one side was the image, on the other a series of coded letters and numbers that reminded him of the best fantasies he had for each particular picture. He had hundreds of these cards—by the time the end came, he would have thousands of them. He often picked up an assortment of the cards—he gave them all girls' names, like "Julia," or "Carol," or "Candy." He'd drive around to his various job sites, carrying the cards with him. Later he would write down his activities for the day in a journal he kept, noting, *Today I spent the day with Julia . . .*

He continued with his writing, but he'd abandoned the

story form for the time being. Instead he kept notes—very, very detailed notes. And diagrams. And drawings.

He spent hours cruising the streets of Wichita—"trolling," he called it, looking for someone who fit his "codes." Someone vulnerable, some place where he could get in and get out without anyone seeing. He committed scores of burglaries—taking underpants, jewelry, money, odd knickknacks. It was the sheer pleasure of knowing he could do it that animated him.

In April 1979 he spotted a young woman going into a house in southeast Wichita—a place only a half-mile east of Nancy Fox's house, and less than a mile and a half south of the Otero house. As the month wore on, he moved from the "trolling" to the "stalking" stage. He kept the house on Pinecrest Street under surveillance, and soon realized that the young woman wasn't always there, but that she visited an older woman who lived in the house.

This would be good, he thought. *I can get two.*

On the evening of April 28, 1979, he drove to Pinecrest Street and parked some distance away. He thought one of the women might be in the house, so he wanted to be as quiet as possible. After all the publicity about BTK, he didn't think he'd be able to get away with one of his "russes," as he called them. He could imagine how scared the women would be when he suddenly appeared in the house. That was good.

He went around to the rear of the house. He knew exactly where the telephone line was from his earlier "stalking" phase. Now he snipped it in two with his wire cutters. He located the means of entry he'd already decided upon—a small window into the basement. He removed the screen, taped the glass of the window, then broke it, trying to be as quiet as possible. He climbed in through the window and then began to creep up the stairs, trying to make no noise. But when he emerged on the first floor, he was disappointed. The house was deserted.

He quickly searched the house, looking for the things that fed his "codes"—a scarf, nylons, jewelry, any mementos of his house-breaking legerdemain. *Well,* he thought, *I'm in, so I might as well wait for them to come home.* He settled himself in a closet as he had done at Kathy Bright's and Nancy Fox's.

But the minutes rolled past, and still no one appeared. The killer began to get irritated. He had things to do—the damn social obligations! Why weren't the victims cooperating? Why weren't they behaving the way his stalking phase had said they would? His wife would be wondering where he was—the library would be closing soon.

Sometime after 10 P.M. the killer decided to wait no longer. He let himself out of the house, carrying his booty.

Too bad, he thought.

That night 63-year-old Anna Williams, a recent widow, returned to her house on Pinecrest after a night of square dancing. Almost as soon as she was inside, she noticed that something was wrong. The door to a spare bedroom was open. She was certain it had been closed when she'd left. In her own bedroom she found her jewelry box and clothes dresser rifled. When she picked up the telephone to call the police, the line was dead.

Mrs. Williams knew exactly what that meant after all the publicity from the previous year. She rushed out and went to a neighbor's house. The neighbor immediately called the police.

When the police looked through the house, they found something very ominous on the floor near Anna Williams' bed: a length of wire. What was it that the killer had promised in his letter to KAKE? "#8 Next victim maybe: You will find her hanging with a wire noose . . ."

Besides the wire, there was also a length of rope and a wood broomstick handle.

The Wichita patrolman called the homicide squad assigned to the BTK cases. It was clear that the killer had been in the house waiting for someone to come home. For some reason, however, he'd left. The detectives went through the house, looking for something, anything, that might help identify the intruder. But other than the sinister wire, rope and broomstick, and a neat pile of broken glass in the basement, there was nothing.

That was it for Mrs. Williams, however. She didn't want to spend any more time in the house. She moved in with her daughter and her husband in a small town south of Wichita. From that point forward, her daughter periodically went to pick up the mail at the Pinecrest house, but no one slept there overnight.

On June 15, more than a month-and-a-half later, Mrs. Williams' daughter picked up the mail and found a letter-sized manila envelope addressed to "Williams, Clarence R. CO/ Anna," apparently an attempt to indicate that the envelope contained some sort of official document related to Anna Williams' recently deceased husband. Mrs. Williams' daughter opened the envelope; her mother's missing scarf spilled out, along with some of the stolen jewelry. There was also a poem and a ghastly drawing.

The drawing showed a woman with her hands bound behind her, straddling a broomstick as she bent over a bed. Her ankles were tied together with rope which was tied to the stick. She was gagged, and her face was turned toward the viewer of the drawing. It appeared that her eyes were drawn as mirrors.

ANNA, WHY DIDN'T YOU APPEAR, read the title of the poem. The name "Anna" appeared where the name

"Louis" had been crossed out. Again, this appeared to be something that the killer had plagiarized from another source—the writing was far more elegant than anything the killer had put into his letters; the vocabulary was at an entirely different level. It once again appeared that the killer was trying to pretend to be something that he was not. And there was more—the original title, naming "Louis," suggested that the verse was originally meant for a man. That in turn suggested that the killer was animated by homoerotic feelings.

Well, why not? So far, none of the victims had ever been penetrated. There'd been opportunity for that at the Otero house, at the Vian house and at the Fox house. But all the killer had done was engage in auto-erotic manipulation. What did this suggest, if anything? That the killer was deep in the closet? (Some recalled that he had, indeed, been "in the closet" at the Bright and Fox houses.) The binding suggests that the killer had a strong aversion to women, a need to degrade and control them. Was the killer acting out some long-suppressed hatred of his mother?

The drawing was similar to the crude artistry of the Nancy Fox rendering. The lines were similar, enough so that the Wichita detectives had no doubt that BTK had been in the house.

Now that BTK had apparently decided to communicate again, the police advised the news media to be alert to any new mailings sent to them. The following day, a similar manila envelope arrived at KAKE-TV. The envelope apparently had some clue that it was from the killer, possibly the BTK logo that had first appeared on the February 1978 letter to KAKE. The station turned the envelope over to the police unopened, to better assist the police in checking it for fingerprints.

Once the police opened it, they discovered a copy of

the poem, another scarf taken from the Williams house, and a second copy of the drawing.

That same day, the police announced that the new communications from the killer had been received, and the circumstances.

"It is our opinion that BTK was in fact in her home," Wichita Deputy Police Chief Bobby Stout told reporters. "It is our opinion that had this lady been at home, she would have been killed. We quite definitely believe that that was the intent, and we feel very fortunate that no one was killed."

The *Eagle* noted that fifteen detectives and eight laboratory experts were working on the case, and that efforts were being made to compile a "psychological profile" of the killer.

Someone asked Deputy Chief Stout what the killer really wanted.

"Everybody has tried to second guess what this man wants," Stout said, "and I'm not going to add my name to that list."

Neither the poem nor the drawing was published. Years later, the FBI's John Douglas suggested that that might have been a mistake. He thought that someone who knew the killer might have recognized either the style or merely the fact that he was drawing such violent, degrading pictures.

And as it played out, that's exactly what occurred: the killer's small boy happened on a copy of the ugly drawing one day, about the time it was mailed.

"What's this, Daddy?" he asked.

"Oh, that's just something for school," the killer said. And his son thought no more about it.

Just after the new publicity, the killer got his diploma from Wichita State University. Now he had a degree in criminal justice.

He decided to apply to the police department for a job. He didn't get it. All the records from the application were later tossed. The department only kept the applications of those who had made it.

In the meantime, the killer went quiet again. It would be years before he was heard from once more. When that finally happened, though, the police would keep it secret.

15:

Poets

By the fall of 1979, almost all of the steam had evaporated from the Wichita department's investigation into the murders. The best leads were gone. The only positive thing was that there seemed to be no new murders—except for the narrow escape of Anna Williams. What could possibly explain this interlude? Every expert, including Robert Ressler and John Douglas of the FBI, kept insisting that once a serial killer started, he did not stop until arrested or dead. It was like someone with a bag of peculiarly tasty potato chips, someone said—they couldn't eat just one.

Efforts were made to check the alibis of men who had been sent to prison after February of both 1974 and 1978. If they could only find someone who was incarcerated between the Otero murders, but was out of jail in time for Shirley Vian in March 1977, then was sent back in after the February 1978 letters to KAKE—that would be a perfect fit. There were some in that group—not very many, and none of them was the killer, unfortunately.

Well, maybe the killer was dead. Some detectives thought about matching deaths to the time frame, but that was impossible. There were literally thousands of deaths a year in Wichita alone. Without something more specific to go on, just saying that the killer was probably dead was like holding up a silver cross and waving a garlic clove—it might make you feel good, but it probably wasn't very effective.

In the summer of that same year, 1979, police tried something new: they released copies of the tape of the voice of the man who had called to report the "home-i-cide" of Nancy Fox in 1977.

The tape was played frequently over the air on KAKE's radio station, as well as on television, on August 14 and 15.

"I'm very hopeful for positive results, but I'm very doubtful," LaMunyon told reporters. "Even if you know the individual, to identify him will be very difficult unless he's very close to you."

The tape was originally recorded at very slow speed, which limited its quality. Loewen and KAKE had offered to pay to have the tape enhanced by an expert using a computer; in 1979 this was pretty radical technology.

LaMunyon had to think it over.

"We didn't want to do it just for news," he said. "But we thought there might be some possible benefit to the investigation . . . I discussed it with the detectives and we decided we had nothing to lose. It's a long shot, but there's a possibility."

Loewen and KAKE sent a copy of the tape to Mark Weiss, a professor at Queens College in Flushing, New York. Weiss had developed a computer program to weed out extraneous noises in a voice tape; previously he'd used the program to analyze the Watergate tapes, as well as the Dallas Police Department radio recording to the assassination of President Kennedy in Dealy Plaza.

After two days, the police had received about forty or fifty new tips. But after further investigation, none of the names given turned out to be the killer.

The previous fall, Wichita police were visited by a woman and her husband who claimed that the woman was being stalked. That in itself wasn't particularly unusual—a lot of women, unfortunately, have had the experience of an unwanted man who becomes tiresome, if not obsessed. What was a little more unusual was the age of the woman: 48. Your run-of-the-mill stalker most often was attracted to teenagers or women in their early 20s. But Ruth Finley's husband was a responsible person in the community, a supervisor for the telephone company, and he believed his wife, who also worked for the phone company, so the police did too. What unfolded over the next year, however, was rather more unbelievable.

More than thirty years earlier, as a teenager, Ruth had claimed that an unknown assailant had burned her thighs with a steam iron, leaving a sort of "brand" on both legs. There was, in fact, some minor publicity about the "branding" event—Ruth had the clippings to prove it. Now she told the Wichita police that the unknown stalker was trying to extort her—suggesting that he would "tell some people" about her "brand."

What? The whole thing sounded pretty weird to the detectives, who after all had their hands full with the hunt for BTK. But then, beginning in late November 1978, Ruth began receiving threatening letters. By the end of the month, the stalker was sending her threatening poems.

Poems?

Yes, and not very good ones, either:

Where ever you go on water or land
You still got to pay or I tell about yur [sic] brand
I am smart and no [sic] things to do
You talk to people I despise
Like police Lt & tele[phone] spies

By late January 1979, Ruth claimed she had been abducted, but escaped. Police put her under surveillance, and nothing happened. Her case was featured on a Wichita radio station—police hoped that the stalker might call in, to no avail. Then she claimed to have received a telephone call at her job, telling her that a surprise was waiting for her in the lobby of her telephone company office building. Police searched the building and found a knife in a phone booth in the lobby.

Two days later, the woman received another poem in the mail:

There was a female named Ruth
Who thought nothing of calling a sleuth
I have no doubt
My call was checked out
I didn't tell you your present was in a booth.

The style of the bad poetry was very different from the BTK poems. For one thing, the BTK poems were obviously ripped off from some published source, and these appeared to be, well, original work. While it wasn't very likely that BTK had suddenly gotten (a little) smarter about poetry, the possibility couldn't be overlooked. What if Ruth's stalker was in fact the long-sought killer?

The most striking aspect of what would come to be called "the Poet case" in Wichita was that there were so many parallels between what had been published about BTK and the things that happened to poor Ruth. Too many things, some thought—like coincidences of anniversaries, or the bad poetry. And while some thought this was BTK branching out to extortion, others were convinced that Ruth was doing this to herself—and using the anxiety over BTK as the envelope to package it. But then Ruth was admitted to the hospital with three stab wounds in her back. As it happened, the stabbing took place the day before KAKE and the "home-i-cide" telephone call. The stabbing had come even as the TV station was hyping in advance its forthcoming broadcast of the killer's voice.

Poetry? Stab wounds? And now, just as the call was about to be so publicly disseminated? It was enough to make a homicide detective wonder whether the killer was after Ruth.

By the summer of 1979, the police had no other BTK leads to follow—at least, they had none that had been developed with the paucity of information they had disclosed about the crimes. As a result, it was decided to put a full-court press on Ruth's "poet," if for no other reason than to identify him, and if possible, eliminate him as BTK.

Over the next two years, more than fifty letters were sent to Ruth and her husband, and all of them were examined minutely by the police. As later documented by Bob Beattie, the harassment got weirder and weirder—calls from a mortuary, saying they'd been contacted about Ruth's imminent need for their services, an arson fire at the couple's house, the telephone line being cut at least twice, eggs and feces being smeared against the walls of the house. Eventually, even the news media began to get mail from Ruth's stalker.

Despite all their efforts between 1979 and 1981, the detectives were unable to establish the identity of Ruth's violent stalker. He seemed to be a will-o'-the-wisp, as phantomlike as BTK. But after two years of watching and detecting, some Wichita investigators had reached a solution to the case—Ruth was doing this to herself for some reason.

Then, in early September 1981, police received a letter that essentially asserted that Ruth's "poet" and BTK were the same person. The letter said that Ruth would be "#8," and that Chief LaMunyon's wife would be "#9."

That did it. The next day, LaMunyon carted home all

fifteen volumes of reports on Ruth's "poet," and read them. As far as he could tell, nothing about the case made any sense—the only actual witness was Ruth herself. There seemed to be no corroborative information that indicated there really was a stalker. A meeting was held among the detectives and LaMunyon. Opinions remained split on whether Ruth's "poet" and BTK were one and the same, as well as on whether someone really was stalking Ruth.

"The first thing we have to do," LaMunyon told them, "is eliminate the Finleys." Once that was done, and only when that was done, could the detectives begin to consider the other possibilities.

Three days later the police rented rooms in a Wichita hotel, from which they could keep Ruth's house under twenty-four-hour surveillance.

The surveillance was maintained for nine days. Nothing done by Ruth or her husband seemed out of the ordinary. Then, on September 17, 1981, a helicopter following the Finleys observed them dropping letters into a mailbox. Detective Garrison, following surreptitiously in a car, pulled up to the mailbox just after Ruth and her husband had driven away. He propped up the hood of his car as if he were having engine trouble, and kept guard over the mailbox. The detectives called postal inspectors, and when they opened the mailbox, they found two letters from Ruth's "poet."

Meanwhile, Ruth was seen mailing more letters, and when this box was checked, more letters from the "poet" were found. Then, after obtaining a warrant, the detectives searched Ruth's home and office. Still more materials related to the "poet" were found.

Ruth had been stalking herself for almost three years.

When she was confronted by the police with the evidence, Ruth appeared to have no idea that she'd been doing this to herself. She was admitted to a psychiatric hospital. A few days later, a psychiatrist at the hospital attributed Ruth's behavior to an unconscious, almost unreasoning fear of BTK. By making herself a victim before she became a victim, Ruth in effect surrounded herself with a battalion of badge-carrying bodyguards, and did it so well that at least half the police department had been fooled.

LaMunyon later estimated that the police had spent $370,000 investigating Ruth's stalker, mostly in the hope that it would lead them to BTK. But instead, it was a fatal diversion—fatal for at least three more women.

16:

Ghostbusters

The "poet" case had been a disaster for the Wichita police. Two years and hundreds of thousands of dollars had been poured down the drain, and the investigators were no closer to identifying BTK than they had been the morning after the Oteros had been murdered. LaMunyon had lost face; he'd also lost confidence in the existing homicide squad. The thing to do, he decided, was to start from scratch.

In 1982, he decided to form a special team within the department, composed of detectives who had not worked on any of the BTK cases before. LaMunyon's idea was that the new team would be free of any of the biases that had crept into the investigation from all the years of frustration. And he had a gift for this new team—the additional resources of the FBI.

By that time, the BTK murders had received a substantial amount of national publicity, and why not? Here was the ultimate urban nightmare—an unknown killer who broke into people's houses at random, and strangled them to death. No apparent connection between the victims, and no viable suspects. It could be anyone, and anyone could die. It was any police chief's worst scenario.

By the early 1980s, the FBI's Behavioral Science Unit was up and running. Douglas, Ressler, Hazelwood and a variety of other specialists were studying serial crimes reported from across the country, attempting to identify patterns among the crimes, and among the perpetrators. A new tool was in place at Quantico—essentially, a lengthy questionnaire that would attempt to identify the keys to solving serial crimes. Called the Violent Criminal Apprehension Project, or ViCAP, the questionnaire was the end result of work done years earlier by legendary Los Angeles Police Department Homicide Detective Pierce Brooks. It was Brooks' idea that serial predators tended to follow patterns in all their crimes. Statistical analysis of the patterns might in turn lead to better methods of identification of the criminals.

To get the ViCAP system running, two cases were selected for input into a computer—the Atlanta child murders supposedly committed by Wayne Williams, and BTK.

With the FBI ready to assist, LaMunyon moved to activate his new crew of investigators. For the next four years, they would work with the FBI in an effort to use the latest in computer and scientific technology to winnow the killer's name out of the darkness.

To head the new unit—soon to be nicknamed the "Ghostbusters" after the popular movie of the era—LaMunyon picked Captain Al Stewart. Stewart had been commanding the department's internal affairs division, the cops who investigated other cops. Seven others, all men, were also selected; none of them had worked on BTK before.

At the first meeting of the group, LaMunyon instructed them that they were never to tell any other police officer what their assignment was. According to Beattie, LaMunyon told the members of the new unit that if any one of them ever revealed their assignment, he would fire them all. By this point, given Douglas, Ressler and Hazelwood's earlier assertions about the wannabe-a-cop characteristics of the killer, LaMunyon had to consider the very real possibility that the killer actually *was* a cop. It would explain a lot, he thought.

LaMunyon was also determined to get qualified outside help from the academic world to assist in the project. By the time the Ghostbusters were done, the advice of mathematicians, psychologists, biologists and even astrologers and numerologists had been solicited. An Air Force general associated with the super-secret National Reconnaissance Office, the spy satellite controllers, would be consulted. But mostly the work was collecting and analyzing the reams of paper that had already been generated. The answer had to be in there somewhere—it was just that they couldn't recognize it.

In 1984, three FBI agents—Douglas, Hazelwood and Ron Walker—met with a detective from the Wichita Police Department to give him their collective impressions of BTK. Sitting in on the session, which was tape recorded by the Wichita detective, was the legendary Pierce Brooks, the retired Los Angeles Police Department detective who had been instrumental in getting ViCAP launched. As it happened, one of Brooks' early cases with the LAPD was none other than Harvey Glatman—BTK's claimed idol "Harvery" Glatman.

As recalled by Hazelwood, the Wichita officer later transcribed their taped remarks, and provided each man with a verbatim, hand-written record of what had been said. No formal written report was ever produced by any of the FBI men, or Brooks, according to Hazelwood. But each profiling expert provided some educated guesses as to what sort of person BTK was.

"There were some points of departure among us," Hazelwood recalled, referring to the opinions provided to the Wichita detective, whose name Hazelwood could no longer recall two decades later. "But we were all pretty much in agreement that what the killer was after, what motivated him, was control." The murders weren't personal, all agreed; the killer had no anger toward the victims, or even a desire to have conventional sex with them. What got him going was the process—looking for a victim, stalking them, planning, anticipating, followed by the execution. All thought the killer was married, probably lower to middle class economically, attracted to pornography, an underachiever, and someone prone to thinking of himself as better than everyone else—a classic narcissist with a mostly hidden streak of sadism.

One of the bureau's most insightful profilers, Hazelwood had substantial experience profiling sexual predators. He first became interested in violent, serial sex crimes when, while in training as a military policeman, an instructor lectured about the Glatman case.

"I kept asking why?" Hazelwood recalled. "Why did he take pictures of the victims? Why did he do this or not that?"

"It's not important," Hazelwood said he was told by the instructor. But to Hazelwood, it *was* important. Later, he met Brooks, who gave him considerable insight into Harvey Glatman's history, including that killer's early bondage experiences and penchant for auto-erotic hanging.

As a sexual sadist who was excited by bondage, BTK had been practicing bondage for some time, not unlike Harvey Glatman, Hazelwood thought. The bondage fetish had probably begun when the killer was between seven and ten years old. As an adult, the killer, Hazelwood thought, collected bondage tools such as ropes, chains and handcuffs, along with detective magazines that featured bondage cases. He had an interest in psychology and criminology, and probably frequented adult book stores. He was articulate and intelligent, but an underachiever, and someone adept at convincing people they knew him, when they really didn't. He saw himself as a "lone wolf" type, and for him, the primary motive was to have control over someone. It wasn't sex that drove the killer so much as the stalking, the planning, the capture, the execution of the crime. He was angry at women, but not at the victims personally. They were just props necessary to his desire to demonstrate his control. He carried a gun and a knife, but he preferred to kill his victims by hand, which was more satisfying to his desire to show his control. BTK, Hazelwood said, considered himself intellectually and emotionally superior to everyone else.

Future cases, Hazelwood said—and he believed there would be more—would be marked by the combination of sexual bondage and strangulation.

"I can't stop it so the monster goes on, and hurt [sic] me as well as society," the killer had written. "It's hard for me to control myself. You probably call me 'psyhcotic [sic] with sexual perversion hangup.' When this monster enter [sic] my brain, I will never know. But, it here to stay. How does one cure himself?" The killer himself believed there was no cure, that he would keep on killing for as long as he lived.

The toxic self-love was what drove the killer to send the communications. He absolutely had to get the publicity for his actions, or his life would lose all meaning.

This tape-recorded profile was augmented with some observations by a clinical psychologist, Dr. John Allen. Allen told the Ghostbusters that they had to put aside their preconceptions of the sort of sex predator they were looking for. The man they sought wouldn't have tattoos, he wouldn't linger around school playgrounds, he wouldn't drool or expose himself, and he certainly wouldn't cavort with ducks. The predator they were looking for was someone who seemed utterly normal on the outside, in fact, someone who was absolutely self-controlled. That would be the exterior of the personality, Allen suggested—the shell. Carefully erected, assiduously maintained, the shell would carry BTK through society like a suit of armor, concealing the raging narcissism within. For proof, Allen pointed to Kevin Bright's description of the behavior of the man who was trying to strangle him—that the strangler was calm, matter-of-fact, but deliberate. Or the Relford children—the man who'd come to the door seemed well-dressed, and had said he was a detective.

No, the cardinal thing to remember about BTK was that he wore a mask—a mask that made him seem just like any other person.

Even a detective.

17:

"PJ Cookie"

The years had passed quite pleasantly for the killer. He and his wife and their two small children—his "social obligations," as he thought of them—lived in contentment in the house they'd acquired in the Wichita bedroom community of Park City, some eight miles north of downtown Wichita. No one from the police had ever questioned him—not about anything. He knew they had absolutely no reason to.

His son was now a Cub Scout. That was good—it gave him another alibi for getting out of the house. The library wasn't any good anymore—not since he'd graduated. Maybe that was one reason he hadn't tried to kill anyone since 1979—he couldn't get out of the house because of his "social obligations." Without a wife, without children, he thought, he would have killed many more people. But he had to have the cover, and he was patient—something would come up.

And then something did. It shocked the killer as much as anything—the person he wanted to kill lived only a few doors away. *This is bad*, he thought. *A serial killer should never act in his own neighborhood.* But if he could pull it off—if he could really get away with it—wouldn't that be something? That would make him one of the greatest serial killers of all time—no one else would have dared.

He began to keep an eye on his neighbor, a diminutive, 53-year-old widow named Marine Hedge. When she came home from her job, the killer would wave at her, and she would wave back. They were neighbors—it was the friendly thing to do.

This will be complicated, the killer thought. *The trick will be to be someplace else when it happens. The transportation will be the hard part.*

But as he kept an eye on Marine, a plan began to form in his mind. He worked it out—just how to kill his own neighbor in such a way that no one would ever suspect him. He would use the Cub Scouts as his cover.

On the evening of April 26, 1985, a Friday, the killer was wearing his scoutmaster disguise, as little boys from all over Sedgwick County gathered for a camp-out north of the city. As the boys cooked their hot dogs and sang songs around the campfire, the killer told the other fathers that he had a very bad headache, and he had to get some sleep. No one noticed as he got into his car and drove some distance away. In the darkness by the side of a deserted road he removed the scoutmaster suit and pulled on his "hit clothes"—dark pants, a dark jacket, a watch cap. Then he drove to a bowling alley in northeast Wichita.

"So I parked my car at the bowling alley," the killer said later, "and pretend that I'm really having a good time. I go in and order a beer. And I don't drink it, just put some on my face and I splash a little on my clothes so the taxicab driver that picks me up knows I've been drinking, and he can smell it."

The killer acted drunk. He called for a cab and told the driver that he needed someone to drive him home. The cab took him back to his own neighborhood, but the killer told the driver to stop before they reached his house.

"I need to exercise, I need to walk," he told the driver. "I need to wear this off . . . I need to walk a little bit." He tried to slur his voice. The driver let him out. He paid the driver and turned to walk away.

As soon as the cab was gone, the killer cut through a park that was behind his own house, as well as the house of his in-laws. This was about as close to home as he could get. After moving as stealthily as he could, the killer came up to the rear of Marine's house. He could see her car was there. He thought that meant she was home. That meant he had to be as quiet as he possibly could in getting inside the house.

He snipped the telephone wire. At the back door he used a long screwdriver to pop it open. Once inside, he realized that he'd been wrong—Marine was not home. He looked through the house, locating the usual things—nylons, scarves, articles of clothing that excited him. While he was in the bedroom he heard a car door slam outside. He hid himself inside the closet. He heard the door open, and Marine came in with a man.

Shoot! he told himself. He hadn't planned on this. After the fight with Kevin Bright years before, he didn't want to have any more confrontations with men. He certainly didn't want to try to strangle a man like he had with Kevin. This time, if he had to, he'd shoot first.

Eventually the man left. It was after 1 in the morning. The killer continued to wait in the closet. He heard Marine get ready for bed. It was getting close to midnight. Still he waited. He wanted to surprise her in her sleep.

At length, when he thought that Marine was asleep, he crept out of the closet as quietly as he could. He approached the bed—yes, it looked like she'd dropped off to sleep. He turned on the light in the adjacent bathroom. She didn't wake up. The killer climbed onto the bed, and this did wake her up.

"What the hell is going on?" Marine asked.

The killer put his hands around her throat and began to

choke her. Marine struggled to get loose, but the killer outweighed her by almost ninety pounds, and had all the leverage, since he was on top. Marine passed out.

He turned her over and cuffed her hands behind her back. He wrapped his belt around her neck and choked her again until she was dead. He resumed looking through the house. He found her purse and emptied its contents, taking her driver's license and car keys.

He returned to the bed and removed her nightgown, then wrapped the body in the blankets from the bed. He picked up the wrapped body and took it outside to Marine's car, opened the trunk and put it in the back. The killer was surprised at how heavy the body was. It was the first time he'd ever moved a dead person.

The killer started Marine's car; by now it was after 2 A.M. He drove out of the neighborhood, heading for his church, located across the street from his old high school from twenty years earlier. He had keys to the building, because he was one of the church leaders—hell, everyone trusted him, he was one of the pillars of the community. He pulled into the parking lot, opened the trunk, and removed the body. He put it down under a line of fir trees outside. He unlocked the church doors and went into the basement. He had sheets of black plastic hidden down there. He retrieved the plastic and used thumbtacks to secure it over the windows, so no one would be able to see any light coming from the basement. He turned on the lights, then went back outside to see if any light was showing through the plastic. There was none. He picked up the body from the ground and carried it downstairs into the basement.

He removed the blankets from the body, then began tying it with ropes, pausing periodically to reposition the body and to retie the ropes. He fitted the body with high-heeled shoes, bound it with nylons, used other props he had brought with him, including gags. Over about three hours he did this many times, taking a photograph of each new position—thirty pictures in all—with his Polaroid camera.

It was beyond macabre—it was as grisly as it was ghastly. "I had my time with her," he said later.

By then it was beginning to get light outside.

Oh shoot, he thought, *I got to hurry.* He'd taken too long, indulged himself too much. He had to get everything cleaned up, but he was running out of time. He had to untie the body, wrap it in the blankets again, carry it back upstairs to the car, then get rid of it someplace where it wouldn't be found right away. Then he had to come back to the church, finish cleaning up, get rid of the car, then get back to the Cub Scout camp by 7:30 in the morning to perfect his alibi.

He drove Marine's car east and then north, finally stopping by the side of a field well out of town. A culvert paralleled the road. The killer took her body out of the trunk and dumped it in the culvert, then covered it with some loose brush. This was a place, he knew, that was occasionally used by people getting rid of animal carcasses; and in fact, there were the remains of two dead dogs nearby.

He went back to the car and realized he'd locked the keys inside.

He found a rock and broke the windshield, managing to reach in with his hands to retrieve the keys. He drove back to the church to take down the black plastic and hide it, and clean everything else up. The sweat was pouring off of him.

He left the church and drove Marine's car back to the area near the bowling alley, where he'd left his own car. He parked, got out, shut the door, locked it and went to his car to drive back to the Cub Scout event.

He made it. No one had even missed him.

It was Saturday morning, April 27, 1985. And tomorrow he would go to church. He was sure no one would notice the tiny holes from the thumbtacks he'd used to put up the plastic to cover the windows. And he was very, very sure that no one would ever suspect what the church basement had been used for that night.

Which gave him a real charge.

18:

Linkage Blindness

That same day, Marine did not show up for her job at a local hospital—she worked in the cafeteria there, and would have told someone if she'd had to miss work. In fact, she never *had* missed work. It was completely uncharacteristic of her, so her supervisor called Marine's son-in-law, Rod Hook. Hook drove to Marine's house, but soon decided that she was not home, because her car was gone. It was odd that she would leave without telling anyone, and especially not telling someone at her job, Hook thought.

The next day, April 28, still not having heard from his mother-in-law, Hook was really worried. He called the small-town Park City Police Department to tell them Marine had disappeared. He drove out to Marine's house, and was joined by a Park City police officer. Both men discovered the severed phone line, and noticed that the back door appeared to be jimmied open.

Soon, the Park City police tracked down Marine's date from Friday night, and discovered that she had had dinner with him Friday night at the Red Coach Restaurant north of the city, and that he'd left her alive and well about 1 A.M. on Saturday morning.

Despite the cut telephone wire and the evidence of forced entry; despite the fact that Marine's bed had been stripped of sheets and blankets; despite the fact that her car was missing—the Park City authorities initially listed Marine's mysterious disappearance as a missing persons case. This was not a good way to get the attention of Stewart's Ghostbuster crew, who were even then searching high and low for some sort of trail to BTK.

But even if the Park City police had immediately notified the Ghostbusters of the cut telephone line, outside of that there wasn't much to match with the BTK cases from the 1970s. First of all, the victimology was all wrong—BTK's victims had been young women, not 53-year-old widows. Anna Williams *was* 63, but as far as the Ghostbusters were concerned, the real target there had been Anna's granddaughter.

And even if BTK now was targeting older women, there were other problems with the case, at least as far as tying it to BTK. For one thing, there was no body. In all the other cases, the killer had left the body at the scene. But Marine was missing, and even if she had been murdered, that was very different.

Most important, though, Marine Hedge lived in Park City, eight miles away from the scene of the BTK crimes. Neither the Park City police, nor the Sedgwick County Sheriff's Department, which eventually took over the investigation of the case, ever seriously considered that BTK was at work in their jurisdictions.

Four days later, Marine's car was located in a parking lot near the bowling alley. It was obvious from the windshield that it had been broken into. A security guard's log showed that the car had been there since the previous Saturday morning. A Wichita police detective came to the parking lot. A locksmith was called to open the car. In the trunk of the car, the Wichita detective discovered two bed covers, a purple bedspread, a tan curtain, and a pink Sears electric blanket. Marine Hedge's bedding had been found, but she was still missing.

Three days after that, Park City Police Chief Ace Van Wey decided to stop at a place where he knew that people sometimes disposed of animal carcasses. This was some distance to the east from where Marine and her male friend had eaten dinner on Friday night. Accompanied by the city's animal control officer, Van Wey clambered down to the culvert and discovered Marine Hedge's body. An autopsy on the decomposing remains showed that she had been strangled to death.

But no one believed—well, at least officially—that BTK had gone outside the city limits for a new kill.

Effective serial homicide investigation involves casting a broad net, followed by the mind-numbing drudgery of elimination. It's the opposite of most criminal investigation, where a likely culprit is identified at the start, followed by efforts to prove the person guilty sufficient to convince a jury.

"It's like looking for a needle in a haystack of needles," one police commander once said of another such long-running serial murder investigation. In such a case, all-inclusiveness is a virtue, not a drawback. The small-bore approach simply will not work in random homicides where the killer has no connection to the victim. Nevertheless, the sheer size, complexity and expensive, time-consuming effort to reel in a large net of potential suspects, and then to eliminate them one by one, is all too often beyond the resources of a local police department, if not its imagination; certainly, the political leaders who budget the resources needed all too often have their eyes focused on the short term. In a sense, it's doing everything backward from the usual police investigation method, a reality that is often not understood by the money appropriators.

But it's the only way. And in that regard, every extra pair of eyes and ears on the street can help, because the serial murder problem is not so much a crime problem as it is a public mental health problem. That's one of the main reasons why keeping the details of such crimes secret is counterproductive. The more information out there, the better the chances are that someone will recognize the links.

As the mid-1980s rolled by, Stewart's Ghostbusters pulled out every stop they could think of to identify the killer, constantly looking for some anomaly that would jump out at them. The fact that they had to be aware that the person they were seeking was someone who seemed to be, to the outside world, just like them, made the job very much more difficult. It was only the fact that they remained convinced that the killer had to be someone intimately familiar with the east Wichita neighborhood that prevented them from considering that the killer might be wandering farther and farther afield as he grew older and more experienced in murder.

Stewart had broken his group into teams—two detectives each for the Oteros, Shirley Vian and Nancy Fox, and two others for Kathy Bright and the Anna Williams break-in. They examined the records of every male adult who lived within a quarter-mile of each crime scene. Everyone had recognized that the killer seemed drawn to a particular section of the city, the southeast quadrant. There the houses were all similar in age and type, as were many of the residents. It seemed possible that the killer had grown up in that area, or that he'd lived there for many years. Of course, that meant there were literally thousands of potential suspects. It wasn't enough to simply review the BTK files, the detectives realized—they had to go through virtually all of the department's recent reports on peeping, or exposure, or impersonating a police officer, or other burglaries in the southeast part of the city. On at least one occasion, according to Beattie, the detectives even disinterred the dead in an effort to compare biological evidence.

Detectives checked with the telephone company for records of cut telephone lines—it turned out that there were many more of those than anyone had expected. Was this the work of the killer? Had he cut those lines and waited inside, as he had at Anna Williams' house, only to give up and leave before someone came home? One address turned out to be just down the street from the Vian house—at the house Steve Relford had seen the killer visit before coming to the Vian house instead. The review of the department's reports on breaking and entering showed a number of incidents that had occurred in other houses near the known victims' homes. It seemed very likely that there was little about the victims themselves that precipitated the attacks—the similar break-ins suggested that it was the date and the location that was determinative. The killer had made up his mind to kill someone—anyone, but preferably a woman—on a certain date, and if the original target wasn't home, he improvised by attacking someone else in the immediate neighborhood.

The Ghostbusters also developed one of the first attempts in the country to computerize data for the purpose of sifting through huge numbers of suspects. They were able to obtain book-borrowing information for patrons of the public library, as well as lists of Wichita State University students and faculty; they rounded up lists of employees of the phone company, Dillons grocery stores, plumbers, window installers, natural gas company employees, just about anyone with some superficially legitimate reason to be at work in the southeast section of the city. They did not, it appears, check with firms that installed burglar alarms—there simply weren't very many of those in the affected neighborhoods.

The FBI, meanwhile, rounded up details on other bondage homicides committed in other parts of the country—to them, at least, it was perfectly plausible that the killer had murdered in other jurisdictions besides Wichita.

Over time, the Ghostbusters visited prisons and mental health facilities to interview men, and collected even more biological samples. The DNA era had not yet dawned—the semen samples taken from the crime scenes could only be typed in the most general way. Nevertheless, the blood and tissue type of the suspect was shared by only six percent of the male population. This narrowed the field considerably and provided the detectives with a sure way to eliminate almost nineteen out of twenty possible suspects. But it still left a very large number of possibles—6 percent of 100,000 Wichita area men eligible by age and race was 6,000 suspects.

Then, in 1985, after DNA testing became technologically feasible, Stewart's investigators decided to put some of their best suspects to the test. The object was to identify DNA taken from the semen samples at the Otero crime scene, and compare it with DNA taken from the suspects. According to Beattie, the very first person to have his DNA tested in a criminal investigation in the United States was a Wichita police officer. The officer was not the killer. Eventually, after a number of expensive and time-consuming tests of 225 of the best suspects, a dozen names remained: five men who refused to provide their samples, and seven others whose samples showed they were the same blood and tissue type as the killer—in other words, in the six percent group—but whom the rudimentary DNA testing could not eliminate.

Stewart also had the idea of seeing if the military's supposedly vaunted spy satellites might have recorded a vehicle near the Nancy Fox house. Stewart reasoned that since Nancy's house wasn't too far from an Air Force base, and because arms control agreements might require the base to be under satellite surveillance, it was possible that the killer's car might have been observed from overhead. He managed to wrangle an appointment with an Air Force general. The general said no, absolutely not—he couldn't confirm or deny that such satellites existed, let alone whether it might have photographs showing Nancy's house on the night in question. Then, according to Beattie, Stewart showed him pictures of Josie and Joey Otero. The general then twisted arms in the Pentagon, and eventually some surveillance photographs from the eye in the sky were produced. Unfortunately, they were of no help.

By 1986, the Ghostbusters had spent nearly half a million dollars on the hunt for the killer—someone who hadn't been heard from since early in 1978, seven years earlier. The politicians were growing restive about the time and money being spent. Wasn't it likely that the killer had left town? Or that he was dead? What if he simply couldn't be identified—couldn't that money be used for the living? It was reminiscent in a way of the scene in *Jaws*, when the mayor tells the police chief that the shark is gone.

The Ghostbusters were summoned to a secret session at the Wichita city manager's office, one attended by prosecutors. There they gave a briefing on what they had done so far, and what they still had to do. The next morning, the politicians pulled the plug—the Ghostbusters were themselves busted. It was too expensive to continue to look for someone who had seemingly vanished, and if Hannon were to be believed, had never really existed.

Stewart was disgusted at the wishy-washy politicians who balked at the difficulties. Just because it was hard didn't mean they shouldn't try. But the political wind was against him. Not long after this, he decided to retire. The Ghostbusters' effort would be the last time anyone tried to solve the BTK puzzle—until Beattie, almost twenty years later.

19:

"PJ Piano"

But if the police had quit, the killer hadn't. Even as the Ghostbusters were boxing up all their files for storage, he continued to prowl the city, always trolling for new "projects." He continued to build his homemade pornography collection, and found new and better ways to conceal his predilections from his "social obligations." He cut a hole in the flooring of his closet and made a sort of safe there to store the tools of his trade; he did the same with false bottoms in drawers, and found places to secrete damning items at the home of his mother and father not far away. By day he drove around the city with his index-card, letter-coded "girls," "trolling" and "stalking." Sometimes he stalked several women at once. He wanted to be prepared to improvise. By night he played the role of the stolid husband and father of two. His wife and his children still had no idea of who he really was.

Late in August 1986, the killer found himself with a lot more time on his hands. His employer, the burglar alarm company, had been bought by another corporation, and the management was in a state of flux. The local managers were in and out of the office, and no one was paying very much attention to what the employees did. "When the cat is away, the mice will play," the killer said later.

One day he found himself driving in northwest Wichita, far from his usual hunting ground. As he drove his company's burglar alarm van down West 13th Street, he noticed a young woman getting out of her car. His "codes" triggered, he began his stalking phase that day. Over the next three weeks he kept the young woman under covert observations, relying on the anonymity afforded by his company van to conceal his presence. He noticed that she often played the piano—she became, in the killer's mind, "Project Piano."

Vicki Wegerle was 28, and a mother of two children: Stephanie, 10, and Brandon, a little over 2. Her husband, Bill, also 28, worked as a self-employed maintenance man for an apartment building. The family didn't have a lot of money, but they were very happy. Vicki was a member of St. Andrew's Lutheran Church in northwest Wichita, and was the child-care supervisor at a nearby Methodist church. She was, by all accounts, a woman who loved children and someone who had everything good about life to look forward to.

But the killer didn't care. In fact, he didn't even know her name.

On September 16, 1986, he decided he was ready. He drove his own car to a shopping center across the street from the target house. He put on a yellow hard hat he'd stolen from his company, one he'd modified by gluing the telephone company's logo on the front. He carried his briefcase with the usual "hit kit," including cord, plastic bags, a knife and his gun, along with his camera. He also had a telephone headset, intended to convince someone he was a bona fide telephone repair person. He'd made a fake telephone company ID card to flash to allay suspicions, and carried an official-looking telephone repair manual. He did not go directly to the target house, but stopped first at the house next door, which was occupied by an elderly couple. He wanted to give more credibility to his "russ," as he referred to it, mispronouncing "ruse." He didn't want the young woman to be suspicious that he was only interested in her house, in case she was watching through the window.

As he approached the target house, he could hear the piano playing. He readied his headset and knocked on the door. The piano went silent, and Vicki Wegerle came to the door. The killer explained that he'd been sent out to check the telephone line for static. Vicki politely said she would bring the family dog into the house from the back yard so he could check the line in the rear of the house. But the killer told her he had to check the line inside. Vicki let him in and showed him the telephone line terminal in the dining room. He glanced at little Brandon, playing on the floor in the living room.

The killer bent over the terminal connection, removing the cover. He put on his headset and touched the alligator clips to the wires.

"Well," he said, "it looks like it works." He dropped his headset into the briefcase and straightened up, then pulled his .22 from the case and pointed it at her.

"Let's go into the bedroom," he said.

Vicki tried to talk the man out of this. "What about my son?" she asked.

The killer said he didn't care about the little boy.

"My husband is coming home for lunch very soon," Vicki said. "In fact, I think he's going to call any minute."

"I hope it's not too soon," the killer said, motioning with his pistol. He took her purse and removed her driver's license and her car keys. Vicki began begging the man to leave them alone, but he ignored her.

He herded her into the bedroom with the gun. He tied her hands behind her with leather laces, then her ankles. He shoved her down onto the bed. He removed one of his cords from his briefcase, and Vicki realized that the man was going to kill her. She began to pray. He reached out with his cord and began to choke her, but the cord broke. Vicki managed to free her hands. She began to fight for her life. The killer tried to get control of her hands again, but Vicki wouldn't let him. They rolled off the bed and onto the floor, Vicki kicking and clawing at him with all her might. She scratched him on his neck and face, drawing blood. The killer punched her in the head, momentarily stunning her. He reached into a dresser drawer and pulled out a pair of nylon stockings. He wrapped one of them around her neck and pulled it tight. He held her in place with his weight as he pulled. Outside, the dog was barking furiously.

After some minutes, the killer eased up on his pressure. Vicki Wegerle was dead. The dog was still barking. The killer began to worry that Vicki had told him the truth—that maybe her husband would come through the door at any minute. From his surveillance he knew that "there was a husband thing," as he put it later. He momentarily considered the idea of killing the husband when he got home, but decided not to take the risk.

Quickly he retied the nylon around the front of Vicki's face, covering her mouth. He pulled up her blouse and pulled down her pants. He removed his camera from the briefcase, posed her in several different positions, taking photographs each time.

I have to get out of here, the killer thought. *I'm always having to hurry up.* It was disappointing.

The killer knew that Vicki's car was an 8-year-old Monte Carlo parked in front of the house. He went to the front door. Little Brandon was still on the living room floor, but now he was crying.

The killer got into the Monte Carlo and started it up. He pulled out onto 13th Street and headed west.

As he drove, another car went by in the opposite

direction—Bill Wegerle coming home for lunch. It was just before 11 A.M.

"That's weird," Wegerle thought, as he saw a car just like Vicki's go by. It was being driven by a man. Wegerle decided that someone else must have a car that looked like Vicki's. He pulled into the driveway and noticed that Vicki's car was gone. He went into the house and found Brandon crying on the floor. He decided that Vicki had had to go out for some sort of emergency—it was very odd that she would have left Brandon alone. He expected her to come back any minute.

The killer stopped Vicki's car at a convenience store at West and West 13th Streets, and tossed his briefcase into a Dumpster. He got back into the car and drove north on West Street, then came to a muffler shop, where he dumped the hard hat, stripping it first of the telephone company logo. He had the gun in his belt. He drove farther north on West, to 21st Street, then headed east, trying to get back to the area where he'd left his own car.

Bill Wegerle was getting more and more worried over the apparent absence of his wife. Ten minutes went by, then twenty. After thirty minutes he was very worried. At forty minutes he knew something terrible had happened.

All this time, Bill had been in the living room, comforting Brandon. Now he decided to look through the rest of the house—maybe he might find some explanation of where Vicki had gone. He went into the bedroom and discovered her body lying on the floor, concealed behind the bed. He saw that her face was covered with the nylon stocking. He tried to untie it, but couldn't. He pulled out his pocket knife and cut off the nylon and a leather thong that was also around her neck. Vicki wasn't breathing.

At 11:54 A.M. he called 911.

"Vicki, Vicki, oh God, no," he was saying as the 911 operator came on the line. "Come quick," he told her. "I think someone's killed my wife."

The fire department reached the Wegerle house just after noon. They found a distraught Bill Wegerle on the front porch.

"If I could've been here five minutes earlier I could've done something," the firemen heard him say.

They went into the bedroom. Vicki's body was lying in a three-foot space between the bed and the wall, hidden from view through the bedroom doorway. That was why Bill Wegerle hadn't noticed it when he'd first come home. The firemen checked Vicki for vital signs, but realized that she was gone. They nevertheless decided to try CPR. Within a few minutes she was being rushed by ambulance to a nearby hospital, where she was pronounced dead even as Wichita homicide detectives were arriving at the house.

As it happened, this was the same day as Al Stewart's retirement party. Halfway through the festivities someone called to tell the assembled guests that another bondage murder had taken place in Wichita that very day. But Stewart shouldn't worry, he was told—the police already had a good suspect.

Bill Wegerle.

Since BTK was, by general consensus, either dead or departed from the city, or alternatively, had never really existed, Wegerle became the detectives' prime focus in the murder of Vicki. In one way, that's simply a matter of procedure—the husband is always the first one to be looked at. In the Vicki Wegerle murder, Wichita detectives had another reason for their suspicion—the forty-five-minute gap between Bill's return home for lunch and the time he'd called 911.

Bill tried to explain about the man he'd seen driving Vicki's car. Not only that, he said, he thought that maybe someone had been "casing" his house in recent weeks. He'd seen a van across the street in the shopping center parking lot a number of times. He told the police they needed to be looking for Vicki's car and the brown van.

Shortly before 12:30 P.M., the news of Vicki's murder was broadcast by one of the city's radio news stations, along with the fact that the police were searching for her missing car. A man who was listening to the broadcast pulled into a parking lot in front of a meat market at West 13th and North Edwards Street. There, parked on the street in front of him, was the very car the police were looking for. The man went into the market and called 911. It was just a few blocks from the Wegerle house.

Bill took little Brandon over to his sister Glenda's house. Both he and Glenda tried to find out what had happened from the 2-year-old. All they could learn was that some strange man had come to the house. After making arrangements for Glenda to take care of Stephanie, who was still at school, Bill went to the police station. He told the detectives what Brandon had told him—that a strange man had come to the house.

By 8 P.M. that night, one of the detectives actually accused Bill of murdering his wife. Bill at first didn't get what the detective was saying—what about the brown van? How could he drive two cars at once, his and Vicki's? But it was simple, the detectives told Bill: he'd come home from lunch, had an argument with Vicki, had strangled her, and had then taken the Monte Carlo himself, leaving it a few blocks away. Then he'd walked home and called 911. That accounted for the forty-five-minute gap.

The detectives wanted Bill Wegerle to confess. He became very angry. He'd told them what had happened and what they needed to do, but they weren't listening to him. They had to look for the guy in the brown van who'd been casing the house, he said.

No, the detectives insisted, you're the guy.

Finally Bill Wegerle realized he wasn't going to get anywhere with the detectives.

"Am I under arrest?" he asked.

No, police said. At that point Bill walked out of the police station. When he got to his sister's house, he told her what had happened. Neither could believe that the police had accused him. He soon hired an attorney. After that, the police asked him no more questions.

But they weren't looking for the killer, either—they thought they knew who had done it. They thought it was Bill. They just couldn't prove it.

At Vicki's autopsy, the pathologists removed some human tissue from under her fingernails; it appeared that she had scratched the killer during the fight. The scrapings were placed in a preservation tin, but not submitted for DNA comparison to the semen samples recovered from the Otero, Vian and Fox murders. What was the point? It was expensive, and besides, the police already "knew" who'd killed her. Of course, that didn't explain why they didn't perform the DNA testing in order to *eliminate* Bill Wegerle. If they had, they might have learned that the person who'd killed Vicki Wegerle was the same person who had killed the Oteros, Shirley Vian and Nancy Fox, the same person who was definitely not the latest victim's husband.

20:

"Another One Prowls"

Two days after Christmas, on December 27, 1987, Mary K. Fager returned to her home from a brief visit with relatives in Emporia, Kansas. Mrs. Fager's husband, Melvin, was a successful CPA and a financial analyst for the Boeing company. They had two daughters—Kelli, 16, and Sherri, 9.

As she went through the front door of their upper-middle-class house in east Wichita—located a little over a mile northeast of the Otero house—Mary Fager was horrified to discover the body of her husband dead on the floor of the entry foyer. He had been shot twice at close range, once in the back. It appeared that the shooting had taken place just after he'd come home; he was still wearing his overcoat.

Downstairs in the basement, Mary discovered the bodies of Kelli and Sherri. Both of them were in the family hot tub. Sherri had been bound with black electrical tape; it appeared that she had been strangled first, then drowned in the tub. Kelli had also been strangled, but she'd died hours after her sister.

Semen was found at the scene.

The *Eagle* raised the specter of BTK in its initial reporting on the awful murders, drawing parallels to the Otero killings more than twelve years earlier. But Police Chief Richard LaMunyon discounted any links, although he said the possibility would have to be investigated.

It wasn't long, however, before the detectives focused

their attention on a man who had been doing some construction work at the Fager house. The man seemed to be missing. Police discovered his van not far from the house. They also realized that a Fager family car, a three-year-old Volkswagen was missing. An all-points bulletin was issued for the arrest of the construction worker, who soon surfaced in Florida—driving the Fager car. The man was arrested and charged with the Fager murders. He denied any involvement and said that he'd had some sort of amnesia—he had no idea of what had happened, or how he'd come to be in Florida.

The police did not believe this. They brought him back to Wichita to stand trial for the Fager murders.

Then, on January 5, Mary Fager received an envelope in the mail.

The envelope contained a typed poem, and a crude drawing of a young woman whose hands were tied behind her, with her ankles tied together. The poem was all in capital letters.

OH GOD HE PUT KELLI SHERRI IN THE TUB
A NOTHER ONE PROWLS THE DEEP ABYSS OF LEWD
THOUGHTS AND DEEDS
AND WHILE HE BUILT THE SPIRITAL [sic] AND
TENSION WASHING REAL . . .

The poem continued, comparing the murders of Mary Fager's daughters to Aztec human sacrifices.

The crude drawing had all the stylistic tics of the Nancy Fox drawing—except for the accuracy. And in case anyone missed it, in the lower right-hand corner, the artist had drawn a version of the BTK logo.

It seemed very clear that the person who had sent the BTK letters of the 1970s had also sent this typed poem.

But it was likewise clear that the person had not been in the Fager house—the drawing was all wrong.

What could be concluded from this? That BTK, if he existed, still existed. That he was still in Wichita. That he had probably not killed the Fagers, but that the acts of the murderer had thrilled him. That he was a very sick individual was evident merely from the fact that he'd had the heartlessness to send Mary Fager this awful poem and drawing only a week after her family had been wiped out.

Later, Beattie was able to obtain a copy of the drawing and poem. The type looked very much like it had come from the same machine used in the 1970s BTK letters and poems, and of course, the logo was a dead giveaway—that had never been published or broadcast by anyone. Like the earlier communications, the Fager letter had been photocopied multiple times in order to blur the idiosyncrasies of the typewriter used, such as chips and cracks. This would make it difficult to trace the letter to any specific typewriter.

When he began his research into the BTK case in 2003, Beattie was very troubled by the police decision in 1988 to withhold public announcement of this letter. Indeed, all the way up until 2004, police had contended that the last time anyone had received a communication from BTK was in 1979. That was plainly not true. To Beattie, it was Exhibit A of the case against the police: they had deliberately withheld the information that the killer was still in Wichita—and if the police had had their way, the public would *never* have been informed about the killer, right from the beginning. It was, Beattie contended, a thirty-year-long pattern of withholding vital information from the public.

"The Wichita police withheld, or tried to withhold, information about BTK's existence from the public in

1974, 1988, and 2004," Beattie said, when interviewed for this book. "This failure to inform the public of this danger struck me as a staggering disregard of what is in the public's best interest. I can see that they could argue that the letters may have been hoaxes, that BTK may not exist, and they could argue that BTK may not commit any more crimes, so there is no reason to get the public in an uproar. But, by that reasoning I suppose they'd argue we should not warn the public of possible incoming tornadoes or hurricanes, because there is nothing that the public could do to stop them."

In June 1988, the construction worker accused of the Fager murders was brought to trial. There were inconsistencies in his story, and in that of the prosecution's theory of the crime. For one thing, his DNA did not match the semen found at the hot tub. The man's lawyer sought to introduce the letter apparently sent by BTK to Mary Fager as evidence that BTK might have committed the murders, but the judge ruled it inadmissible.

In the end, a jury found the man not guilty, and the failure to convict became the main issue when a very attractive, energetic, talkative deputy district attorney named Nola Foulston decided to take on her boss in the next election for DA, and won.

Fifteen years later, it would be the same Nola Foulston who would have the pleasure of prosecuting the real BTK. The Fager letter would be used as evidence, not that he had committed those murders, but instead, of his unspeakable cruelty.

21:

"PJ Dogside"

By January 1991, seventeen years after the slaughter of the Oteros, the specter of BTK had once more faded from most Wichitans' memories. No one had connected the boastful bondage killer of the seventies with the murders of Marine Hedge and Vicki Wegerle. Nor did anyone but the police know about the poem and drawing that had been sent to Mary Fager three years earlier. But by 1991, much of the past had been wiped out by the elements.

To save money, the city management forced the police to move all their stored evidence on BTK six different times in the 1980s, each time to a location with a lower rental rate. Each time it was moved, more got lost, misplaced or stolen. Finally, the remainder of the evidence so patiently and expensively accumulated by Stewart's Ghostbusters was packed off to a storage area in the city's parking garage, located next to City Hall, where it attracted mice and gathered dust. Built by the lowest bidder, the garage had some serious construction flaws. On the night of June 7, 1990, another terrible storm hit Wichita, and one of the garage walls collapsed. Hundreds, maybe thousands of pages of police reports on BTK floated away in the rain and wind, to be lost forever. While all agreed it was too bad, some thought it was fitting in a way—a wet, blustery wind had blown away a blowhard phantom.

But the killer was hardly gone. Instead, he'd been out taking the Census.

• • •

The killer had lost his job with the burglar alarm company in 1988. He wasn't exactly fired, but it was suggested that he find some other work. The ostensible reason was a company retrenchment, but there were some who said that he was asked to leave because he was almost impossible to work with—he was so rigid, so anal-retentive, that it drove his co-workers nuts. He was just too bossy and controlling.

So he'd found a job that suited his roaming desires—he'd become a field supervisor for Uncle Sam's decennial headcount. He'd had some sort of pull to get the Census gig—after all, he'd been a loyal member of the Republican Party for years. That too was part of his cover.

This was actually an ideal job for someone like the killer: he could drive all over, and always have some sort of plausible excuse for his presence in any particular neighborhood. Even better, the supervisory job allowed him to travel overnight out of town.

On one occasion, his "codes" had fired off, and he'd stalked a woman in another town in northern Kansas for the better part of several weeks. Finally he'd broken into her house, "hit kit" at the ready: this would be "Project Prairie." But the woman never came home. "She was very lucky," the killer said later.

Eventually, the Census gig ran out, and the killer was at loose ends for a while; his wife had a job working in a nearby store, and the kids were in school, so he had much of the day free to cruise around, "trolling." He made it a practice just about every day to go to a post office in Kechi, a small community about eight miles north of Wichita, and two miles from his house in Park City. The post office was directly east on East 61st Street. Returning to his house one day after this daily run, he noticed someone who met his "codes." This was 62-year-old Delores Davis, known to her friends and family as Dee.

When he first saw Dee Davis, the killer thought she was a man, she wore her hair that short. He kept her under his sly surveillance for some weeks, and eventually decided that she was a woman. Like Marine Hedge, Dee Davis was small and trim—five-feet-five inches tall, just over 120 pounds. The killer thought she would be easy to kill—best of all, there was no man around.

Early in January 1991, the killer approached her house in the darkness. There was a dog kennel on property to the north, so the killer decided this would be "project Dogside." He approached the house cautiously, trying to decide the best way to make his entry. The doors seemed very secure. He crept close to one of the windows. One of Dee's cats was sitting on the window sill. As he crept closer, the cat suddenly began batting at the window, furiously hissing. The killer got out of there, leaving tracks around the side of the house. Dee thought it was strange—she thought maybe there was some sort of animal outside that had spooked the cat. But the cat settled down, and Dee thought no more about it.

Several nights later, on January 18, 1991, the killer returned to Dee's house. It was a Friday night. Once again the killer would use a Scouting trip with his son as his cover, this time a winter camp-out known as the Trappers' Rendezvous at a rural lake in Harvey County, about thirty miles north of Wichita. The Scouts participated in the sort of activities associated with early American fur-trappers—wrestling, tomahawk-throwing, outdoor cooking.

The killer drove up to the lake on Friday afternoon and helped set up some of the Scouts' tents. The boys would be arriving the following morning. That night, the killer left the camp and drove to his parents' house in northwest Wichita. His parents were out of the house, traveling. There he changed out of his Boy Scout uniform and put on his "hit clothes," as he called them—dark pants and a jacket with commodious pockets, and a watch cap. The dark clothes would conceal him in the winter darkness, the killer believed.

From his parents' house, the killer drove to the nearby Park City Baptist Church, which was the sponsor of the Scout troop he was affiliated with. He had a key to the church, and used it to store some tools for his "hit kit." He left his car at the church, and began walking toward Dee Davis' house. It was about 10 P.M.

Dee Davis, meanwhile, had had dinner with Tom Ray, a friend, at the Red Coach Restaurant—the same place where Marine Hedge had had her last meal with her own escort six years earlier. Ray dropped Dee off at her house around 7:30 P.M. It was the last time he ever saw her alive.

The killer walked about a half-mile east on 61st Street, keeping inside a row of trees to avoid being seen, then angled across an open field to a cemetery north of Dee Davis' house. He stopped for a while in the cemetery, perhaps to put himself in the mood. Then he began to creep up on Dee's house.

Once he got there, he peered in one of the windows. He saw Dee was still up, reading in bed. He located the telephone line and snipped it. He waited for a while, hoping she would go to sleep. Searching the back yard, he entered a small metal shed, where he found a portion of an old cinder block. Sometime just after midnight, he threw the block through a sliding glass door in the rear of the house, shattering it. He reached inside, unlocked the sliding door and stepped into the house.

Dee came out of the bedroom, alarmed.

"What happened? Did you hit my house with your car?" she demanded.

The killer had already decided to use his "wanted man" trick. Before entering, he'd covered his face with a nylon stocking.

"No," he said. "I'm wanted by the cops, they're after me. I need your house and your car and your money. I'm going to tie you up and I'm going to leave you. I'm going to be a little time in here, because I need to— I need to get inside and warm up, but I'm going to take your car and some food."

Dee retreated. "You can't be in here," she said.

"Ma'am," the killer said, polite as any policeman, "you're going to cooperate. I've got a club, I've got a gun, I've got a knife, I suggest you do what I say. You take your choice of how you want it."

"Okay," Dee said.

The killer cuffed Dee with her hands behind her. Then he tied her ankles together with pantyhose.

"Someone's coming over in a few minutes," Dee told him.

The killer wasn't sure if she was telling the truth. If someone really was coming over, he would have to get moving. He forced Dee back into the bedroom. Then he began searching the house, finding the keys to her car, and making noises as if he were looking for food.

He returned to the bedroom. He removed the handcuffs, holding her arms with his hands.

"You say you've got somebody coming?" he asked. He pulled off his mask.

"Yes, somebody is coming."

"Well, they'll find you," the killer told her. "They'll find you and call the police. I'm out of here." The killer was trying to calm her down.

Then he took one end of the pantyhose still around her ankles and began to tie her hands. Dee realized that he wasn't going to leave as he'd told her.

"You're not going to kill me, are you?" she asked. "Don't kill me. I've got kids."

"Too late," the killer said, and he strangled her with another pair of pantyhose.

"I used quite a bit of pantyhose on her," he recalled later.

The killer had planned to take pictures of Dee, but her warning that someone was coming changed his plans. He quickly tossed the house, taking Dee's jewelry box and a camera, and several other items, including her driver's license. Then he used a bedspread to drag her body out to her car, keeping it covered with the blankets and sheets. He put the body and the bedding in the trunk.

He drove Dee's car south on Hillside Street, heading for the 45th Street underpass of I-135, the main route north from Wichita. It was about three minutes' drive from Dee's house. There were two man-made lakes there, one on either side of the freeway, which took some of the overflow from Chisholm Creek, named after the early-day cattleman who had helped put Wichita on the map.

At the east lake he put Dee's body under some bushes. He went back to her car and drove to his own church, Christ Lutheran, where he had once profaned the basement with his abuse of Marine Hedge's dead body. There he stashed Dee Davis' jewelry box and other things he had taken from her house, using a hidey-hole he had fashioned under the floor of a shed on the church grounds. It was wonderful to have the church as a place of refuge.

Next he drove Dee's car back to her house, making sure to wipe it clean of any evidence. No one was there—

no one had come, despite what Dee had told him. He threw the car keys onto the roof, just as he had the Otero car keys seventeen years earlier, almost to the day. Then he walked back to the Baptist church where he'd left his own car. On the way he realized he still had two keys belonging to Dee Davis, so he threw those away in the trees.

The killer started his own car and drove back to the lakes. He'd had a lust in his mind for years: he wanted to pose one of his victims in a barn. Bondage in a barn. Or a silo. His grandparents had owned a farm, and the fantasy of doing whatever he wanted to do to someone in a barn was one of his fondest desires.

At the lake, he reclaimed Dee's body and put it into the back of his own car, a station wagon. Just the sort of car one might expect a family man like him, a Scout leader, to drive. He headed north and west, out into the rural darkness. It was snowing very lightly. He was looking for the barn he'd already picked out, but as the snow got worse, he began to worry. He had to get back to the Trappers' Rendezvous before someone missed him. If he wasn't there when the Scouts showed up in the morning, there would be questions.

He decided to give up on the barn. Too bad. About eleven miles out, just before the county line, he saw a bridge over a small drainage swale. *This will do it*, he thought, and he stopped his car, opened the back of the station wagon and dragged Dee's body out. It fell on the pavement. He dragged the body down into the swale under the bridge and left it with the debris. Then he got back in his car and drove to the barn, where he'd left some things—ropes, his Polaroid camera—he didn't want anyone to find.

He got back to the camp-out before dawn. No one had missed him.

• • •

The next day, just after noon, Tom Ray, Dee's friend, arrived at her house. They'd made plans to get together; Tom had promised to wash her car. But when she hadn't arrived at his house, he'd called her to see if something was wrong. No one answered the telephone.

Worried, Ray drove to Dee's house. He could see that the outside light was still on, and the living room curtains were drawn. That was unusual, because Ray knew that Dee liked to get up early. Not only that, her car was in the driveway—Dee never left her car out in the winter elements. Ray opened the garage door and saw that the interior door to the house was ajar. He went into the house and saw that the telephone line had been pulled out of the wall. As he walked through the house, he saw that the sliding glass door into the family room had been shattered by a cinder block. In the bedroom he noticed that the sheets and blankets were missing, and that Dee's jewelry box was gone.

At that point, Ray had no doubt that something very bad had happened to Dee. He left the house and went to a telephone to call 911. Minutes later, two Sedgwick County Sheriff's deputies arrived at the house. Another search disclosed that keys to Dee's car were on the roof of the house.

That night, a man walking his dog along North Hydraulic Street discovered several blankets and other bed linen in a culvert about a quarter mile to the northwest of Dee's house. They were identified as having come from Dee's bed.

The killer wasn't done yet with Dee Davis. That night, even as the Sedgwick County sheriff's deputies were collecting the bedding from the culvert, the killer was on his way back to the place where he had dumped her body the night before, seven miles to the northwest of the culvert. He made another headache excuse to the Scouts, and drove to Sedgwick, a small town a few miles southeast of the Trappers' Rendezvous. Dressed in his Scout uniform, he stopped at a convenience store to buy a newspaper. He wanted to see if there was any news about Dee Davis. Of course, there was nothing—it was too early.

He drove on, pulling into a highway rest stop just over the county line. In the lavatory, he took off his Scout uniform and put on his "hit clothes." At that moment, a Kansas Highway Patrol officer came into the lavatory, checking it for unsavory activity.

"What are you doing?" the patrolman demanded.

Shit, the killer thought, *I'm done. It's over, this guy's gonna bust me.* His heartbeat started racing.

Somehow he managed to stay calm. He explained that he was on his way to the Scout camp, that he was changing his clothes.

"Well," the trooper said, "when you're done, come outside. I need to talk to you."

Now the killer was really worried. There were things in his car that he didn't want the trooper to see—a mask, for one thing.

But outside, the trooper simply ran his name on the computer to see if there were any wants or warrants on him or his car, a routine procedure, and of course, there were none. The trooper let him go.

Vastly relieved at his escape, the killer drove back to the place where he'd left Dee's body in the swale. It was very foggy—spooky, the killer thought. When he climbed down to look at the body, he saw that small animals had been gnawing on it.

Creepy, he thought. He bent down over the body and

put the mask he had brought over her face. He wanted to "pretty her up," he said later. It was a plain white mask of a man's face that he'd altered by painting it a flesh color, the lips red, and gluing eyebrows and eyelashes to it. He'd put a black line of ink between the crimson lips. The mask had a length of venetian blind cord tied to it. He took several photographs of the body with the mask. Then he decided to leave it with the body—a signature of sorts.

Twelve days later, a boy walking his dog near 117th and Meridian Streets just a few miles short of the county line, discovered the remains of Dee Davis' body. He immediately ran home to call the police. When they arrived, they found her decomposing remains still tied with pantyhose around the neck, knees and ankles. Nearby they found a very weird flesh-colored mask with a piece of venetian blind cord attached.

But by then the killer was back in his snug little house in Park City, miles away, and utterly no one's suspect as the horrible killer known as BTK.

THE RETURN

22:

The Dogcatcher

The years after 1991 passed quietly for the killer. Maybe it was because he was getting older, maybe it was because his children were growing up, but the urge to murder had begun to abate. It wasn't actually necessary, he thought—he had his collection of notes, diagrams, pictures, drivers' licenses, jewelry, underwear and drawings, as well as his homemade collection of porn. He had his short stories featuring "Rex," the bondage killer, whose disgusting adventures almost always replicated what had actually happened, if embroidered to make "Rex" seem even more ominous.

The point was, he could visualize the past whenever he wanted to, especially those moments of someone's terror. He kept thinking of new "Afterlife Concepts" for his victims—this one a slave, that one a housekeeper, another one to be his "primary mistress."

He had his camera, and when he wanted to, he could dress himself up as a victim, tie himself up, and take his own picture. And often did. Once he had dug a grave in the northern part of the county, then climbed down into it wearing one of his grotesque masks, and snapped his own picture.

On another occasion, at another Scouting camp-out, he'd climbed into the back of his truck, inside the camper shell, and tied himself up, for purposes of auto-eroticism. Then he couldn't get loose. He began to sweat, struggling to get out, and began to think that he'd have to call someone, one of the Boy Scouts, to set him free. It would be embarrassing. People would ask questions, maybe get ideas. But eventually he did get loose.

"That was a close one," he said later.

Four months after he'd killed Dee Davis, he'd been hired as the Park City "compliance officer." What he was, though, was the town's dogcatcher.

Later, much later, he would become indignant when people called him that; he considered himself a law enforcement officer, a sort of cop. Besides riding herd on all the town's dogs and cats, he had to make sure that people kept their lawns mowed and had their trash picked up. He had the power to issue citations to residents, which could make them account for themselves in court. This was an almost perfect job—with the ideal excuse to butt into everyone's business, he could cruise the streets of the small town, "trolling," as he put it, and check out their houses. He soon began to rub a number of residents the wrong way, just as he had his fellow workers at the burglar alarm company in the 1980s. But the killer was generating revenue with his frequent citations. No one in the city government paid much attention to him—not as long as he kept the money coming in.

The killer spent a lot of time daydreaming. He'd leave the office in the morning, drive out to some spot in town to keep someone or something under surveillance, while fingering his coded cards of "Julia," or "Priscilla," or "Honey." SBT. No one ever checked up on him.

So the years rolled by, and BTK went from being a puzzle to a phantom, and from a phantom to a myth.

Until Beattie decided to poke at the monster to see if he was still alive.

23:

Double Dates

After the *Eagle*'s January 2004 story on the thirtieth anniversary of the Otero murders, Beattie hoped that the killer would reveal himself. His strategy, of course, was to make the killer think that he, Beattie, would now get all the notoriety from the old murders. Beattie's notion was that the killer, whoever he was, would simply not be able to abide this. If he was still alive. If he'd really existed in the first place.

For the next month after Laviana's story ran, Beattie kept his ear to the ground, waiting for some indication that the killer had made a new contact. By early 2004, Beattie had interviewed many retired cops who had worked on the case, and he was pretty sure that if something happened, they'd find a way to tip him off, even if the current police department wanted to keep a lid on it.

But when a month went by without anything happening, Beattie began to doubt his gambit—after all, if the killer was dead, or he had moved away from Wichita, one story in the *Eagle* wouldn't have come to his attention. So Beattie began trying to drum up more publicity, in part with the idea that perhaps someone who knew something, or had some unexplained item from a deceased father, might come forward. Keeping the story fresh in the public's mind was the only way to do this, Beattie knew.

Of course, the Wichita police weren't happy about this. Ken Landwehr, the lieutenant in charge of the department's homicide squad, had been part of the original "Ghostbusters" back in the 1980s. As an ex-Ghostbuster, Landwehr wasn't one of those who doubted BTK's existence—he *knew* that BTK was real. Over the years, Landwehr had given several public presentations on the murders and the investigation, including one to Beattie's Mensa group in 1995, and shown many of the crime-scene photographs, diagrams and reports, as well as the communications from BTK, including the letter sent to Mary Fager. Landwehr had asked the Mensa people if anyone had any bright ideas, and didn't seem all that impressed with what was suggested, according to Beattie.

"When he met with us, Landwehr acknowledged that the police had already tried talking with outsiders, including 'psychics,'" Beattie told Laviana in early 2004. "I was amused to learn that in helping to solve crimes, in the police department's eyes, the Mensa high IQ society ranked lower than psychics!"

But Beattie soon got word back through the grapevine that Landwehr and the current homicide detectives had a dim view of his book project. Beattie sent Landwehr several emails, asking him about certain innocuous subjects, and Landwehr did not respond. Beattie said he was told that the detectives referred to his activities as "the Beattie problem," and that most considered his interest in publicity purely venal—that is, he only wanted to sell books.

By now, Beattie had assembled a great deal of information about the old murders—some from documents that the retired cops had kept, which wasn't entirely proper, but was something of a godsend, since so many of them had blown away in the storm of 1990. Going over the information, Beattie was struck by the recurrence of certain dates. It was almost as if the killer kept track of the dates, and tried to act again on anniversaries of those dates. Of course, the concurrence wasn't exact, but it was close. Who knew? Maybe the killer had set out one night to commit another crime, say, three years to the day that something else had happened, and something unforeseen had thrown him slightly off schedule. Beattie made a list of the relevant dates for his growing timeline. Making such a timeline is a critical first step to understanding the relationship between complex events, since it often reveals causes and effects that wouldn't otherwise be apparent.

Beattie's timeline, when sorted by month and date but ignoring the year, showed:

1/05/1988	Possible BTK letter to Mary Fager
1/15/1974	Otero family murdered
1/18/1991	Dee Davis murdered
1/31/1978	BTK sends "SHIRLEYLOCKS" poem to *Eagle*
2/01/1991	Dee Davis' body found
2/09/1978	BTK sends "Oh! Death to Nancy" poem, drawing and letter to KAKE
3/17/1977	Shirley Vian murdered
4/27/1985	Marine Hedge last seen
4/28/1979	Anna Williams' house broken into
5/05/1985	Marine Hedge's body found
6/15/1979	BTK sends letters to Anna Williams & KAKE
9/16/1986	Vicki Wegerle murdered
10/22/1974	BTK calls Secret Witness tipline, leads to first letter
12/08/1977	Nancy Fox murdered
12/11/1974	Cathy Henkel *Sun* article

If the profilers' theories were right, and if BTK was in fact a "narcissistic sexual sadist" with compulsive need for publicity, Beattie thought, it was entirely possible that he would choose the anniversary of one of the earlier dates to send a new communication to the news media. That might vastly increase the significance of the communication, and hence its notoriety, if the media noticed the coincidence of the dates.

Looking at the established dates, Beattie could see that this might have already happened on several occasions: BTK's murder of Nancy Fox, almost exactly three years to the day after Cathy Henkel's story in the *Sun*; the murder of Marine Hedge, almost exactly six years to the day of the break-in at Anna Williams' house; and the murder of Dee Davis, almost (well, three days off) seventeen years to the day after the Otero murders. So, Beattie reasoned—maybe the killer will choose to communicate again on one of these other, so-far unpaired dates.

There seemed to be another pairing of dates at the end of January and the first day of February. On the last day of January 1978, BTK had sent the "SHIRLEYLOCKS" poem to the *Eagle*. Thirteen years later, Dee Davis' body had been discovered. But wait—the killer had had no control over *when* the body was discovered. So the discovery date was still unpaired—so far.

The next unpaired date was February 9 with the mailing of the Nancy Fox poem to KAKE. After that came the twenty-seventh anniversary of Shirley Vian's murder on St. Patrick's Day, March 17. If he could just get some more publicity before the anniversaries of some of these dates, Beattie thought, maybe the killer would be goaded into communicating.

By this time, Beattie was on very good terms with many of the retired police officers, particularly those who had worked the case back in the 1970s, when it first began. This was something of an irritation to Landwehr, who really did wish that the old-timers would just shut up, and quit giving Beattie information. But they didn't care—as far as they could see, Beattie was the only one doing anything about *their* case, one that had haunted all of them ever since the day Josie Otero was found hanging in the basement.

As it happened, the retired officers had a small newsletter that was circulated among them: *The ReTIRED COPPER*, it was called. Early in March, former detective John Garrison wrote a story for *The ReTIRED COPPER* on Beattie's book project, noting that he had been invited to give a talk on BTK to the monthly meeting of the retired officers on Saturday, March 20. Beattie added a short article himself on what he was up to, and why he was doing it.

This edition of *The ReTIRED COPPER* was put in the mail around March 10, 2004. Over the next week, the several hundred subscribers got their copies. Three of them had taken new jobs with Park City. One of them read the newsletter, and then pitched the copy into the City Hall recycling bin.

On or about March 15, 2004, the killer fished the copy out of the recycling and read it.

Two days after that, on St. Patrick's Day, the twenty-seventh anniversary of Shirley Vian's murder, he sent a letter to *The Wichita Eagle*. On March 18, it was routinely opened, and dumped into a mail bin for distribution to the newsroom. There was nothing about it that clamored for attention—it was simply a single sheet with what appeared to be four photocopied images on it, and a series of seemingly meaningless letters across the top, along with a stylized logo of sorts in the lower right-hand corner. It was almost thrown away as having no meaning.

Instead, it was picked out of the mail bin by newsroom secretary Glenda Elliott. She turned the letter and the single sheet over to assistant managing editor Tim Rogers. Rogers glanced at it, concluded it was somebody's idea of a prank, and sent it on to reporter Laviana, with instructions that Laviana should pass it on to the police. Laviana made a copy of the single sheet and put the copy amidst all the papers on his desk.

The next morning, Laviana headed over to the police station for the department's regular morning briefing. When he got to the police station, he gave the original of the single sheet to Wichita Captain Darrell Haynes. Haynes tossed it on his desk.

That afternoon, Laviana went home for the weekend. He'd entirely forgotten about the single sheet that had come in the mail. "We get letters like this all the time," Laviana told Beattie later.

On the following Monday, March 22, Laviana decided he really did need to tidy up his desk. He began sorting through various papers that had accumulated there—reporters attract paper like dirty dogs get fleas—and happened to glance at the single sheet. He was just about to toss it out when his eye fell upon one of the images.

It was someone's driver's license. In fact, it was Vicki Wegerle's driver's license.

Laviana hadn't worked on the BTK case in the 1980s without having learned something about the disputes that had churned the police department in that era. With Bill Hirschman, he had co-reported a story on the Ghostbusters of Al Stewart. He recognized that Vicki Wegerle was the name of a murder victim that some—well, a few—suggested might be a BTK victim. He and Hirschman had pressed the cops hard back in 1986 as to whether Vicki Wegerle had been killed by BTK, and had been assured that she had not. They'd also asked about Marine Hedge and Dee Davis, but had again been assured there was no connection.

That's weird, Laviana thought. *Who would be sending us a copy of Vicki Wegerle's driver's license?* And then

Laviana looked at the other images: each appeared to be a copy of a photograph of Vicki Wegerle, on her back, half-naked, and bound. To Laviana, she looked dead.

Laviana picked up the telephone and dialed Captain Haynes at the police station.

"Have you looked at what I gave you on Friday?" he asked.

Laviana could hear Haynes rustling through his own stack of papers.

After a few minutes, Haynes was back on the line.

"I'll call you back," he said, and hung up.

24:

Bill Thomas Killman

The more he looked at the single sheet of paper, the more Laviana was convinced that it really *was* from BTK. For one thing, there was the stylized logo of the initial BTK in the corner, which was similar to earlier logos drawn on the 1978 communications. True, the string of letters across the top didn't make any sense, but there were the photographs. They didn't look like police crime-scene photographs to Laviana—why would the cops have altered the victim's clothing and pose? The clothing that remained seemed arranged differently in each picture. The police wouldn't have done that, Laviana knew.

Several hours went by while Laviana waited by his telephone. He looked at the envelope the paper had come in. In the return address space there was a name and an address:

Bill Thomas Killman
1684 S. Oldmanor
Wichita, KS. 67218

Bill Thomas Killman, Laviana thought—initials B, T and K, for BTK. Oldmanor—there was no such street in Wichita. But there was an Old Manor Street, and it was only a block away from the Otero house.

Laviana's telephone rang. It was Kelly Otis, a detective with the Wichita Police Department. Otis told Laviana he'd been assigned the Vicki Wegerle murder as a "cold case" some four years earlier. He asked a few questions about how the paper had come into possession of the *Eagle*, and who had handled it. He did *not* want the paper to print anything. Laviana said he couldn't make that promise.

"Give me forty-eight hours," Otis told Laviana.

Laviana asked if Otis thought the letter was for real—from BTK.

Otis said he couldn't say.

Laviana said he'd check with his editors to see if they'd be willing to withhold publication if Otis would agree to tell them if the letter was legitimate. Both men agreed to proceed on that basis.

That day, the *Eagle* editors agreed to withhold publication of the news about the letter, and Lieutenant Landwehr agreed to brief them two days later.

On Wednesday, March 24, Laviana emailed Beattie.

"Bob," he wrote, "are you going to be around this afternoon? There may be a big development in the BTK case today. If it pans out, I may want to run something by you."

That same morning, Landwehr told the *Eagle* that the letter was legitimate—it was a new communication from BTK. He wanted the people at the *Eagle* who had handled the letter to agree to provide their fingerprints for purposes of elimination. The *Eagle* editors agreed to this request.

That afternoon, Laviana called Beattie.

"Bob," he told him, "I've got to ask you for a quote. But first I want to tell you what's happened." Laviana told Beattie about the new message. "Landwehr told me that he is one hundred percent certain it is BTK," he added.

Beattie told Laviana that if Landwehr really was "one hundred percent certain," that meant he had to have more information than just the letter. Beattie pointed out that

Vicki Wegerle had been taken to the hospital, and that no crime-scene photos of her body had been taken by the police at the scene.

Of course, that alone wouldn't prove that the letter had been sent by BTK, only that Vicki's killer had taken her driver's license and the disgusting photographs and copied them. Someone else could have found them and mailed them to the newspaper. Beattie's mind leaped ahead: to be "one hundred percent certain," Landwehr was probably admitting that the police had DNA evidence.

"Maybe he licked the stamp or something," Beattie suggested, meaning BTK.

As it happened, Landwehr and Detective Otis did have DNA evidence. When he'd received the Wegerle "cold case" in January 2000, Otis had reviewed everything that had been done eighteen years earlier. At some point in early 2003, Otis realized that scrapings had been taken from under Vicki's fingernails. He knew this would be a potential source of DNA. He and his partner, Detective Dana Gouge, had somehow found the tin containing the scrapings in the police evidence collection, and taken it to the Sedgwick County Regional Forensic Science Center for testing. On August 14, 2003, lab technician Dan Fahnestock reported back: he had been able to extract a man's DNA profile from the scrapings. The profile did not match any known suspect.

But now, with the new letter, they did have a suspect—BTK. The logo in the upper right corner of a paper with pictures of Vicki's body surely showed that BTK had to have murdered her, and now they had his DNA from the crime scene itself. Landwehr immediately made arrangements with the DNA lab to test physical evidence from the other BTK crime scenes, including the Otero and Fox houses. The Vian evidence seemed to be missing. But if the Wegerle DNA matched DNA from the Otero and Fox scenes, that would be proof, "one hundred percent certain" proof, that the new communication was from BTK, his first to the public since 1978, and the first of any kind since the Mary Fager letter of 1988.

BTK RESURFACES AFTER 25 YEARS, the *Eagle*'s headlines screamed the next day.

"A serial killer who terrorized Wichita during the 1970s by committing a series of seven murders has claimed responsibility for an eighth slaying and is probably now living in Wichita, police said." Laviana wrote the story.

He sketched in the circumstances of the arrival of the new letter, including the fact that it contained photocopies of Vicki Wegerle's long-missing driver's license, as well as three pictures of her body.

"The photographs appear to be authentic," Laviana quoted Landwehr. "I'm 100 percent sure it's BTK. There's no doubt that that's Vicki Wegerle's picture."

Laviana took up the issue of the return addressee—"Bill Thomas Killman."

"There has never been a Bill Thomas Killman," he quoted Landwehr as saying. Laviana noted that there was also no Oldmanor Street in Wichita, but that there was an Old Manor Street. He didn't point out that Old Manor Street was a block away from the Otero house, but quoted Landwehr as saying he didn't know the significance of the return address.

Laviana also quoted Beattie, after noting his book project once again:

"The vast majority of police officers thought he was

dead," Beattie told Laviana. "*I* thought he was probably dead. But now you have to allow for the possibility that he's been walking around Wichita, getting his hair cut and acting like a normal person."

Landwehr said he had no idea of why the killer would resume communications after such a long time. Beattie offered a possibility:

"Maybe he wants more publicity than the guy who's writing the book," he suggested.

The apparent return of the killer electrified Wichita. It also galvanized the national news media—here was a story with a mystique: SERIAL KILLER RESURFACES AFTER A QUARTER OF A CENTURY. Beattie was suddenly in great demand. Radio stations began calling him for interviews as early as 6 A.M. the next morning. Retired detective Garrison called him and asked him to write an article for the next edition of *The ReTIRED COPPER*. Beattie agreed, and learned that Landwehr and the police would be giving a press conference that morning at 10. Garrison asked him to see what happened there. Beattie agreed.

He drove down to police headquarters. But at first a police spokesperson wouldn't let him attend the briefing—no book authors, she said, an oblique reference to the department's "Beattie problem." Beattie told her that he was writing an article for Garrison and *The ReTIRED COPPER*. Grudgingly, the spokesperson allowed him to stay. He asked only one question: "Do you deny that the 1988 letter to Mary Fager was from BTK?"

"No," Landwehr said, "I do not deny that."

Over the next few days, Beattie gave more and more interviews to the broadcast media, including the *CBS Evening News*. The phone rang incessantly, and the message machine was so crammed that it refused to take any more calls. He agreed to appear on a number of national television programs. *Dateline* wanted him, Greta Van Susteren wanted him, *48 Hours* wanted him, ABC wanted him. CNN called. He was soon interviewed on *America's Most Wanted*. He was getting as much publicity as the killer. The plan was working.

After several days of this, Beattie met with Detective Otis and others from the police department. He gave them a copy of his timeline, by then seventeen pages of single-spaced entries. Otis and Beattie discussed several suspects whose names Beattie had unearthed during his research.

"What about the prime suspect?" Otis asked.

Beattie shrugged, his face impassive.

"Robert Beattie?" Otis prompted. A tip line set up by police after the news had broken had recorded at least thirty-two suggestions as to the identity of the killer, and every single one was: Robert Beattie.

"I am not a suspect," Beattie told Otis calmly.

Otis nodded, according to Beattie, and agreed. "You are not a suspect," he said.

Beattie then offered to allow the detectives to take a DNA sample from him. Otis said, "Since you offered, we'll take it."

A detective pulled on a pair of rubber gloves, and swabbed the inside of Beattie's mouth. He put the swabs in a test tube, sealed it and labeled it.

"We're going to have a swab-a-thon," Otis told him. And in fact, Beattie was the first of many to give oral swabs to the police over the next eleven months.

He was also the first person to be cleared.

25:

Secrets Long Hidden

By the following Monday, the tip line had received a staggering total of 650 calls suggesting possibilities to be investigated by the police, as well as over 300 emails. One store selling police equipment and other security devices reported selling out of pepper spray, and started a waiting list. The store owner told the *Eagle* that the run was a direct result of the publicity about BTK. An alarm company reported getting eight times the normal volume of calls from people asking about burglar protection devices.

"Yesterday we had our normal day, and today it's kaboom," Chuck Hadsell, of SecureNet, the alarm company, told an *Eagle* reporter. "We're getting a combination of calls from existing customers wanting to add service, and new inquiries. They're referring to the BTK situation directly."

A gun shop and indoor shooting range also saw an upsurge in trade. "This afternoon has just been booming," the owner told the newspaper.

The paper published an editorial commenting on the frenzy, and grimly suggested that this time the killer had gone too far.

"It's unclear what he wants—more publicity for his crimes?" the *Eagle* wrote. "He might get more than he bargained for. He might get justice.

"Somebody knows this person. Anyone with a shred of suspicion should come forward and talk to police . . . BTK apparently likes cat-and-mouse games—and that could eventually be his undoing. He's going to get caught. Sooner or later. And justice will be served."

Reporter Roy Wenzl took a stab at trying to illuminate some of the killer's traits, including his possible description. He noted that after KAKE-TV had received the "Oh Anna" poem in June 1979, an *Eagle* reporter had interviewed a detective who tracked down a postal clerk who had seen the killer drop the package to the station into the mail bin at about 4 A.M. on June 16, 1979. The reporter, Ken Stephens, said his notes from the era included a description of the killer:

"A female postal clerk happened to open a door and a man was standing there," Stephens' notes said. "He said 'put this in the KAKE box' and handed the envelope to her. She didn't think much about it. Later, she described him as about 30 years old, about 5 feet nine inches tall, white. He was wearing a blue jean jacket, jeans and gloves (in June!) He was clean shaven, with hair cropped short above the ears. He had a gap between his front teeth."

Wenzl tracked down Laviana's old partner, Bill Hirschman, to get his ideas about the killer. Hirschman said he thought the killer believed he was smarter than the police.

"Why else would he rise out of his rabbit hole [to] send letters?" Hirschman asked. "He's looking for recognition. And there's careful planning in that, too. Some of the things he did, he did on the anniversaries of his killings. I suspect if we figured the whole thing out, we'd find a reason for every single thing he ever did."

By the first of April, the news about the "swab-a-thon" promised to Beattie by Detective Otis had become apparent. With so many people being asked to contribute samples, it was impossible to keep the tactic secret. The

Eagle contacted Beattie after learning that he'd given the first sample. Beattie told the paper that he'd been told that the police were up to "number 600" by April 1—that was probably an exaggeration, given the fact that only eight days had passed since Laviana had given the police the letter. But it certainly showed that the police were leaving no swab unturned.

"The good news is, they're getting lots of swabs," Beattie told the paper. The bad news: "If they've swabbed 600 men in the last week, that doesn't indicate to me that they've narrowed down any suspects." Beattie said that he'd volunteered for testing, and although the tests had not been completed yet, the very fact that he'd volunteered had considerably damped down the speculation that the man who was so interested in writing about the case might just possibly also be the killer.

The tsunami of publicity over the murders picked Beattie up and cast him high over the arid sand dunes of other would-be authors. By April, publishers and agents were calling him rather than the other way around. He reached a tentative deal with a publisher, but insisted that the book not be luridly titled or illustrated. He felt that he owed that to the families of the victims, most of whom had spoken to him by that point, and to the retired detectives. The publisher's editor agreed to Beatty's preferred title: *Secrets Long Hidden: The 30-Year Hunt for the BTK Strangler*. Beattie took the title from the prologue of Goethe's *The Fable of Faust*:

> Therefore, myself, to magic give
> In hopes through its power and might
> Secrets long hidden
> May be brought to light.

Beattie's idea was that rather than magic, his writing of the book would unearth the secrets of BTK.

The publisher's editor said he saw no problem with this proposed title, so Beattie set to work, writing.

By mid-April, the police were well-embarked on the "swab-a-thon," busy tracking down men who had been suspects as long as thirty years earlier in an effort to eliminate them from the pile. They were convinced that they had the name of the killer someplace in their old lists—hadn't John Douglas, now retired from the FBI, opined that the killer had stopped in the late 1970s because the police had come close to him?

Of course, that was now open to argument—the link to Vicki Wegerle's murder seemed to show that he hadn't really stopped. And it opened the question of whether there were other unsolved murders from the last thirty years that had never been linked to BTK.

Such was the flood of interest in the case that Kansas Attorney General Phill Kline pledged state resources to the investigation. A task force was assembled of detectives from the Kansas Bureau of Investigation, the FBI, the Wichita police and the Sedgwick County Sheriff's Department. Efforts were made to identify unsolved murders that might conceivably fit the BTK m.o., chiefly those involving bondage. Altogether, more than a dozen unsolved murders that had never been linked to BTK were reviewed, among them the murders of Marine Hedge and Dee Davis.

All the publicity about the murders generated an even larger number of cranks. Since it had broken the story of the apparent return of the killer, the *Eagle* got a lot of this attention. The paper had made it very clear that it was cooperating with the police, so some people thought that the best way to put their own oar into the turbulence was to go to the newspaper. An editor there told Beattie: "People were trying to get their work done and couldn't," referring to the incessant telephone calls reporting "suspects." Besides that, editor Rick Thames said, some people kept trying to get into the newsroom without being invited, which was disturbing—who knew if some wacko might try to do something bizarre?

The paper's pages were filled with articles about the case on an almost daily basis. That was hard to do, because after the initial flurry of information from the receipt of the letter, police grew tight-lipped. Hard information about what they might be up to was difficult to come by. The newspaper fell back on the news-you-can-use approach: how to make sure your house is secure, why you should talk to your neighbors, identifying the police department's community service officers, what to tell the kids, why this was such a big deal to people older than 40, another run-through on the sordid history of the murders.

Beattie, too, got unwanted attention. Besides being named as the most popular suspect by ignorant tipsters, he soon realized that his house was now on the city's automobile parade route. Just as teenagers in the 70s had "dragged Douglas," now a steady stream of motorized gawkers gaped at Beattie's dwelling.

Soon people, strangers, actually began stopping at Beattie's house, wanting to talk to him. Beattie, being polite, always answered the door, but quickly learned to regret it. Wichitans might pride themselves on their normality, but that did not mean the city didn't have the usual complement of nuts. And Beattie had another thought: what if one of the strangers was the killer? He told Mary Ann not to answer the door anymore.

Then there were the weird phone calls. Beattie and

Mary Ann stopped answering the telephone, letting the messages pile up. At intervals, when they could face it, they listened to the messages, calling back the people they knew, ignoring the rest. Some of the calls, Beattie later said, were vaguely menacing. There was one, from a stranger, who assumed an intimacy that was creepy: "I'm bored, Robert," the caller said. "I'm bored. Give me something to do." The guy kept calling but never left his name or telephone number.

Then there was the vandal who trashed the Beatties' front yard. The year before, their daughter had brought a sack full of tulip bulbs from a trip to the Netherlands. By the spring of 2004, the tulips were in full bloom. One day after making a short trip to visit Mary Ann's 97-year-old mother, the Beatties returned to find half the tulips torn out, crushed, and strewn over the front yard and driveway. Mary Ann began to cry.

"Why?" she asked. "Why?"

Vandals were also at work other places around town, as well. Graffiti artists spray-painted "BTK" on vehicles and garage doors. The usual gangster tagging was replaced by much more ominous initials.

Beattie made an appointment to interview one of the psychologists who had worked with the Ghostbusters, Dr. John Allen. Before long, "he had me rest on his therapist's couch," Beattie recalled. "He could see I was under stress."

Beattie asked Allen why he thought BTK had finally resurfaced after so many years.

"He pointed at me and said, 'Your book,'" Beattie said.

When he analyzed some of the reasons for his stress, Beattie identified something that had always been present in his unconscious mind, but that he hadn't really thought all the way through—what if the book project stimulated the killer to kill again? Would he be responsible for that? And in more concrete terms, would he have any legal liability? What if the killer murdered again, and sent a new communication: "Here's the last chapter for Beattie's book"?

This worried Beattie a lot. After some time he decided to consult with a lawyer in New York over the liability issue.

"I paid quite a lot of money," Beattie recalled, "to the law firm of Satterlee Stephens Burke & Burke, specifically to attorney Bob Callagy. Because I needed the question answered. The legal opinion was that I have no legal liability, but whether legally accountable or not, the stress that I felt over this possibility . . . was enormous."

While all this was going on in the last week of March and the first few weeks of April, unbeknownst to the public or even Beattie, the technicians at the Sedgwick County Regional Forensic Science Center had made an important breakthrough. On April 2, 2004, the lab informed Landwehr that the DNA extracted from a semen stain on a blue robe at the Nancy Fox murder scene matched the DNA found under Vicki Wegerle's fingernails. This was actual, scientific proof that BTK existed—and also, the first indisputable link that the same man had killed both Vicki Wegerle and Nancy Fox. One week later, the lab matched the same DNA to DNA recovered from the Otero house more than thirty years earlier. BTK had killed the Oteros, too, exactly as he had always claimed.

26:

Thomas B. King

Late in April, a source telephoned Beattie with some odd news. The DNA tests that had just been conducted on all the major suspects in the investigation from the preceding three decades had all come back negative—every single one of them.

"They don't know what to think," the source told Beattie, meaning Landwehr and the detectives. All those years, the experts kept insisting that the detectives had the right guy, somewhere in their files, they just needed to prove it. Now they had the killer's DNA, which meant they *could* prove it, only none of the major suspects matched. Could they have been that far off, all along? It hardly seemed possible.

The detectives went back to their lists. If it wasn't someone they'd already investigated, it had to be someone they hadn't. They checked old Coleman records for the names of male employees between 20 and 50 years old at the time that Kathy Bright and Julie Otero were working there; they checked former Wichita State students who'd been in the folklore class of Professor Wyatt; they checked post office workers from the 1970s. They began checking the DNA of the retired cops.

Some were insulted, but most were glad, they told Beattie. If it helped solve the case, it would be worth it.

Then, on May 5—the nineteenth anniversary of the day that Marine Hedge's body was discovered—the killer sent another message.

• • •

The envelope came in the mail to KAKE-TV. Opened just before noon, it contained three pages. By that evening, the story was on the air. Jeanene Kiesling, a KAKE reporter, told the audience that the station had given it to the police.

"Here's what police say we can release," she said. "The first page [read], 'The BTK Story.' It was typed, and included titles for a list of chapters. The second page had the title 'Chapter 8,' and was a puzzle filled with letters in vertical rows. Some spelled out words, some numbers were intertwined. The third page has what appears to be two ID badges. The first is of a Southwestern Bell employee. The other is for a Wichita Public Schools special officer."

Even before this broadcast, one of the station's other reporters, Chris Frank, had called Beattie for his reaction, and offered to show him the letter. Beattie was doing an interview with retired Wichita Patrol Officer Lowell Hollingshead, who, with John DiPietra, had discovered Nancy Fox's body more than twenty-seven years earlier. Beattie asked Frank to describe the letter. As described by Frank, the letter did not have the BTK logo. Beattie told Frank he didn't think the letter was legitimate, but didn't tell him why.

That afternoon, Beattie watched as the station aired reporter Kiesling's piece, illustrated by footage of the KAKE news director turning the package over to Detective Otis.

Later that day, "I heard through the grapevine," Beattie recalled, "that the police were leaning toward a conclusion that the letter was genuine." That night, Beattie began receiving faxed copies of the letter, because KAKE had begun faxing its copy to others, who in turn faxed it to Beattie. After first looking at the letter, Beattie thought it might be another hoax, not unlike that perpetrated by the "poet," Ruth Finley, in the early 1980s. Beattie thought the first page, "The BTK Story," was the work of someone who had studied the case—perhaps had even attended one of his talks on the subject. He noted that all the other communications from BTK had the logo, as well as graphic details of the murders. This one had neither.

Looking at the first page of the communication, Beattie was struck by one thing that did seem consistent with a mailing from the killer, however. "The BTK Story" might easily be taken for an outline of a book, or even chapter titles. Like other mailings, it was all in capitals. It read:

THE BTK STORY

1. A SERIAL KILLER IS BORN
2. DAWN
3. FETISH
4. FANTASY WORLD
5. THE SEARCH BEGINS
6. BTK'S HAUNTS
7. PJ'S
8. MO-ID-RUSE
9. HITS
10. TREASURED MEMORIES
11. FINAL CURTAIN CALL
12. DUSK
13. WILL THERE MORE?

Was this the killer's attempt to take back the publicity from Beattie—to indicate that he, and he alone, knew the real truth—that Beattie's book would be a pale imitation of his? And what, if anything, was the significance of thirteen chapters? Beattie had a vague notion that 13 meant something to the killer.

He inspected the second page, the puzzle. This could be the letter-writer's "8. MO-ID-RUSE," a simple grid pattern of letters and numbers, it appeared to have headings for MO, ID, and RUSE. Some of the rows were not well-aligned—more evidence that the killer, if indeed it was he who had sent this letter—was not a skilled typist. The grid held some words that seemed to be spelled out. At a glance, Beattie could make out "realtors," "insurance," "id ruse," "fantasies," "telephone co.," "a serviceman," "victim," "details," "for sale," "vend," "vise" and possibly, "JPL," maybe an abbreviation for "Jet Propulsion Laboratory." And these were just in plain view in the vertical rows.

The third page was a photocopy of an open wallet, one containing two identification badges, one for the telephone company, the other for a school district security employee, each in different names.

Beattie noted the return address on the envelope was Thomas B. King. Instead of BTK, this was TBK. As in the March letter to the *Eagle*, the address was fictitious. Then Beattie realized that people with similar names lived on the streets where the fictitious addresses were. If the letter was genuine, Beattie thought, the killer was trying to lead them astray. He realized that the fictitious addresses weren't selected by the street name, as had been thought, but by the similar names of the residents who happened to live on that street. All the letter-writer had to do was open the telephone book and find individuals with names that spelled out B, T and K, not necessarily in that order.

By the following Friday evening, Beattie was no longer convinced that the letter wasn't genuine, even if it didn't have the logo. He convinced KAKE news director Glen Horn to let him take the puzzle to the monthly chapter meeting of Mensa. Beattie invited one of the retired detectives, Arlyn Smith, to join them. For about an hour the Mensans pored over the puzzle, with KAKE taping them. Many members thought the puzzle should be published or broadcast to give the public a chance to solve it. Some, including Beattie, eventually concluded that the puzzle actually had the killer's name and address embedded in it.

On Monday, May 10, 2004, Ken Landwehr held a news conference. He did not release the puzzle or the identification badges. He did say that his detectives were interested in hearing from the public about anyone posing as a telephone company employee or a school district worker who had attempted to gain entry to anyone's home in the years 1974 to 1986. He said the new letter had been given to the FBI for further analysis.

By this time, the detectives had done their own puzzle solving. They saw that it appeared to be divided into thirds, vertically. The top third began MO, apparently for *m.o.* The middle third began ID, apparently for *identification*; and the bottom third began RUSE, for *ruse*. They picked out the names used on the identification badges, and realized that numbers in the puzzle coincided with numbers on the ID badges. The far right-hand column, read all the way down, had the heading "PJ," which some thought might refer to Professor Wyatt. The letters under that column were harder to make sense out of.

Throughout the rest of May, Beattie continued to give interviews, including one to *Los Angeles Times* reporter Stephanie Simon. She asked if he thought the latest letter was on the level.

If it wasn't, Beattie told her, he was sure the real killer

27:

A Very Nice Guy

Early in June, Beattie composed a Letter to the Editor for the *Eagle*. It was his fondest hope that the killer would read it.

Noting that some people had been criticizing the police for their failure to identify the killer, Beattie wrote that as far as he could tell,

> The BTK investigation has been thorough and exhaustive. The story is the same today as it was 30 years ago; it's about the incredible suffering of the victims, the almost pathological frustration of the public, and the investigators' stoic endurance when faced with their inability to solve a case that obsesses them . . .
>
> If at the end of this storm we have protected the many innocent while hunting the single guilty party, if we have maintained our poise and decency in the face of indecent horror, then we can be proud of ourselves. That is a goal worthy of great community.

"I CAVEd my own words in that letter," Beattie said later. "I wanted the killer to read it and think that it was possible that he could continue to communicate with impunity, safely. And at the same time I wanted to demonstrate to him that his power over the rest of us was very small . . . Because my message here is about the community. He thinks we're trapped here with him, but he's trapped here with us. And we have to behave decently with each other, because there's this tremendous amount of suspicion, everybody's calling in their neighbor, every eccentric in town is getting reported to the tip line, [along with] every ex-husband and ex-boyfriend . . ."

As Beattie saw this, it would be a challenge to the killer—the community against one man. He didn't think the killer would be able to resist his narcissism: he would feel compelled to respond to Beattie's us-against-you put-down.

Three days after the letter was published, June 9, a man named Michael Hellman was driving to his job when he noticed a clear plastic Ziploc bag duct-taped to a stop sign at 1st and Kansas Streets in downtown Wichita. For some reason not made clear later, Hellman decided to remove the bag. Inside was a brown envelope. He threw away the bag and the tape, and went on to his workplace. There he looked at the outside of the envelope, and saw the lettering: "BTK Field Gram." Inside were three typewritten pages.

Hellman showed his discovery to his work supervisor, who advised him to call the police. Landwehr came to pick it up. Inside the envelope were three pieces of paper. Two pieces of paper contained the photocopier-reduced texts of six pages headed "C1: Death on a Cold January Morning," along with a drawing of a naked, bound and gagged female figure. There was a caption to the drawing: "The Sexual Thrill is My Bill," it read. There was a BTK logo on the page. The last page enclosed in the package had the same list received by KAKE-TV the previous month. This time, however, "8. MO-ID-RUSE" was blacked out. It seemed clear that BTK was saying he'd already sent number 8.

A date at the end of the story indicated that the killer had originally written it on February 3, 1974, a little more than two weeks after the Otero murders. In it, the killer

"Rex" described exactly what he had done to the Otero family. The account read like a very badly written novel, some thought—an amateurish attempt at horror storytelling.

The interesting thing about this, however, was the attempt at publication—duct-taping a "BTK Field Gram" to a stop sign in central Wichita wasn't exactly guaranteed to get publishers racing into town. In fact, the limited attempt at distribution showed something of the paucity—indeed, the narrow locality—of the writer's imagination. This should have been another tip-off that the killer was home-grown, and was someone who was acutely tuned to the local information media. But the Wichita police decided not to let anyone know that the killer had communicated again.

A week or so after the package was posted on the sign, Beattie had telephone and/or email contact with Detective Otis, Lieutenant Landwehr and former FBI profiler Roy Hazelwood. Beattie tried to explain his CAVEing concept to each of them, and his ideas about Daniel Kahneman's theories of economics—the five-dollar bill concept.

All this was part of his strategy to induce the killer to come out of hiding after so many years, Beattie tried to explain. But to Beattie, Landwehr, Otis and Hazelwood all were mesmerized by their tendency to look for a traditional motive on his part—Beattie had to want money. Right? Why else would he be doing any of this? To them, it was police work, looking for the killer. It was *their* job, not Beattie's, or anyone else's. The fact that they'd so far spent thirty years and hadn't gotten anywhere simply didn't factor into the equation. As far as they could see, Beattie was simply a problem, not the possible solution. And as for CAVEing or Kahneman's economic theories, to the police, it was just so much pointy-headed intellectualism. Or so Beattie believed the police thought.

Afterward, Beattie began hearing from retired cops that Landwehr was asking people not to talk to Beattie. The lack of a DNA match to any of the old suspects had flummoxed the investigators, as had the continued communications. From the police perspective, it was time to put out even less information, not more. It was clear that the killer wanted something, but what? If they did the wrong thing, said the wrong words, who knew if it might not set the killer off? The best thing to do—and the FBI agreed—was to keep it quiet for the time being, and think of a way to encourage the communications without driving the killer to prove himself by killing some more.

"The cops didn't know what to think," Beattie recalled. "So they were shutting down even more. They wanted to shut down everything and try to get a handle on it."

But the police were about to do just what Beattie was doing—only Beattie was doing it from outside the tent, not inside. He was "the Beattie problem."

On June 24, Landwehr held a new press conference, admitting that the May 5 KAKE communication was probably from BTK, and announcing that a new communication—the stop-sign Baggie—had also been received, and was considered genuine.

"We truly feel that he is trying to communicate with us," Landwehr told reporters. Landwehr wouldn't give any details about the new communication, except to say it concerned the Otero murders.

The underlying message of Landwehr's statement was an attempt to induce the killer to communicate directly with the police department. "Communicate with *us*," of course, meant the police, not the news media, or certainly not some civilian who happened to pass by a stop sign. Landwehr was attempting to develop an intimacy with the killer—"he" and "us." But interposing the police department into the communication chain meant trying to assert the power of censorship over the killer's communications. So far, the news media had largely cooperated with the police in censoring the communications, but Landwehr knew that over the long term this was a chancy proposition. Sooner or later, as the public interest continued to build, one media outlet or another would refuse to play along. So he wanted to encourage the killer to communicate directly with the police. That way, he hoped, the police could retain control of the situation.

The news people noticed the reticence of the police in supplying details of the new communication.

"One mystery about the case is the secretiveness with which police have conducted the investigation," the *Eagle*'s Laviana reported. "Many have speculated that police think the lack of publicity will prompt BTK to send more letters." He asked Beattie what he thought.

"It's pretty clear they don't want to deal with the press," Beattie told him, not directly answering the question.

But the killer *did* want to deal with the press. He wanted the press to make the announcements of his "field grams," not the police. He wanted to drive the news media into a frenzy. That was much of the fun of the thing. After taping his latest communication to the stop sign, he'd called KAKE-TV and the *Eagle* to tell them where to go to pick it up. Every time he called, he announced himself:

"This is BTK," he'd begin, and then the person on the other end of the line in the newsroom would hang up on him. They'd gotten so many crank calls from people claiming to be BTK, who then made such outlandish pronouncements, that no one took it seriously. This frustrated the killer enormously.

For some reason he'd decided to stop using the mail, perhaps because he now realized that it was possible for the police to obtain DNA from his envelopes. But from June on, he would use dead drops for all his communications, followed by the calls to the news organizations. He just couldn't understand why no one believed him when he called.

On Saturday morning, July 17, James Stenholm, an employee of the Wichita Public Library, emptied the outdoor book return bin at the library's main branch in downtown Wichita. At the bottom he found a plastic bag. Through the plastic, Stenholm discerned the letters BTK. Without opening the envelope, he called the police. Detective Otis came to collect the bag.

Inside, Otis discovered five pieces of paper. One was titled "BTK Flash Gram," and the following two pages contained a short narrative titled "Jakey." This referred to the death of a young man named Jake Allen who had apparently killed himself two weeks earlier by lying on the railroad tracks not far from his home in Argonia, Kansas, about thirty-eight miles southwest of Wichita. The second page of the narrative included a BTK logo and the notation: "CC: BTK Files."

The last two pages included four pictures of young males in bondage poses.

"I had to stop work on Chapter 2," the killer wrote. "I was so excited about this incident that I had to tell the story."

The killer claimed that he had lured Jake Allen out to his death by posing as a private investigator in a computer chat room, who needed Allen's help to catch BTK. The killer implied that he had killed Jake, and also, that the young man ". . . had fantasies about Sexual Masturbation in unusual ways with Bondage and Homosexual thrills."

He provided a description of Jake Allen's death, and added "While I peck this out my Sparky is going hard."

There was more:

"I have spotted a female that I think lives alone and/or is a spotted latchkey kid. Just got to work out the details. I'm much older (not feeble) now and have to conditions [sic] myself carefully. Also my thinking process is not as sharp as it uses [sic] to be . . . I think fall or winter would be just about right for the HIT. Got to do it this year or next! . . . time is running out for me.

"Now back to Chapter Two. May not made [sic] the July deadline, be patient."

Police asked the library to delay opening for an hour or so while they worked on the latest package. But they refused to disclose its contents.

Two days later, on Monday, July 19, they confirmed that a package had been collected, but again declined to discuss it. Left without any sources, the media turned to Beattie, who was happy to comment.

"If this is a package," he told Laviana, "as opposed to a letter, this might be a way to deliver it without going through the mail." Beattie was thinking about the notion of DNA on stamps—by now he had heard through the old grapevine that the police *had* recovered DNA from either stamps or envelopes from the older communications—in fact, they'd had this DNA profile since the fall of 2003, or so the story was told. If BTK knew that they'd collected his DNA, that might explain why he'd apparently abandoned the postal service.

Landwehr's decision to withhold the contents of the latest communication was consistent with the department's policy of censoring all the communications, going back to Hannon's decision in 1974 with the first letter found at the library. From his perspective, assisted by the

FBI's evaluation, it appeared that the killer was trying to direct the investigation. For some reason, he wanted them to look at Jake Allen's death. But why? The best guess was that it was a blind alley—something spun off by the killer to send them off on a wild-goose chase. The police examined Jake Allen's computer. There was no evidence that Allen had ever conversed with someone in a computer chat room about BTK.

For Landwehr, disseminating the contents of this communication could serve no useful purpose, other than to get people stirred up, and to profane the memory of Jake Allen. So he elected to keep the subject of the communication secret. Much more disquieting was the killer's apparent threat to murder again.

"I have spotted a female . . ." he'd written.

The thing to do, Landwehr decided, was to acknowledge that a new communication had been received, and to warn the public that the killer was still at large, and advise the public to take precautions. Meanwhile, the police checked Jake Allen's computer for evidence that he'd ever communicated with anyone about BTK, and found none. Still, the news that BTK was communicating again ennervated many people.

"Landwehr specifically said anyone living alone should make a habit of using dead-bolt locks, keeping the outside of their homes well lighted and not opening their doors to strangers," Laviana reported.

Laviana noted that Landwehr was no longer answering any questions from reporters, and that that posture had stirred up considerable criticism on computer chatboards.

Laviana tracked down former chief Richard LaMunyon to get his reaction to the news blackout.

"I don't know that it's a matter of being secretive," LaMunyon said. "I think it's a matter of being prudent . . . there's a fine line between what should be released and what should be withheld to maintain integrity of an investigation."

But deciding where to put that line was at the core of the BTK problem, and always had been. Keeping all the information to themselves was the natural police instinct, just as taking all the responsibility for solving the case was their instinct, even when, in a serial homicide case, the more leads one can generate, the better. In the case of the Jake Allen package, some judicious editing would have accomplished *both* purposes: the police could have said that the letter concerned Jake Allen's death (after all, the death had generated earlier publicity, hence BTK's familiarity with it), and—more to the point—the sentence, "While I peck this out my Sparky is going hard," would have been very useful to publicize. It was obvious from the context that "Sparky" was a possible nickname for the male sex organ, and a somewhat unusual one at that. The chances were quite good that someone other than the killer might be familiar with this colloquial usage. This is the sort of thing that can be productively employed in the search for a serial killer—idiosyncratic characteristics that don't directly come to bear on evidence. If forty men were said by tips from the public to use the nickname "Sparky" for their penis, that would be forty new needles for the haystack, most of which could be eliminated by discovering that they had legitimate alibis for any of the by-now connected murders. Keeping the information back did nothing to assist the investigation, but instead possibly hindered it.

As far as Beattie was concerned, the main thing that withholding the information accomplished was to frighten the wits out of the community.

By August, it appeared that the police had finally worked out a strategy to communicate with the killer, although one on their terms rather than his. Since the plan was to encourage the communications from the killer, there had to be something more useful than "no comment" from the police. Relying upon recommendations from the FBI, the police began assisting the media in developing stories about the case—but stories of their choosing, not the killer's. The *Eagle* published discussions about DNA testing, and located Charlie Otero, now 46 years old, in an effort to put a more human face on the victims. The possible link to WSU Professor P. J. Wyatt was brought to the surface publicly for the first time, along with the suggestion that the "PJ" on the May KAKE letter might refer to Professor Wyatt, who had died in 1991.

"Friday, police Lt. Ken Landwehr said FBI profilers have confirmed BTK investigators' conclusion that there's a connection involving the professor, the late P. J. Wyatt. What's needed, Landwehr said, is for the public to help provide missing pieces between Wyatt and the killer," *Eagle* reporter Tim Potter wrote.

Now, at last, the police were getting the hang of how to use the public to assist them. It wasn't necessary to put out all the details of the crimes and communications, just those that might tend to narrow the public's focus. A secondary tactic was to make Landwehr the sole spokesperson for the police department, and to identify him as the man in charge of the case. That way, BTK would know who to communicate with if he wanted to deal one-on-one with the police.

"Here are the critical details police want the public to know," Potter continued, and established that a poem sent—Potter didn't say to whom—had "adapted lines from a folk song called 'Oh, Death.' "

"We are looking for the public's help on identifying anyone who has used this obscure folk song and had contact with Dr. P. J. Wyatt," Landwehr said.

There was more. Former FBI profiler Robert Ressler

was contacted. Ressler told the newspaper that almost thirty years earlier, he and John Douglas had theorized that the killer was a student, and possibly a criminal justice student. He was someone who had studied serial killers, and had familiarity with their names and crimes.

"Friday's announcement by police is not the first time connections have been made between the killer who dubbed himself BTK . . . and WSU," Potter added. The Ghostbusters of the 1980s had been able to establish that the killer used a photocopy machine at the university for the "Oh Death" letter in 1978.

"He reportedly made a reference to the school's campus to the survivor of one attack," Potter wrote, and "This past May 5, the killer sent a letter to KAKE-TV with the heading 'The BTK Story' and a chapter titled 'P. J.s.' "

This, finally was news the public could use. Regrettably, however, it was too little. What should have been added by the police in this effort to get focused help from the public were other facts: that the killer was a very bad speller, often switching letters around, as if he were dyslexic; that he was probably now around 60 years old; that he was close to six feet in height, and at the time of the attacks had weighed around 180 pounds; that he owned at least two handguns; that he was probably a practiced burglar; that he had most likely grown up in Wichita; that he was familiar with an old serial killer named Harvey Glatman; that he probably was around children (from the "SHIRLEYLOCKS" poem and the child's printing set); that he was proficient with knots; that he watched KAKE-TV and read the *Eagle*; that he had a penchant for superficial, almost pedantic precision; that he was white, and almost certainly not a white-collar worker, such as a banker or lawyer; that he had a preoccupation if not an obsession with abbreviations; that he identified with the police; and that he was so rigid in his methods as to be seen by others as almost anal-retentive. Juxtaposed with the notion that the killer had likely been a criminal justice student at WSU in the 1970s would have really narrowed down the field, and certainly have produced some very solid leads.

This method of narrowing the focus of the public's eye, however, is usually not recommended by the FBI and other experts, who say that making the profile too narrow runs the risk of causing the public to dismiss likely candidates from consideration.

Nevertheless, a wider profile brings in too many generalized suspects; use of a more focused profile can instead bring in more of the sort of suspects that are really worth investigating. The trick is to disseminate this quality of information once the parameters have become clear, not too soon and not too late; and then to be able to use the information still held back, such as specific movements and actions at crime scenes, to eliminate the false confessors by making them *prove* their guilt, while using the same information to put the non-confessing suspects under stress.

So by that August, some experts approved the idea of finally putting out profile information, even if it was too limited in scope. Greg McCrary, a former FBI profiler, offered a possible reason for the change in policy. He suggested that police had already exhausted all their leads having to do with WSU, and hoped the public could give them more.

"He also had advice for anyone who might be able to provide police a vital link," Potter said of McCrary, "but might be reluctant:

" 'There's a tendency for people to be in denial about having any valuable information about who a suspect could be,' McCrary had said. " 'Chances are this person is in many ways a nice guy—on the surface, anyway.' "

Reading this, the killer had to agree. *That's me*, he thought. *I'm actually a very nice guy.*

28:

"Uno-Dos-Tres"

By the end of August 2004, the police had disseminated more information about the killer, including the "Oh Anna, Why Didn't You Appear" poem rip-off that had been mailed to KAKE and Anna Williams twenty-five years earlier. Again, the plan seemed to be to trigger someone's more specific recollection, another example of providing the public with a narrowed profile.

Then, in early September, another card was played.

DEATH PENALTY UNLIKELY FOR BTK, the *Eagle* headlined. Here was yet another proactive effort to establish contact with the killer. In effect, this told the killer that he might avoid execution if and when he was arrested, which had the effect of lowering the stakes somewhat in continuing to communicate.

The *Eagle*'s Laviana queried a number of legal experts on the topic, and the consensus seemed to be that since all of the BTK murders had taken place during an era when the state of Kansas did not have a constitutionally conforming death penalty, the killer would likely not be executed. The key paragraph was provided by Sedgwick County District Attorney Nola Foulston.

"You prosecute under the law that exists at the time of the crime," she told Laviana. Which meant that since the death penalty law did not exist in Kansas at the time of the murders, BTK would not be executed.

The media kept the pot stirring for the next month, although they began to run out of things to write about or broadcast. A complimentary profile of Landwehr appeared in the newspaper; this, too, was part of the strategy, to put a human face behind the name associated with the investigation in order to ratchet up the level of intimacy the killer was supposed to feel with his pursuer.

A psychic came to town and toured some of the sites, eventually declaring, "This is no weirdo . . . This is an ordinary guy who has moments of madness. It could be your next-door neighbor, and you'd have no way of knowing it. He's just an ordinary man." That was hardly a conclusion that required ESP, though. The killer couldn't have lived for thirty years in Wichita without being "an ordinary guy," at least to everyone except his victims.

Then things grew quiet—too quiet, for the killer.

NEW LETTER MIGHT BE FROM BTK, POLICE SAY, the *Eagle* headlined on October 27, 2004.

Once again, the police were withholding information, it appeared. This time, a letter was left near a United Parcel Service drop box at a downtown Wichita office building. The package was actually left on October 22—exactly thirty years after the original communication about "those two dude" that had first revealed BTK's existence in the library letter of that same date in 1974.

The police confirmed that a communication had been received after television stations KAKE and KWCH reported it; the stations got their information from employees in the office building, who had heard about it from the police.

This was a particularly odious communication, some thought.

A UPS driver, Eric McRae, arrived at the Omni Center at 2nd and Kansas Streets, one block away from the June drop, around 7:30 P.M. He noticed an unsealed manila envelope inside the drop box. Opening the envelope he found a plastic bag containing another envelope, with the words "BTK FIELD GRAMS" on the exterior. Inside that envelope he found eight three-by-five index cards. Some of the cards were filled with what the driver thought was gibberish—combinations of letters and numbers that made no sense. Others were filled with some sort of writing. The last appeared to be a collage of photographs of pictures or drawings of children apparently cut from magazines. All of them had hand-drawn bindings or gags.

McRae did what anyone else would do: he called the cops.

Afterward, an analysis of the contents of the latest communication showed that it contained, besides the chilling drawings, two principal components, each validated with a BTK logo: first, four cards that contained some sort of description of BTK's personal history; and second, on two cards, some sort of stream-of-consciousness ranting headed "THREE: 1-2-3: UNO-DOS-TRES: THEORY." This too had a BTK logo. The last card showed "The BTK Story" list with Numbers 1 and 8 lined out. What was also clear was that BTK had been enjoying himself with photocopy machines again. The cards represented reduced reproductions of full-sized, typed pages.

If one and eight had been lined out, that suggested that this "THREE: 1-2-3: UNO-DOS-TRES: THEORY" represented #3 on BTK's list: "FETISH," as he had listed in the May letter to KAKE. There was an explanation of some sort proffered by the killer:

"The BTK World, Works in Threes and is base [sic] on the Eternal Triangle," he'd written. He'd provided a helpful example of an equilateral triangle nearby, one with a base made up of three dots.

It was hard to make anything sensible out of this, however, except that everything that followed seemed to be in threes:

Universe (God)-Cosmos (Holy Spirit)-Elements (Son)
Elements-Light-Heavy
Heavy-Gravity-Space
Space-Galaxies-Solar Systems
Solar Systems-Planets-Suns
Sun-Heat-Light
Light-Photosynthesis-Carbon
Carbon-Fuel-Air
Air-Water-Food
Food-Plants-Animals
Animal-Non-primate-Primates
Primates-Non-Human Type
Human-People-Persons
Person-Man-Women
Women-Man-Sex
Sex-Birth-Family
Family-Parent-Child
Child-Mothers Love-Dad's Love
Love-Good-Bad
Bad-Physical-Mental
Mental-Normal-Abnormal
Abnormal-Controlled-Psycho
Psycho-Serial Killer-BTK
(BTK) Bind-Torture-Kill
Kill-Death-Spirit-Soul
Soul-Dust-Planets
Planets-Solar System-Sun
Sun-Heat-Gravity

Gravity-Space-Universe
Universe-Cosmos-Elements

This descent and ascent by categories of threes was followed by another bit of assistance:

Example of cardinal number one more than two theory:

BTK-Victim-Police
Police Dept.-Officers-Detectives
Detective-Others-Landwehr
Be:
Victim-No Go-Go
Go-PJ-Details
Details-Time-Hit
Hit-Thrill-Kill

The next card continued:

Three-Continue:
Etc.
PJ-Board Water-Details-Time
Time-Day-Hr
Hr-Thrill-Capture
Bind-Torture-Kill
Kill-Erection-SBT
SBT-SX Release-New High
New High-Brain Video-SX Fuel
Etc.
PJ Little Key-Details-Time
Time-Day-Hr
Hr-Thrill-Capture
Bind-Torture-Kill
Etc.
Torture-Mental-Physical

Physical-Rape-Sodomy
Sodomy-Sparky-SBT
Etc:
Details-Turn Key-Alone
Alone-No-Yes
Yes-Break in-Await
Await-Thrill-Capture
Etc.

There were several striking things about this seeming stream-of-consciousness voiding. First, in clarion contrast to the earlier communications, there were no misspellings in this one. Second, the typeface was completely different—in fact, it appeared that it had been composed on a word processor. That probably explained why there were no misspellings—the computer had automatically corrected them. "Photosynthesis," for example, was a word that was almost certainly beyond the killer's rudimentary spelling ability.

Second, from this the killer was apparently attempting to indicate something of the origins of his behavior—almost suggesting, in fact, that he was some sort of alien. The only place in the first part where he'd not used a trio was in "Primates-Non-Human Type." The killer seemed to be suggesting that he was non-human, and that torture and murder had some sort of cosmic power or significance.

The part of this meandering message that caught the detectives' most earnest attention, however, was the part that referred to them: "BTK-Victim-Police." Was the killer saying he was a victim of the police? Or was he saying the police would be his next victim? The killer's use of Landwehr's name—"Landwehr / Be: / Victim."

Was it likely that the killer would try for Landwehr or his family? That couldn't be discounted. From that point forward, Landwehr's house was put under extra police protection.

The second card offered some additional fodder. First, there were the initials PJ again—three times overall in the two cards. And two with uppercased terms after them: "Board Water," and "Little Key." And after these, the same general pattern of lists: details, time, day, hour, and similar expressions. This suggested that the two PJs were of a type, perhaps alternatives. SBT was incomprehensible to the police, but it was adjacent to "Sparky," "Sodomy," and "Rape," as well as "SX" and "Release," not to mention "Kill" and "Erection," which certainly indicated that SBT had something to do with violent sexual predation.

And there was one more thing: the killer seemed to be manifesting his list-making habits, his follow-the-manual way of organizing his mind.

Police confirmed the receipt of the newest communication with a terse acknowledgment saying only that it had been sent to the FBI for further analysis.

Then things grew quiet again.

29:

"Doll-o-Gram"

After studying the latest communication for more than a month—and without hearing further from the killer—Landwehr in consultation with the FBI decided that a little gentle prodding might do no harm. The first part of the October 22 communication, the four cards that purported to relate something of the killer's claimed personal history, might be publicly disseminated with possibly good results. Of course, there was every chance that this was more misdirection—another attempt to lead police astray, as in the Jake Allen letter. But even liars sometimes use the truth, so it was decided to put some of the claimed characteristics out to the public in the hope that it might generate more tips.

On November 30, the police issued a carefully crafted press release.

In BTK DESCRIBES HIS BACKGROUND, the police noted that the killer had provided number of facts about his background, but did not say exactly how or when these statements had been made. The word "claims" was in boldface, indicating that the public should maintain skepticism about the accuracy of the information. The police provided the following list of claims:

- He claims he was born in 1939, which would make his current age 64 or 65.
- His father died in World War II, and his mother raised him.

- His mother was forced to work, so his grandparents cared for him.
- His mother worked during the day near the railroad.
- He had a cousin named Susan, who moved to Missouri.
- His family moved a lot, but always lived near a railroad.
- His grandfather played the fiddle and died of a lung disease.
- His mother started dating a railroad detective when BTK was around 11 years old. This relationship would have occurred during the years 1950–1955.
- In the early 1950s he built and operated a ham radio.
- He has participated in outdoor hobbies including hunting, fishing and camping.
- As a youth he attended church and Sunday school.
- He had a female, Hispanic acquaintance named Petra, who had a younger sister named Tina.
- Around 1960, he went to tech military school. He then joined the military for active duty and was discharged in 1966.
- He has a basic knowledge of photography and the ability to develop and print pictures.
- In 1966 he moved back in with his mother who had re-married and was renting out part of her house.
- His first job was as an electro-mechanic, requiring some travel.
- After attending more tech school, he worked repairing copiers and business equipment; this sometimes required travel and he was away from home for extended periods.

- He admits to soliciting prostitutes.
- He has a lifetime fascination with railroads and trains.

The decision to release some of this supposed background information was applauded. The *Eagle* quoted former FBI profiler Greg McCrary as approving the release. McCrary noted that there was a chance that at least some of what the killer claimed might be true, and that it should help people to think about the person who had committed the murders. But McCrary cautioned that serial killers tended to be notorious fabricators, and that some had a penchant for borrowing backgrounds from other people. He suggested that the police had decided to put the information out because they had once more run out of leads.

Another retired profiler, Bob Ressler, agreed with McCrary.

"One has to consider the fact that this guy is a gamesman," Ressler told the *Eagle*. "He likes to play with authorities." The very fact that there were so many supposed details about the killer's past made him suspicious that the killer was making it up, Ressler said. "This whole scenario could be contrived just to set out false leads and keep the police running." Still, he said, the police had to put the information out.

"It certainly would be less than responsible for law enforcement not to share this with the public," he said. "The key could be there. There could be something that leads to this guy's apprehension."

Ressler said he had an idea that the killer had stopped murdering years earlier as his killing urge waned with age. Based on the descriptions of the man in the first murders, the killer would probably be nearly 60 if not older,

Ressler pointed out—in fact, the killer claimed to have been born in 1939.

"I for one, have never heard of a man in his 60s who's a serial killer," Ressler told the *Eagle*. "This guy could be the exception." But Ressler thought it was far more likely that the killer was simply trying to relive the days when he *had* murdered by whipping up a public frenzy.

"To see their deeds played up in the media is very exciting and very ego-rewarding," he said, speaking of serial killers generally.

Former chief LaMunyon thought that the increase in self-revelation on the part of the killer presaged a possible decision to turn himself in.

"He's becoming more and more open with information, and it's logical to assume that the next step will be to identify himself or maybe even come forward," LaMunyon told the newspaper. "I'm hopeful that will be his next step . . . I could be wrong, but I just truly believe that this is an individual who doesn't want to go to his grave without telling us who he is."

But over the next few days, reporters reached people in the military and other occupations for their reaction to the killer's claims, and some of the air begin to leak out of the balloon. Veterans and others familiar with military jargon thought that either BTK was lying about his military service, or was changing his story so as to avoid detection. Wichita Mayor Carlos Mayans, a native of Cuba, thought it was odd that the killer would claim to have an Hispanic girlfriend named "Petra"—it was a very uncommon name for a girl of Hispanic descent, he observed. The man who had the contract to service WSU's typewriters back in the 1970s noted that most of the photocopying machines—

fairly rare in that era—were serviced by the manufacturers directly. That seemed to suggest that the claim was bogus—surely the police would have obtained a list of names of people who serviced such machines in Wichita in the 1970s, and it was doubtful it would be much larger than ten or fifteen names. If the list was that small, the police almost certainly could have arrested or otherwise identified the man without having to put out the list of background attributes. So it was probably a bogus claim.

Then, on December 1, 2004, the police made an arrest.

Later, the origins of this move were shrouded in some secrecy. It appeared that after the list of background "facts" claimed by the killer was publicly disseminated, the police received 350 new tips. And while Landwehr later would not confirm it, or indeed, provide any comment on the episode, it appears that something in these tips focused detectives' interest on a 64-year-old south Wichita man after keeping his house under surveillance for most of the day. Beattie learned that at least two of the new tips named the man, asserting that several points of the man's background matched the list provided to police by the killer. Detectives began an intense scrutiny of the man's past, and soon concluded that he indeed matched the profile they were expecting.

"We got him," one detective was reputed to have exulted, at least according to one of Beattie's sources.

A search warrant was asked for and approved, and the police took a DNA sample from the man, while arresting him on at least one warrant for a misdemeanor—trespassing, according to Beattie.

The word of the surveillance, search and arrest leaked almost immediately, even as the events were unfolding. The networks' camera crews raced to the man's house and took shots of unidentified figures, presumably police, going in and out.

Then the word came back to the detectives from the DNA lab—there was no match. The 64-year-old was definitely *not* BTK, and had the genes to prove it. The police kept mum about this, however, and by noon the following day, the network trucks were out in force in the parking lot near police headquarters, located in the Wichita City Hall. By that point, the entire world was waiting for the word that the long hunt was over, that BTK was identified and under arrest.

It fell to newly appointed Wichita Police Chief Norman Williams to face the incredulous news media.

"We have not, and I repeat, we have not made an arrest in connection with BTK," Williams said. The chief's credibility was clearly strained by the snafu—especially by his implication that they'd only made a routine misdemeanor arrest, and that it was the fault of the media for going hog wild on the story.

Soon a lawyer for the arrested man was giving a statement to the press: a DNA test showed his client "is not BTK," he said.

"The WPD has now confirmed that DNA testing has excluded him as a suspect in the BTK investigation," the lawyer said in a public statement. He said that Landwehr himself had told him the results. The police would not confirm the lawyer's statement, for some reason, saying only that it was a WPD policy never to discuss results of forensic testing.

The embarrassing and all-too-public flub of the man's arrest and release, especially if it *was* the result of the killer's dubious list of claims as to his background, as it seemed to be, would probably cause the real killer great merriment, former profiler McCrary told the newspaper—he'd pulled another fast one on the cops.

But the killer wanted to make sure that the police got the message. He had another anniversary present planned for them.

On the evening of December 8, 2004, exactly twenty-seven years after Nancy Fox's murder, a man telephoned a convenience store near the corner of Hillside and Harry Streets in southeast Wichita. This store was not far from the former location of the jewelry store where Nancy had worked on the night of her murder. He'd already tried calling KAKE and the *Eagle*, but again they'd hung up on him.

"I'm calling to tell you of a BTK package at Ninth and Minnesota, on the northeast corner," the man told the clerk who answered the telephone. He gave precise instructions to the clerk, telling him to write the directions down, then read them back. The clerk thought the man was being a jerk, and told him he wouldn't do any such thing. The man lost his temper and hung up. Afterward, the clerk thought about the call, which he considered someone's idea of a bad joke. He told his supervisor, who told him to call the police. The police came and interviewed the clerk, who tried to remember what the man had told him. Based on this information, the police went to 9th Street North, near Murdock Park in downtown Wichita. Playing their flashlights all around, the police could find nothing, and gave the job up as the prank of just another nutball.

Five days later, a man walking through the northeast corner of the park saw a white trash bag near a tree. He passed it by, but on his return trip, William Ervin saw a shooting star, which he took as a good luck omen. He decided to pick the bag up to see what it held. Inside he found a clear plastic bag with an index card attached, with the word "Doll-o-Gram" printed on it. Inside the plastic bag was a doll, some papers and Nancy Fox's driver's license. Ervin's mother recognized that Nancy Fox was the name of a BTK victim. In fact, she'd seen this on KAKE-TV. She called KAKE, and a cameraman came out and videotaped the package. Then the station called the police, who came and collected the two plastic bags and their contents.

The doll was gruesome. It was tied with yellow tape around its ankles, and red tape on its hands. The colors matched the colors of the pantyhose used to tie up Nancy Fox. The doll had a blouse but no pants, just as Nancy had been found. Her driver's license—the original, not a copy—was tied to the doll's ankles like an i.d. tag.

Inside the inner bag was a two-page typed document: "CHAPTER 9: HITS: PJ FOX TAIL—12-8-1977," it read.

This apparently was meant to be a portion of Chapter 9 of the killer's book, and again, as he had with "Death on a Cold January Morning," he described in detail how "Rex" had murdered.

One more piece of paper was headed "The BTK Story," again with the chapter list. This time, numbers 1, 2, and 8 were lined out. There was an additional paper with the letters "PJ Bell."

This time the police announced the discovery only two days after it was found.

30:

"Rex, It Will Be OK"

After the dreadful "Doll-o-Gram," the pace of communications from BTK began to quicken. The killer was sure they could hear him now.

Unfortunately, the unreliability of the dead-drop system continued. There was no way to insure the packages would be picked up, or at least, picked up in a timely fashion. Still, it was safer in the killer's mind—he'd become worried that somehow the postal service could narrow things down to the time and place where his efforts were sent from, so he avoided the U.S. Mail.

On January 8, 2005, the killer prepared a special communication for the police department. Using an empty box of Special K cereal as a container, he prepared one two-page document titled "BOOM." The first page of this described what the killer referred to as his "lair." His "lair" was a three-story house with an elevator, he said; on one floor there was a special "kill room" called "BTK's DTPG & BONDAGE ROOM." His fondness for abbreviations and acronyms was unabated, maybe growing worse. In his mind, DTPG stood for "death to pretty girl," although the police could not know this. The next page was an apparent wiring diagram for a homemade bomb, which he'd placed in the basement. He indicated that if the police tried to search his "lair," the bomb would go off.

A second document was headed "COMMUNICATION." In this, he included a list of "PJs"—"PJ - Little

Mex, my 1 big hit . . . a good start as Serial Killer," "PJ - Fox Tail . . . Nancy J Fox, My best Hit." He also listed another "PJ"—an attempted abduction at Twin Lakes Mall in 1974.

The killer also had a question he wanted to ask the police.

"Can I communicate with Floppy and not be traced to a computer? Be honest." If so, if a floppy could not be traced, the police should put a classified ad in the *Eagle*: "Rex, it will be ok." The killer said he'd undertake "a test run" in the near future.

That night, on January 8, 2005, three days after the seventeenth anniversary of the Mary Fager letter, the killer drove his SUV to the parking lot of the Home Depot store on North Woodlawn near Route 96 in north Wichita. He cruised around the parking lot for a while, sniffing the air for possible danger. Then he pulled in next to a pickup truck, got out of his car, threw the cereal box into the bed of the pickup, got back in his own car, and drove off.

For the next week, the killer looked through the *Eagle* want ads, searching for "Rex, it will be ok." But it was never there.

Well, the killer thought, *something must have happened. The bozo who owned the truck must not clean the bed of his truck out, or if he does, he probably threw my message away.*

He decided to try again.

On January 17—the one-year anniversary of the Hurst Laviana story about the thirtieth anniversary of the Otero murders—the killer prepared another communication, this one in a Post Toasties cereal box. *Ha Ha*, he thought. *Cereal killer—get it?* He was such a card.

This one was another "Doll-o-Gram." Inside this box, he put a plastic doll painted to look like Josie Otero. Around her neck he fashioned a noose, and tied the noose to a small piece of pipe.

That ought to get their attention, he thought. This box he stuffed with more papers. He drove to North Seneca Street, not far from where he'd grown up, and left the box next to a road sign that read "Curve." He tied a red streamer to the box, and weighted it down with a brick. He circled the "T" in *Toasties* and marked a "B" and a "K" around it. Inside the box he put several pieces of jewelry that had belonged to his victims, and some portion of "#7 PJs."

Another week went by—still nothing. The dead-drop method wasn't working. He had to get someone's attention. Finally he broke down and sent a postcard to KAKE.

As Landwehr had feared, difficulties were now beginning to crop up between the police and the news media. The local television stations, now that the story had gone national, were less likely to do whatever the police wanted. That had already been evident when it turned out a reporter from KAKE had kept back part of the Murdock Park package—the index card that read "Doll-o-Gram." True, it had only been kept back for a day, but it showed a growing restiveness from the reporters, less of a willingness to cooperate.

On January 25, 2005, Glen Horn, the news director at KAKE, called the police media information spokesperson, Janet Johnson, and demanded to speak to Chief Williams. Johnson wanted to know why. Horn told her that the station had received another communication from BTK. But he wanted to talk to Williams, not Landwehr or one of his detectives.

Words were exchanged, and finally Horn and reporter Larry Hatteberg agreed to meet with Detective Otis. Otis picked up the postcard that seemed to be from BTK.

Addressed to KAKE, the postcard had a sender name of "S Killett," and a return address that was the same as the Otero house. The rear of the postcard read "COMMUNICATION #8," and described the location of a Post Toasties cereal box on North Seneca Street.

"Let me know some how if you or Wichita PD received this," BTK had written. There was also a question about "#7 at Home Depot Drop Site 1-8-05."

Horn told Otis that he'd already sent a camera crew to the place where the Post Toasties box was supposed to be. They found such a box, he told Otis.

Otis was not happy. Horn told him that no one had touched the box. Otis called in, and soon two other detectives were on their way to the location. When the two detectives arrived, they found the KAKE personnel "surrounding" the box. Otis arrived a few minutes later and took possession of it.

When he opened the box, Otis discovered the awful doll and the pipe, along with a copy of "#7 PJs." Reading this, police understood for the first time that the letters "PJ" had nothing to do with Professor Wyatt.

Also inside the box, Otis found "CHAPTER 9 HITS: PJ-LITTLE MEX-01-15-1974," "The BTK Story" chapter list, with chapters 1, 2 and 8 lined out, a two-page paper titled "BTK's Haunts," and a list of the killer's favorite acronyms, including DTPG. There was also some jewelry in the box. The "PJ-LITTLE MEX" papers described the Otero murders.

Because of the question about the Home Depot, a detective drove to that store and contacted the manager. A search of the store and parking lot was made, but nothing was found. Afterward, the store management posted a notice in the employee break room, asking if anyone had discovered an unusual package recently. One employee said, yeah, his roommate had found a Special K box in the back of his truck. The box had several pieces of computer paper in it, along with some blue beads. The roommate had decided someone was playing a joke on him, and threw the box out. By now, said the employee, the box was probably at the dump.

But two days later the roommate called the police. The trash hadn't been picked up yet. He still had the box if they wanted it.

They did.

A detective now reviewed a security videotape for the night of January 8. The roommate's truck was clearly visible. At some point that night, a dark vehicle pulled into the lot, made several turns, and then parked next to the roommate's truck. A shadowy, indistinct figure emerged from the dark vehicle, walked around to the rear of the truck, and threw something into the back. Freezing the frame, detectives tried to measure the ground clearance and length of the vehicle. They concluded it was probably a Jeep Grand Cherokee—one of about 2,500 registered in the county.

The killer had been caught on tape—it was just that the image was too dim to identify him.

On January 28, the police secretly placed an ad in the *Eagle*—"Rex, it will be ok."

Now, the police had to hope that the killer was really as ignorant about computers as he seemed to be.

"We were really hoping he would buy that," Detective Otis said later.

31:

"Thank You for Your Quick Response"

Postcards seeming to be a reliable way of directing attention to his communications, the killer adopted that method again in early February. On February 3, KAKE-TV got another postcard from BTK.

"Thank you for your quick response on #7 and 8," the killer typed. "Sorry about Susan's and Jeff's colds." Two of the KAKE anchors had recently complained of the usual winter respiratory affliction.

Under a heading he made—"business issues"—BTK advised, "tell WPD that I receive [sic] the newspaper tip for a go. Test run soon. Thanks."

That night, on the air, KAKE reporter Larry Hatteberg addressed the killer directly, telling him that his message had been received and passed on to the appropriate parties.

The discovery of the two cereal boxes in north Wichita sparked speculation that the killer had expanded his base of operations from downtown Wichita to the outlying areas. Beattie was asked what he thought it meant. Not much, he said. He pointed out that most of the locations for recent drops had been fairly close to I-135, the major freeway that bisected the city. The only significance of the locations, Beattie suggested, was that it was quick and easy to get off and back on the freeway after making a drop, thus lessening the chance of being caught in the act.

Others, however, wondered if the killer might have some connection to the northern part of the city, or even its outlying suburbs. The *Eagle* noted that Park City had had two murders, both strangulations, in the past two decades: Marine Hedge in 1985, and Dee Davis in 1991.

Both murders bore some similarities to the BTK killings, reporters Tim Potter and Hurst Laviana noted, including some apparent bondage. But they differed in that all the known BTK murder victims had been left in their residences, while both Hedge and Davis had apparently been kidnapped before being murdered. Beattie, in his research for his book, had already decided that the characteristics of the Hedge and Davis murders, with the obvious bondage, were so similar to the known BTK cases that they had to be the work of BTK, despite the public denials by the police, who discounted any connection because the bodies had been moved.

"In retrospect, both the Marine Hedge and Delores Davis murders should have stood out under the glare of lights," Beattie said later. "Their bodies were bound, moved miles away from their homes, but were *not* buried." The bodies of several other female murder victims in the Wichita area, Beattie realized, had been moved, but in those cases, the bodies *were* buried. Not in the cases of Hedge and Davis—Beattie thought that was significant.

"Why?" Beattie wondered. Why would the killer take the time, trouble and risk of moving two victims, when previously he was perfectly content to leave them where he killed them? It was only later that the answer became obvious: the killer lived in the same neighborhood as the last two victims, and wanted to get those crimes as far away from where he lived as he could.

"I imagine future geographic profilers might add Dennis Rader's behavior to their analysis," Beattie said later. "If a body is moved, ask 'Why?' Is it because the murderer lives or works near the victim?"

But if the police were in agreement with Beattie's reasoning at this point, they weren't letting anyone else in on it.

Then the killer mailed again.

On Wednesday, February 16, Marcine Andrews, a receptionist for KSAS-TV—the Fox affiliate in Wichita—opened a large padded envelope that had come in the mail. The envelope contained three index cards, a gold chain with a locket, and a purple computer disk. The sender identified himself as "P.J. Fox," and listed a downtown Wichita return address.

Andrews took the envelope and its contents to station manager Tom Gdisis. Gdisis recognized this as a probable mailing from BTK, and immediately called the police.

A WPD detective, Dana Gouge, retrieved the envelope from the television station. One index card contained a photocopy of the cover of John Sandford's novel about a serial killer, *Rules of Prey*. Another card had the title "COMMUNICATION-11," and contained a list of communications #7 through #11. Apparently the killer didn't want anyone to miss anything.

The last index card referred to the computer disk, and provided further instructions for future communications through more newspaper advertisements. "Test Floppy for WPD review," the killer had identified it.

This was what the detectives had been waiting and hoping for. The disk was taken to an expert in the department's computer crimes section, Detective Randy Stone, who discovered that it held only one file: "TestA.rtf." Opening the file, Stone read the words on the screen:

"This is a test. See 3 × 5 Card for details on Communication with me in the newspaper."

The killer did not seem to understand that every computer file contains a record of who created it and when. Stone examined the "properties" section of the file. And there it was: the author name "Dennis," and the owner of the computer—Christ Lutheran Church in Park City.

Stone put "Christ Lutheran Church" into the Google search engine, and came up with a webpage for the church. The Congregational President was a man named Dennis Rader.

A further computer search showed that Dennis Rader lived in Park City. In fact, some noticed, he lived only a few houses away from Marine Hedge's address in 1985.

Rader, detectives now discovered, was employed as the Park City "compliance officer." A compliance officer enforced the city's ordinances—an almost-cop, exactly as had been predicted for nearly thirty years.

In other words, Dennis Rader, apparently the man who had written "This is a test," and promised further communications by way of ads in the newspaper, was the town dogcatcher.

He was also BTK.

Maybe.

Was it possible that the congregation president of a long-established church in suburban Park City was really a secret serial killer? A quasi–law enforcement officer? What if someone else had used his name to gain access to the church computer? It was certainly possible. Before rushing out the door to put a respected member of the community in handcuffs, the detectives had to make doubly sure. True, Rader was 59 years old—the right age for BTK. And he'd graduated from WSU with a degree in criminal justice in 1979. He'd previously worked for a burglar alarm company in Wichita—exactly the sort of occupation that might give someone access to people's homes. But this was on paper—in reality, Rader seemed like the last person anyone would suspect of being a homicidal maniac. And the police department was still smarting from the December fiasco, when Chief Norman Williams had had to eat crow in front of a national television audience.

More information was needed before detectives could be sure.

That afternoon, Detectives Clint Snyder and Tim Relph cruised by the Rader home in Park City. There, parked in the driveway, was a black Jeep Cherokee—registered to Rader's son.

This fit. Obviously, the son couldn't be BTK—he would only have been a toddler when the Oteros were killed. From this point forward, detectives put Rader under loose surveillance—not only to prevent him from escaping in case he got wind of their interest, but also to make sure he didn't kill again.

At the same time, the detectives cast around for a way to get Rader's DNA. After some research and consideration, the detectives decided to get a court order to obtain a biological sample from Rader's daughter. The court order allowed them to obtain the sample from her medical files without her knowledge. This sample was submitted under conditions of great secrecy to the Kansas Bureau of Investigation forensic laboratory in Topeka on February 22, 2005. The lab analysis showed that the DNA from Rader's daughter matched in a statistically unique way

32:

"I Am BTK"

At 12:15 in the early afternoon of February 25, 2005, a team of police officers pulled Dennis Rader over in Park City as he was on his way home for lunch, driving his city-owned dogcatcher's truck. A KBI agent, Ray Lundin, who had been assigned to the Otero case almost a year earlier, pulled him out of the truck and threw him to the ground. Surrounded by eleven officers, all with guns drawn, some wielding shotguns, he was made to lie face down on the ground while being handcuffed. He looked up at the officers, very calm.

"Let my wife know I won't be home for lunch," he said.

Rader was put into a police car for transport to the FBI's offices in Wichita. As the rear door was opened, he leaned in and saw Landwehr.

"Hello, Mr. Landwehr," he said, obviously recognizing the lieutenant who had been the main spokesman for the police over the long years of the hunt.

At about a quarter to 1 that same afternoon, detectives read Rader his Miranda rights. He readily agreed to waive his right to a lawyer, and said he'd be happy to talk. Landwehr and FBI Special Agent Bob Morton conducted the first interview. They also served him with a search warrant that permitted them to take his DNA; they wanted to be absolutely certain that Rader's DNA matched that found at the murder scenes. Two samples were taken by swabbing the inside of his cheeks, and sent off to two different labs just in case something went wrong. Other detectives, meanwhile, were serving other warrants on Rader's Park City office, his house, the Park City library, and Christ Lutheran Church. A small army conducted the searches—215 officers and agents altogether, the police said later.

At first, Rader seemed to want to banter with his interrogators. He never asked why he had been picked up—it was obvious from his recognition of Landwehr that he knew exactly what was on the table.

"Have you been following the BTK investigation?" Rader was asked.

"Yeah," Rader said. "Yeah. I've been a BTK fan for years, watching it."

"Do you know why we've taken your DNA?"

"Well," Rader said, "I assume I'm a main suspect."

"What's going to happen if your DNA matches the DNA we've got from the crime scenes?"

"I guess that might be it, then," Rader said.

"What do you remember about the Otero murders?"

"Four—" he started, then amended, "Well, whatever was in the paper. Four members were killed. A man, and a wife, two kids. And the way the paper dictated, it was pretty—pretty brutal. Yeah. You know, spent quite a bit of time looking for the guy."

"Why the Oteros?" Landwehr asked.

"Well, if you take that murder and some of the others, I would say you've got a serial killer loose . . . When was the last one? What year was that? Yeah, well, they think BTK did it. 'eighty-six. 'eight-six. Oh, Vicki."

" 'Vicki'?"

"Well, you got to remember," Rader said, "I have read quite a bit about the cases."

Landwehr and Morton asked what sort of person Rader thought BTK was.

"Kind of like a lone wolf . . . Kind of like a spy or something."

They asked him if he knew very much about DNA.

"See, it's always—it's always intrigued me," he said. "I assume this person left something at the crime scenes that you guys could match up with DNA. But after all of these years, they still have that stuff?"

Assured that they did, Rader for the first time seemed worried.

Morton and Landwehr showed Rader the purple computer disk, the one that had come from the church with the name "Dennis" in the "properties" section of the software.

"There's no way I can weasel out of that, or lie," Rader admitted.

Rader asked if it was really true that BTK would not have to face the death penalty. He wanted to know what sort of prison sentence BTK would get if there was no death penalty. He thought BTK would have a hard time in prison because "BTK has killed some kids and stuff."

About three hours into the interview, Morton looked directly at Rader and told him:

"Say who you are."

"I'm BTK," Rader admitted.

"You guys have got me," Rader said. "How can I get out of it? . . . [There] Isn't any way you can get out of the DNA, right?" Landwehr and Morton assured him that DNA didn't lie. Rader now decided to give it all up, just as the FBI had predicted he would, years earlier.

Tell us about it, Landwehr and Morton urged.

"It'll take a while," Rader said. "We can start with one and work the others."

Landwehr noticed the phrase, "work the others." That was detective jargon, "working a case." This was validation of one of the FBI's oldest predictions: BTK thought of himself as a cop, or at least identified with law enforcement. He decided to play along with this mindset of Rader's, thinking it would facilitate the confession.

Rader was still worried about what might happen to him in jail, though.

"Now, are they going to—if—am I going to be in a special section of the jail—or am I going to be thrown in with a bunch of the loonies?" he asked. Landwehr and Morton assured him that he'd be protected while in jail.

But before he began to admit anything definitive, Rader wanted to clear something up. Tapping on the computer disk that was on the table in front of him, Rader looked at Landwehr.

"I need to ask you," he said, "how come you lied to me? How come you lied to me?"

"Because I was trying to catch you."

Rader said he was surprised and disappointed that Landwehr and the police had lied to him about not being able to trace the disk.

"I thought we had some rapport," Rader said, referring to the communications that had gone on over the past year.

Morton and Landwehr asked him about the nonsensical letter strings that were on some of the communications. The FBI had worked on this, but had been unable to find a solution to the code, if indeed it was a code.

The letters were a German "fractional" code he had learned when he was in the Air Force, Rader told them. But when asked to explain it, he couldn't.

Why had he made all the drops over the previous year? Why had he given up Nancy Fox's original driver's license, and various items of jewelry?

The reason for that, Rader explained, was that he'd decided to get rid of all the evidence. He was going to retire from murder, and since he knew he was going to get rid of the stuff, he thought he might as well have some fun with it. His plan, he said, was to scan everything into a computer, then put it on a CD-ROM. He'd put the CD-ROM in a safe place, and then when he was dead, someone would find the disk and realize the truth. It tickled his imagination to think of that day, he said.

This was so close to what Beattie had originally suggested might happen back in January 2004 that it seemed very likely that Rader had read the Laviana story about Beattie's proposed book, when Beattie had suggested that the children of the killer might one day run across his "mementos." In fact, the code string atop the Vicki Wegerle letter he'd sent to the *Eagle* in March 2004 meant "Tell Beattie for the Book," Rader claimed, although he was unable to show how the otherwise nonsensical letter combination spelled that out.

And with that, Rader began his detailed confession. Altogether, it would last thirty-two hours over three days. And by the end, it would be more bizarre than anyone could ever have predicted.

33:

"Something's Happening"

That same day, February 25, 2005, Beattie had a 1:30 P.M. appointment to see Larry Hatteberg, the KAKE reporter. For the past few weeks, Beattie had sensed a quickening pace for the BTK investigation. There were rumors that some detectives were working as late as 3 A.M., and that one suspect was under continuous surveillance. Beattie also heard a story that suggested the police were examining a security camera videotape from a Home Depot store in north Wichita, "frame by frame," as Beattie put it later.

As Beattie entered the KAKE-TV studio, Hatteberg pulled him into a side room.

"Bob," Hatteberg told him, "something's happening." He stared at Beattie meaningfully—they'd already previously agreed that this would be their signal in case either Beattie or Hatteberg discovered that an arrest had been made or was imminent.

"Really?" Beattie asked. "It's happening now?"

Yep, Hatteberg told him—either it had already happened, or was going on right that minute.

"Check your sources," Hatteberg advised.

Beattie immediately left the studio and began to hit the telephones.

At approximately the same moment, Dennis Rader had just embarked on his confession to Landwehr and Morton.

"The goal was to get Rader talking and keep him talking," Sedgwick County Assistant District Attorney Kevin O'Connor said later. "Rader accommodated, and was easily manipulated by law enforcement's feeding of his incredible and narcissistic ego. Rader displayed an infatuation and obsession with himself to such a degree that he actually believed that the law enforcement officers were his friends. Rader felt so comfortable that, at one point, he told an officer to put 'BTK on the lid' of his cup before putting it in the refrigerator." It was as if Rader saw himself sitting around the stationhouse with his friends and co-workers, the detectives.

He'd prepared and mailed or dropped all the communications, beginning with the letter in the library, Rader admitted. In fact, he'd been working on a new communication, one that recounted the murder of Shirley Vian, just the night before. He'd recently thrown away one of his guns.

"I shot Bright with it, Kevin Bright," Rader said. He described the gun as a .22-caliber Colt Woodsman, "a target pistol, that's what it was. A hair trigger on it, that's why I missed . . . Anyway, when we were fighting—Well, first of all, I think I had him tie his sister; I took her to the room, I come back to do him, do him in, and I got the lariat around his neck and it snapped, and I think he broke his bonds, and he got out. And he's a big old guy [Kevin Bright was actually very slight in stature]. So I just quickly, just like you do in the Westerns, just without hardly thinking, I grabbed my backup, which I think I had that with me, and I pointed it at his head and fired. Well, it—I think it wounded him." At the time, Rader said, he thought he'd killed Kevin.

"Then I went back to—to do my thing with . . . Kathy, yeah . . . She fought me like hell." When he went back to check on Kevin, "he jumped up and grabbed me. Well, he almost got me right there, because he reached for what he thought was a weapon. I was going to shoot him with the second [gun a second] time, but it was actually my magnum, I had my shoulder holster, and that sucker was pointed right at my heart, and he stuck his hand in there, and I said, *Oh, shit, I'm going to die right here.* But I got my finger in the trigger guard, and I fought him off. I either bit him or hit him and knocked him loose and fired again, but that didn't take."

Morton and Landwehr realized that Rader wasn't confessing so much as he was boasting—bragging about his "fast draw," his narrow escape, as if he were the hero of the movie.

After shooting Kevin, Rader said, he returned to finish off Kathy Bright. "And I completely lost control of that, so I just stabbed her," he finished.

During his communications over the years, he admitted, he often tried to lead the police astray. In fact, in one of them, he attempted to convince the detectives that he had been a student of Professor Wyatt—because that's what the police seemed to think, at least according to the news media. But this was just "blowing smoke," he said. "I never knew her, never met her." The message about Jake Allen was "really blowing smoke," he said. "And you guys did go—You took it for a while, because you went down there and took his computer and everything. But I said, 'search deep.' And I know you went and searched deep. I bet you went through his house, his computers. And they kept everything real quiet down there, real quiet, so I knew you guys were—took it line, sinker and hook, and all, for a while."

As Ressler and others had predicted, this game-playing with the police was part of Rader's charge.

He admitted murdering his neighbor, Marine Hedge, and seemed to want admiration for this. "Marine Hedge was really complicated, so we'll get that out." He'd also killed Dee Davis, he said.

"I assume the county is going to get involved in this," Rader said, referring to the Sedgwick County Sheriff's Department, which has jurisdiction over the Hedge and Davis cases. "I think it's good, because if we're going to go open, we might as well clear everything out." Once again, it was as if Rader was giving the detectives advice on how to proceed.

Asked what made the Hedge case so complicated, Rader explained: the big problem with Marine Hedge was the transportation—all the switching of cars, the various locations, including his church.

The church? Morton and Landwehr asked.

Yes, Rader said, he'd taken Marine Hedge's body to his church, "to the church, Christ Lutheran . . . when the church was not like it is now. And I had my time with her. And—and I just took her back to the east until I thought I found a nice place and dumped her . . . And I had a mess with that car; I got the keys lost. Broke the windshield . . . When I dropped her, I put the keys up on the dash, and they slid down, just right against the window, and I couldn't get them . . . could not get them. And here I am, *Gee, without a key, I can't get out of here.* I think I broke the glass and reached in and got the keys. So if you read the report, you may find the windshield was broken."

That was exactly right—just the kind of factual detail that the police needed to keep back to verify a confession.

Morton and Landwehr asked Rader to tell them the order he'd killed his victims.

Rader listed the four Oteros, then Kathy Bright, Shirley Vian, Nancy Fox, Marine Hedge, Vicki Wegerle, and last, Dee Davis.

"And that's it. Now, I had a whole bunch that I followed . . . I almost got . . . I almost got—" a number of others, he said, people who had no idea of how close they had come to being murdered.

Morton asked if Rader had killed anyone in any other states.

"This is it. I've got ten people," Rader said.

Having decided to confess, Rader now began to play the role Ressler, Hazelwood and every other expert had long anticipated: he became a cop, and explained to Morton and Landwehr exactly what they had to do to make their case. He told them where to find the evidence.

"You'll find quite a bit at the office," he said. Rader's dogcatcher office in Park City was where he kept most of his murderous records. He called this cache "the motherlode." All they had to do, he said, was open his file cabinet. They'd find everything in there: originals of pictures he'd taken at various scenes, Vicki Wegerle's actual driver's license. He really wished he'd had a camera when he'd murdered little Josie Otero. "I asked her if she had a camera," Rader said. But he had other pictures, including many of himself.

"Basically self-bondage," Rader said. "Just a thing I have." Rader seemed to sense that Landwehr and Morton were thinking he was very weird.

"I have— I have real good sex with my wife," he said. "But [it was] more fun if it was different . . ."

Actually, Rader said, the police and public were lucky he'd been married. If it hadn't been for his "social obligations," such as his wife and children, he would probably have killed many more people.

"Personally, I would like to live by myself, be a lone wolf, completely," he said.

Rader admitted that he'd been stalking an intended eleventh victim just before his arrest.

"Project Broadwater or Boardwater," he said, a reference to his rantings in the "Uno-Dos-Tres" communication. "I tried to hit on her the day I dropped the [communication] at the UPS box. It was a run, it was a go and everything, but they were working on the roads. They were working on the curbs. One of those things you don't foresee . . . So what in the hell do you do? You just do a backup and wait for another day. I was going to try it in the spring or fall."

"Project Board Water"—actually "PJ Waterboard" in the "Uno-Dos-Tres" letter—was picked because "she had a routine. People that have routines are trouble with me. That's what I am always looking for, is routines."

Morton and Landwehr asked about the communications—why had Rader felt the need to send them?

"Because once the media thing started going, I had to feed the media," Rader told them. "The media, you know, it's like, you know, it's like one of the things that the newspapers said, 'serial killer,' like it's your fan club."

He'd planned to commit one more murder, he said, then stop.

"You know, I thought I would pull it off and retire and have mementos; it didn't happen—you guys outsmarted me." Rader complained to Morton once more about the trick with the computer disk. He was convinced that the detectives had pulled some sort of fast one on him. "I checked the 'properties' and the other stuff," Rader said, "and there was nothing there, nothing. So you guys had to do something else. And I talked to some other people, they said, 'Oh, floppies can't be traced, floppies can't be traced.' And I thought, *Should I take a gamble? Take a gamble?* And I knew I was taking a big gamble."

As for Landwehr's deception on the floppy question, Rader thought that "Ken" would never be dishonest with him because of their "rapport." "And I really thought—I really thought—*I know he's trying to catch me.* I really thought Ken was honest when he gave me—when he gave me the signal [that] it can't be traced, and I really thought that . . . the floppy did me in."

34:

The Motherlode

As Rader was talking to Morton and Landwehr, other members of the BTK task force were serving the search warrants on his Park City house, his office at the Park City City Hall, the Christ Lutheran Church, the Park City public library, and on several vehicles associated with the Rader family. The searches were assisted by Rader's advice, telling police exactly where to look. Nevertheless, they evacuated the neighborhood around the Rader residence, reasoning that anyone who had previously threatened to blow them up during a search might actually mean it. Rader's wife and son were whisked away, as much to protect them from the public and the news media as for questioning.

"I don't want you to go messing up my house," Rader said. "I'll tell you where the stuff is." The most important of these caches could be found in his office at the Park City City Hall, he said. That, he told them, was "the motherlode."

"You're going to find a whole bunch of stuff here, pictures, you might even find some victims' type stuff, and newspaper clippings. I don't know what you're going to find there, but you're going to find a lot of stuff."

Once inside this office, detectives found a small, two-drawer filing cabinet. Opening the lower drawer, they discovered seven three-ring binders, and more than two dozen hanging folders. Lying flat beneath the drawer containing these folders was yet another manila folder, this one containing scores of colored drawings of women being bound and tortured by various devices.

The binders and folders held additional material: one three-ring binder contained original local newspaper clippings about the BTK murders, as well as cut-outs of articles in national magazines. Another binder was labeled "MASTER BOOK," which held more clippings, a copy of the composite drawing of the unknown man in the Otero murders, and an original of the table of contents of "THE BTK STORY"—a copy of which had been sent to KAKE in May 2004, and periodically included in subsequent communications, with various "chapter numbers" lined out—in other words, the contents of BTK's supposed "book." This "MASTER BOOK" folder contained a number of original chapters, separated by dividers, most with handwritten changes.

Still another binder labeled "COMMUNICATIONS" contained a complete list of all the messages that had been sent in 2004, including the original of the page sent to the *Eagle* about the Vicki Wegerle murder in March 2004—the one that included copies of Vicki's driver's license and the three pictures of her on the floor.

Yet another binder included more notes, copies of the communications and newspaper clippings. But this binder also held a plastic bag containing a dozen original Polaroid photographs of Marine Hedge, dead, bound and lewdly posed in the basement of Christ Lutheran Church. Besides this, the binder included several typewritten descriptions of the attack on the Brights, the murder of Vicki Wegerle, the original copy of the poem sent to Anna Williams, a copy of a drawing of how Rader imagined Mrs. Williams would have looked had he succeeded in tying her up, and three photographs of Dee Davis' body in the place where it had been discovered—including one in which she was wearing the macabre mask that had been found near her body. The binder also included a hand-drawn map of the Dee Davis house, including routes drawn in before and after the murder.

This binder also included the original of the letter sent to Mary Fager in early 1988.

Other folders contained yet more material: one held a number of magazine pictures of various celebrities—Meg Ryan and Halle Berry among them—many with gags and other bindings crudely drawn in. Others contained drawings or photographs of women being attacked or tied up, many from low-grade detective magazines.

And detectives discovered hundreds of three-by-five index cards, each with drawings pasted on them—obviously, reductions made by photocopy machines. Each of the drawings contained images of women or children in various forms of bondage, all with arcane strings of letters and numbers—Rader's "codes," which he would subsequently admit comprised his shorthand for whatever particular violent fantasy he had with the image. These image cards, he later said, had unique names—"Monique," for example. Rader usually referred to these cards by these names, as in "I spent the day with Monique."

Next to the filing cabinet was a large green plastic container with a lid. This storage tub contained still more images of bound women and children.

Even without Rader's admissions to Morton and Landwehr, this "motherlode" of evidence seemed to clinch the case. The truly astonishing thing was that it was there to be discovered at all. Like any detective, Rader had documented all of these cases thoroughly—the difference was, he was both the suspect *and* the investigator. It was an astounding moment. The idea that the killer sought for so long, at so much time and expense and frustration, would have all this material neatly organized and just sitting in a file drawer in a publicly owned office in a Wichita suburb was mind-boggling, as was the realization that it had been in that drawer for more than a decade without being observed by any other person until that day.

While these searches were going on, Rader continued to talk. Morton and Landwehr gave way to other investigators. An agent of the Kansas Bureau of Investigation, Larry Thomas, wanted Rader to describe something of his life before his first murders, those of the Otero family. Where did all this behavior come from?

"It started in grade school," Rader said. "I used to make sketches even back then. Annette Funicello was my favorite fantasy hit target when she was on the Mouseketeers . . . she was a dream girl for a lot of guys . . . I had these imaginary stories of how I was going to get her, kidnap her, and do sexual things to her in California." From that early point, the fantasies grew ever more violent and complex over the ensuing years into adolescence and then adulthood.

Rader said he had a thing for mummies—that is, dried and bound corpses. "Mummy was always a big favorite, they bound people up."

Rader could see that Thomas wasn't sure what to make of this.

"You're going to be talking to a guy that's really weird and has these dreams," Radar told him.

Thomas asked Rader if he'd ever tortured or abused animals—an interesting question to put to a professional dogcatcher.

"I have—yeah, I have killed some animals," Rader said. "To get off, I guess. I would get a cat or a dog and tie them up and strangle them."

Thomas asked about Rader's first sexual experiences.

"I learned all that in the service," Rader said. "That's where I got my knowledge of sex." This was a curious disconnect—after admitting that he'd had sexual fantasies in grade school, and that he'd strangled small animals "to get off"—asserting that his first experience with sex was in the military suggested that Rader had thoroughly disassociated "normal" sex from his fantasy life.

He had compiled many scrapbooks over the decades, Rader continued, most of them with what he called "slick ads"—cut-outs of young female models in underwear taken from catalogs or newspapers.

"Now, my scrapbooks are slick ads," he said. "You probably don't know about those yet. You'll find them. But they are slick ads. They are models, girls. They are usually pretty cute-looking. And sometimes I would draw them in bondage pictures." Sometimes, he said, he'd lick the ink off the ads in order to get rid of the underwear image to make the models seem more nude.

He'd concealed these scrapbooks in his house, Rader said. He drew the detectives a diagram, a floor plan of the house, to show them how to find these materials.

"Right here is what you call a cupboard, where you put all of your dry goods. Okay, the bottom drawer, you take that out, the bottom one, you'll see a false bottom." Inside the false bottom were still more index cards, he said.

A nearby closet contained another plastic tub with the collection of "slick ads," Rader said. The closet contained spare uniforms from his dogcatcher job. He drew in the location of this closet on his diagram.

"In the bottom of this closet is a plastic tote case; that's full of mostly slick ads. Slick ad stuff. There might be some of my fantasy three-by-five-cards. The 'slick ads' are almost like treasures to me. I've been saving these things for years."

Over the previous year, Rader continued, he'd been

slowly moving material out of the house to his Park City office.

"Basically what I was doing is phasing the stuff out, because I was shutting this down in about a year. If I got through it, once the story was done, I might get—I might do another hit, and I might not do another hit. It's just, I tried— I have been working on this one girl for over two years." He planned to scan all these papers and copy them onto a CD-ROM, he said. Then he planned to get rid of everything, dropping the actual bits of evidence in various places to keep the BTK pot stirred up—"feeding the media," as he called it.

What about the "hit kit," his weapons and strangling gear?

He kept that at home, Rader told Thomas. He sketched in a spot in the bedroom closet.

"In this corner, you'll find my basic hit kit, okay? And I know it's not anything like it used to be, but it's probably pretty incriminating. And you'll find my—my twenty-five [caliber] auto, okay?" Rader meant an automatic pistol. "That's another one of my backups, okay? They're in a little black bag."

A shed in the back yard had a cache of bondage materials: ropes, pantyhose, chains, handcuffs, belts, sash cord, duct tape. All of these he used to tie himself up from time to time, Rader indicated.

The detectives followed this up—what did he mean? He'd had a fetish for self-bondage ever since he was a child, Rader said—he used to go down into the basement of his parents' house on Seneca Street and hang himself from a pipe there, just as years later, he'd hung little Josie Otero. As the decades went by after his adolescence, he enjoyed fantasizing that he was hanging a woman. He'd dress himself up in women's clothes, then hang himself, using a cable release to take a picture of the event. Later, he'd look at the photograph, using the image to fire his imagination. He probably had hundreds of such pictures at his house, including some of him in a grave he'd dug in northern Kansas.

At one point, a Sedgwick County detective who'd investigated the Dee Davis murder showed him the plastic mask that had been found near her body.

"That's my mask," Rader said.

"*Your* mask?" The detective was taken aback. Yes, Rader said. He'd had it for years, using it to take pictures of himself posing as a bound woman. The mask assisted his erotic imagination. When he killed Davis, he put the mask on her, took photographs, and then left it at the scene.

The attic of his house had old detective magazines, Rader continued. "And they all tend to be toward bondage. You know, in the fifties, they usually string up the girls, the girls there [on the old magazine covers]. And they tie them up, you know." Just like Harvey Glatman, in fact, who had lured some of his victims by pretending to be a photographer for a pulp detective magazine. It was clear that the photography angle was deeply embedded in Rader's deadly fantasies.

In the back of Rader's car, detectives would find a collection of dolls. He'd intended to use them for his future communications. He'd planned to send one with the Shirley Vian message he'd been working on the night before.

"Shirley was going to go in the box, the doll . . . And she was going to be naturally nude, and she was going to have assimilated [sic] bindings on her, with a white plastic bag over her head, and a pink—pink something on her head."

The "Shirley doll" would be included with another "bombgram." He wanted the police to face a choice:

Would they blow up the communication rather than risk death or injury by trying to defuse it?

"I was going to wire this sucker with the four wires and I was going to run it over to a cardboard box and [label it] 'BTK Bombgram' . . . And I thought, *Well, this will give the bomb squad a little— They know who it's from, they don't want to destroy this, this will really give them something to think about.*" He'd also intended to include another poem, he said.

He'd worked on the package the night before the arrest. Park City had night court, and as the town compliance officer, he'd had to attend. That was an excuse for getting home late.

"We had court last night . . . That's a two-hour type thing. So that gives me a chance to do my BTK thing . . . Yeah, basically I'd work on it a little bit in the afternoon or in the evenings, whenever I can fudge a little bit, getting home late, doing BTK. It's a riot."

35:

"The Bottom Line"

As Beattie later realized, the word about another BTK arrest spread rapidly through the news media community on Friday, February 25, even as Dennis Rader was being questioned at the FBI's Wichita offices. Officially, the police put out only a cursory statement:

> Wichita Police Chief Norman Williams has announced that a briefing on the BTK investigation is slated for 10 AM Saturday, February 26, in the City Council Chambers.
>
> Distinguished guests will include Mayor Carlos Mayans, City Council members, District Attorney Nola Foulston, Kansas Bureau of Director [sic] Larry Welch, Federal Bureau of Investigation Special Agent in Charge Kevin Stafford and Congressman Todd Tiahrt.

The fact that such an array of political luminaries was scheduled to appear could mean only one thing—the case had been solved.

Or had it?

The *Eagle*, for one, reacted cautiously. After all, there'd already been one arrest that had left everyone embarrassed.

On the other hand, they couldn't very well downplay the news—not after the events of the last year.

The following day, the paper split the difference:

POLICE TO TALK ABOUT BTK TODAY, the paper headlined. NEWS CONFERENCE FOLLOWS MAN'S DETENTION IN PARK CITY RAID.

Eagle reporters Hurst Laviana and Dana Strongin carried the ball for the paper. They noted that "a flurry of police activity in Park City" had resulted "in the evacuation of a neighborhood and questioning of a man who lives there."

The paper pointed out that the forthcoming press conference was to be attended by the area's congressman—who had helped land a $1 million federal grant to finance the latest BTK investigation—and Nola Foulston, the Sedgwick County district attorney, as well as Wichita Mayor Carlos Mayans. The politicians' proposed appearances clearly suggested that something momentous was about to happen—the reporters noted that this was the first time that Foulston had ever participated in a BTK press conference, to say nothing of the congressman, the city council members, or the mayor. The paper also said that family members of the victims had been invited to attend a pre–press conference briefing.

But the paper did not name Rader. It said that police had refused to release the arrestee's name, or explain why he had been arrested. A comparison was made to the December fiasco: "The scene in Park City on Friday afternoon was similar to one in south Wichita after the Dec. 1 arrest of a man as the result of a tip made to BTK investigators," Laviana and Strongin reported. "That man, formally arrested on misdemeanor charges, was later ruled out as a BTK suspect, but television crews did live shots outside his home on the day of his arrest and crowds of curious residents gathered."

The Wichita bomb squad had appeared at the scene, the paper added, along with two SWAT teams. A helicopter overflew the area. The neighborhood soon was besieged by gawkers, and something of the atmosphere of a public event unfolded. "Dozens of onlookers gathered to take pictures, and motorists clogged the streets as they drove by the scene," Laviana and Strongin reported. "One onlooker brought a lawn chair, and at least two brought their dogs."

At 10 the next morning, at a nationally televised press conference in the Wichita City Council chambers, several hundred people gathered, including members of the Fox family and other survivors of victims, along with Landwehr, Otis and most of the rest of the detectives.

The killer, police said, was Dennis Rader, the Park City compliance officer. They refused to say what evidence they had that Rader was in fact the killer. But they noted that Rader had been talking freely since the arrest the day before. The implication was that he had not asked for a lawyer, and the further implication of that was that he was providing a confession. They did note that in addition to the seven official BTK murders—counting Kathy Bright—they'd now officially determined that three other cases were also connected: Vicki Wegerle, Marine Hedge and Dee Davis. The latter two, officials acknowledged, had happened well outside the city limits, in the jurisdiction of Sedgwick County.

"The bottom line: BTK is arrested," said Wichita Police Chief Norman Williams, to the applause of many of the victims' family members who attended the press conference.

Kansas Attorney General Phill Kline also made a somewhat theatrical appearance at the gathering, advising all present that, "in a few minutes, you will look face-to-face with pure evil . . ."

And with that, a photograph of the face of BTK, Dennis Rader, was publicly flashed on a screen. Kline was still talking: "Victims whose voices were brutally silenced by the evil of one man will now have their voices heard again." Kline, who had recently been severely criticized as attorney general for attempting to obtain the medical records of women who'd had abortions in Kansas, was a born-again Christian. For him, "pure evil" was a real thing, a force of the supernatural abroad in the world—a palpable manifestation of Satan himself. It also played well in the rural areas of the state, Kline knew, where his abortion stance was usually applauded, and here was Exhibit A in support of Kline's assertion that the Devil did exist: BTK, aka Dennis Rader.

Beattie sat in the rear of the council chambers while the politicians crowded the front of the room. Earlier that morning, he'd had breakfast at a south Wichita café with numerous members of the ReTIRED COPS Every one of them had shaken his hand. As far as they were concerned, the politicians might claim the credit, but if BTK was really in jail after thirty-one years, there was no doubt in their minds that it had been Beattie who'd smoked him out.

As they filed out of the council chambers, Wichita reporters knew that while the police had reached a logical climax with the arrest, their job was just starting. Because now the question was: who *was* this man, Dennis Rader?

What seemed clear, even in those moments of triumph declared by officialdom, was that until just before the arrest, none of the police had known who Dennis Rader was. He was not, despite all predictions, ever included on any of the voluminous lists of suspects compiled by detectives and haphazardly monitored by reporters over the years. He was, in fact, a suspect from so far out of left field as to be a complete, shocking surprise. And he certainly was no transient assailant on his way to New York or California, no person of "foreign extraction." Nor was he particularly "swarthy" in his appearance. In fact, at least one thing was obvious—Dennis Rader was one of Wichita's very own.

Some reporters—and legal experts—soon criticized Chief Williams for his unequivocal statement: "the bottom line is, BTK is arrested." That certainly damaged the arrested man's right to a fair trial, some thought.

But the prevailing opinion was that BTK had in fact been arrested. Why else would he apparently be blabbing away, somewhere in police custody? Didn't that mean the police were getting a confession? In contrast to the December arrest—*that* man had howled in outrage and had hired a lawyer—this Dennis Rader seemed to be cooperating with the police.

Certainly no lawyer had as yet surfaced, complaining of police misconduct in the arrest, or even asserting his client's innocence. In itself, that spoke volumes, the news media collectively concluded. So the question for the media now was: who was this face of "pure evil," as Kline had described him? Who the hell was Dennis Rader?

Reporters from the newspaper and the city's broadcast stations fanned out across the flatlands in search of anyone who could shed light on this new mystery. If for thirty years the media had cooperated with the police during all the killer's depredations and communications, now all bets were off.

The first two places reporters went looking for information about Dennis Rader were his neighbors, and his job. They weren't alone. In the aftermath of the nationally televised press conference, a caravan of motorized rubberneckers was soon streaming by the Rader house in Park City, trying to get a glimpse at the place where the accused—make that notoriously accused—murderer had lived for thirty-odd years. Neighbors of the Rader family were in a state of disbelief—how could this man they'd known for so long be BTK? It was simply mind-boggling. Worse, some realized that as the city's compliance officer, Rader had been in and out of their houses and legally authorized to poke around their yards for years. If it was true that Dennis Rader was BTK, the killer had had ample opportunity to case them for more than a decade. It gave virtually everyone the creeps.

Reporters quickly learned that the Raders were devout Christians, that they had attended church for years—Christ Lutheran Church. Soon the newspeople were at the church, pressing for more information about the Rader family. Mike Clark, the church's pastor, told them that Dennis Rader had been a member of the parish for nearly twenty-five years. Not only that, he had just been elected the congregation's president.

The church, Clark said, was giving support to Rader's wife, son and daughter.

How are they doing? one reporter asked.

"How *would* they be doing?" Clark responded to the inane question. "They're having trouble with it, feeling very confused."

By that afternoon, the *Eagle* had sketched in the briefest of outlines of Dennis Rader's life, and soon posted these cursory facts on its website: Rader was 59 years old, and had worked as a compliance officer, then as a compliance supervisor, for Park City for approximately fifteen years. That meant he was in charge of animal control, petty nuisances, vehicles junked in front yards, and general municipal code compliance, such as lawn length, or trash-can maintenance, which gave him the right of access to people's private property.

The paper reported that Rader had served in the military during the Viet Nam War era, that he had worked for Coleman after getting out of the service—"as did two of BTK's early victims," the paper noted—and that he'd had a job in earlier years for a security alarm company in Wichita.

He'd also attended Wichita State—"long linked to the BTK case," the paper noted—and had graduated in 1979 with a degree in Administration of Justice.

"He is married and has grown children," the paper concluded.

The next day, Sunday, Pastor Clark gave a sermon to his congregation, which was still reeling from the news of the arrest of their president.

As Christians, he said, they were all now faced with a severe test—whether the devastating news would eviscerate their faith, or bring them together and even strengthen them.

It was normal for people to feel confused, he said, by such senseless acts that surpass understanding.

He'd written a sermon the prior week, Clark said, but everything changed on Friday, so he'd junked it. When the police had come to the church that day with a search warrant, when they'd told him they had reason to believe Dennis Rader was BTK, it was as if everything he'd thought was true had been turned upside down. But as he thought it through, he realized this was a true crucible for faith.

"I propose that we choose to let this be a time of strengthening, of renewing and healing," he said. "As we continue to let Christ's light shine in our world, let us become the stronger in faith, in love and in hope."

He asked his congregation to pray for the BTK victims, and their still-grieving families, for the police who had spent so many years of their lives trying to solve the case, for Dennis Rader's wife and his children, and for Dennis himself.

"As we continue on as a body of Christ, it is important that we show compassion and love towards Dennis," he said. "If what is claimed is true, we should be about the business of asking for God's help in healing of heart and soul." He asked the congregation to pray to bring Rader's family members peace as the uncertain future unfolded.

But each new day would bring forth more horrors for Pastor Clark, and the challenge of loving, and trying to heal a man who had profaned everything Clark believed in had to be one of the hardest things he'd ever had to do, however Christian the desire to do it.

36:

The Three Faces of Dennis Rader

The next week brought still more portraits of Dennis Rader into the light.

LIKED BY MANY, LOATHED BY SOME, the *Eagle* reported on the same Sunday Reverend Clark gave his unplanned sermon. And over the next week, the *Eagle* and other newspapers strove to define the human conundrum that was Dennis Rader.

It soon appeared that there were at least two Dennis Raders, according to an account written by *Eagle* reporters Fred Mann and Les Anderson—one man who was genial, helpful, a Boy Scout leader, a church official, a willing volunteer, a pillar of the community, a man who was conscientious and meticulous almost to a fault; and a second man in the same skin who was seen as "arrogant, by-the-numbers, rude and confrontational," an officious ass who took pleasure in harassing others for the sheer pleasure of throwing his weight around. Or possibly even three Dennis Raders: the church leader, Boy Scout volunteer, devoted husband and father; the officious, nasty city official; and the man who police claimed led a secret life of murder for more than thirty years, and so successfully that even his wife and adult children never had the slightest notion that he was, underneath it all, a monster.

Piecing the various accounts together gave something of a picture, although it was obvious that something important was missing. Rader had been born in Pittsburg, Kansas, March 9, 1945, the oldest of four sons. When he was 4, the family moved to Wichita, where his father, a Marine in World War II, was employed as a power plant control operator for an electric utility. The family settled into a neatly kept house in a middle-class neighborhood of northwest Wichita. Some thought his mother doted on her first-born, perhaps dreaming of making him a child star: there were recollections of Dennis being a participant in a children's show then broadcast live by KAKE, the city's first television station.

The family was religious, others recalled, faithfully attending a local Lutheran church—the same church, some noted, that had years later been attended by the Wegerle family. Rader attended local Wichita schools, and worked at a local market after graduating from Wichita Heights High School across the street from Christ Lutheran Church in north Wichita in 1963. His mother also worked at the market.

A former classmate contacted by the *Eagle* expressed incredulity at Rader's arrest as the BTK murderer. "It's just overwhelming to me," Richard Crusinberry told the paper. "I can't believe it. In a room of 15 people, you just wouldn't notice the guy . . . He was very bright, good in school, nice to everybody, nice smile, a great person. I just can't believe it."

Others who had grown up with Rader had similar reactions: John Davis, for instance. He'd been Dennis Rader's best pal since they were 5 years old. Their fathers had worked together, they'd lived near each other, gone to the same schools and joined the same Boy Scout troop.

"He spent as much time at my house as I did at his," Davis told the *Eagle*. "He was an all-American boy."

Davis even recalled when Rader saved another boy's life. On a Scouting trip in canoes down the Arkansas River in 1959 or 1960, heavy rains had swollen the river far above its normal size. Ahead on the river, the paddling

Scouts could hear the roar of what sounded like a waterfall. When they got closer, they realized that it was the current flowing over the top of a dam. All the Scouts made for the riverbank, but Rader's canoe, with only a smaller boy accompanying him, couldn't make headway against the current. Grimly paddling with all his might, Rader finally managed to make it to shore. Had they gone over the dam, Davis recalled, Rader and the other boy would probably have been severely injured and drowned. Dennis was lauded as a hero for saving both their lives.

Another early playmate, Margaret Roberts, recalled that Rader played Joseph in the third-grade Christmas play in elementary school. "It was just so sweet," she told *Eagle* reporters Roy Wenzl and Hurst Laviana. She recalled that the neighborhood had a close-knit group of a dozen kids who spent hours with each other. Rader was one of the quietest in the group, she recalled. She trusted him. In fact, she thought of him almost as a brother.

"He would be someone I could count on," she said. "He would keep a confidence. He did well in school, and I admired that." When she'd heard that Dennis had been arrested as BTK, she burst into tears.

One of Rader's three brothers was certain that the police had made a terrible mistake. "They've got the wrong guy," Jeff Rader said. His brother simply wasn't capable of committing such crimes. It simply didn't fit. The FBI, Jeff added, had asked him whether there was any sexual abuse in the family. "I told them no," Jeff Rader said. "And that's the truth."

In 1965, Rader joined the U.S. Air Force, where he was trained in security system installation and maintenance. There was no evidence, however, that he'd ever served in the same place with Joseph Otero, who was in the Air Force at the same time. According to the *Eagle*, Rader had postings to a variety of Air Force bases in the

1960s, including assignments in Korea, Turkey, Greece and Okinawa.

After leaving the Air Force as a technical sergeant in 1969, Rader returned to Wichita and took a job in the meat department of the market. In 1971 he'd married his wife, who was said to be well-liked by everyone who knew her, and who loved to cook. The couple bought a house in Park City near his wife's parents and a few miles away from Dennis' own mother and father, who continued to live in the northwest Wichita house until Rader's father died in 1996. Rader then worked at Coleman as an assembler in the same department that had employed Kathryn Bright and Julie Otero, although not at the same time. In 1974, he enrolled in the criminal justice degree program at Wichita State, and also took a job with the alarm system company.

A son born in 1975 was followed by a daughter in 1978. In 1979, Rader had graduated from WSU with a degree in Administration of Justice. He continued to work at the alarm company until 1989, when he was laid off. He took a supervising job in the 1990 federal Census in Kansas, and in 1991, was hired as Park City's compliance officer, for which he was paid a bit over $16 an hour.

Some recalled Rader as a nasty boss to work for at both the alarm company and at Park City.

"I don't believe the gentleman was well liked at all," said Mike Tavares, who worked with Rader at the alarm company in the 1980s. Tavares told the paper that Rader was often insulting to co-workers, giving the impression that he thought he was better than everyone else. The alarm system job, Tavares pointed out, would have given Rader a lot of opportunity to case people's homes for the purpose of burglary, or worse. Others thought Rader had a violent temper; one recalled him smacking the hood of a truck during an argument with another worker. After work, he sometimes drank at a local tavern with other employees; while some said they couldn't remember Rader drinking to excess, and saying he'd had to rush home to be with his wife, others recalled a few occasions in which he'd had so much beer that he could barely walk.

In his Park City job, some called him a "control freak" who abused his authority. But others thought of him as a conscientious employee, as organized as he was courteous. One of Rader's jobs was to enforce the Park City ordinances regulating property maintenance, including sign display, or licenses for garage sales, or dogs. Several complained that Rader persecuted them unreasonably, even unfairly, while others contended he was simply doing the job he was hired to do. Several complained that he had impounded their dogs, and had them put to sleep after they had been caught running loose in the town.

A friend of Rader's since high school days, Ray Reiss, told how he'd received a letter from Compliance Officer Rader, demanding that he spruce up a rental property he had in Park City.

"It was not a hostile thing," Reiss remembered. "He was doing his job. He was telling me to tell the renters to clean their act up. He's just a very low-key, nice person—just a regular person."

But, said Reiss, "If it *is* him, I'd just like to say: 'What were you thinking? How do you get to that point that you do this?' . . . He deserves his day in court, but wow, this is just shocking. It's trite to say that he's such a nice guy. Well . . . he is nice."

A city councilwoman in Park City said she'd known Rader for almost a decade.

"He always treated me with respect, was never abrasive with me, which I think he was sometimes with other people," Dee Stuart said. "I know he was a compliance officer . . . and as far as I know, we didn't have a lot of dogs running loose in Park City."

The week following his arrest, though, the Park City City Council voted to fire Dennis Rader. They said the reason was that he'd failed to report for work.

The reason he didn't report for work, of course, was that Dennis Rader was locked up in the Sedgwick County jail. After telling his tale to relay teams of detectives throughout the weekend—covering every one of the BTK murders with often chilling detail—the authorities had lodged him in a high-security section of the jail to await a decision on charges by District Attorney Nola Foulston. Neither his wife nor his children had tried to contact him, it appeared. By now, they were well away from the immediate area, still stunned at this incredible turning point in their lives. Friends stuck by them, though: the owner of the market that had employed Rader's wife as a bookkeeper for many years, Brent Lathrop, told the *Eagle*, "You'll never find a more wonderful person" than the accused killer's wife. On the day of the arrest, Lathrop said, Rader's wife was obviously under a tremendous amount of stress. She'd been escorted to an interview with police, and it wasn't clear if or when she'd be back as an employee. Still, Lathrop said, "I would love for her to come back, and I think eventually she will."

Customers who had been in the store since the arrest had offered "nothing but support" for her, Lathrop told the *Eagle*. "They all have [said], 'If there's anything we can do for her, let us know.' "

Indeed, it appeared after some rather intense interviewing of the tearful Mrs. Rader by police that the double life of her husband was a stunning shock to her. It seemed hard at first to believe that Rader could have had so much bondage material—his ropes and belts and handcuffs and "slick ads"—lying around the house without her having discovered it over thirty years, but this seemed to be the case. Dennis had his secret places, unknown to his wife and children, and too, there were certain storage containers that seemingly had to do with Rader's work, so the family never bothered to look in them. Now the three other Raders were in hiding, mostly from the news media, as they tried to fathom the dimensions of the catastrophe.

One who did try to contact Rader was Michael Clark, the pastor at Christ Lutheran. He'd told his parishioners that the test of their faith was now at hand—would they abandon their fellow congregant, or would they do what they could to pray for him, to heal him? Rader had sent a message, asking to see him, and on Sunday after his sermon he'd tried to visit Rader at the jail, but was told by corrections officers that to visit, he'd have to bring his ordination certificate and fill out paperwork permitting the visits. Eventually, Clark would spend many hours with Dennis Rader. To Clark, it didn't matter as much whether he was able to "heal" Rader as it was that he try—that was his own way of healing, of trying to cope with the enormity of what had happened.

On Tuesday, March 1, Rader had his first court appearance. Clad in a red jail jumpsuit, unshaved, he looked the roughest of characters. Sedgwick County District Court Judge Greg Waller read the charges: ten counts of first-degree murder. The previous day, Waller had held a meeting in his chambers with prosecutors, and apparently, some prominent Wichita criminal defense lawyers. Some thought that the police might have gone too far and denied Rader access to a lawyer after the arrest, but the police proved that Rader had knowingly waived his rights. Now, all that remained was for Waller to make sure that Rader understood what he was facing, and to appoint someone to represent him.

After a few brief preliminary questions, Waller asked Rader, "Do you understand that you're charged with ten counts of first-degree murder?"

"Yes, sir," Rader said.

"All right," Waller said. He scheduled March 15 as the date for another hearing, appointed the Sedgwick County Public Defender's Office to represent him, and set a bail of $10 million. But at that point, even if Rader had had $10 million in his back pocket, Waller would have reset the bail to, say, $20 million. If he'd had $20 million, Waller would have set it at $30 million. There was simply no way anyone was going to let Dennis Rader go, not after thirty-one years.

As soon as these formal, legal charges were filed, Beattie's book publisher was on the telephone. They wanted him to write a very quick final chapter for the book, one that reflected Rader's arrest.

"They said, 'Okay, we need an epilogue about the arrest of this Dennis Rader,'" Beattie recalled. "I said, 'Okay, I can get it in in a week or two weeks.' They said, 'No, no, no, we've got to have it by eleven A.M. Friday morning.'"

By this point, Beattie was weary of the struggles over his book; apart from people who questioned his motives—such as the police—he'd gotten involved in a squabble with the publisher over, of all things, the title. As far as Beattie was concerned, he had agreed to write a book with the title *Secrets Long Hidden*. Then, when the last communication from BTK had come in to the television station in mid-February, the publisher had arranged for him to appear on *Larry King Live* on CNN. That was when Beattie discovered for the first time that someone at the publisher had junked the *Secrets Long Hidden* title as "too literary." The publisher wanted to title the book *Bound in Terror: The Hunt for the World's Most Elusive Serial Killer*.

So Beattie said no. He'd promised everyone he'd interviewed that the book would not exploit their tragedies, and would not glorify the killer. Now the publisher wanted to do just that, or so Beattie thought, with the *Bound in Terror* title.

Beattie refused to appear on *Larry King* unless the title was changed.

Consternation now ensued at the publishing company in New York. An editor there had worked on the book—Beattie had earlier turned in a 557-page single-spaced manuscript—and asked for some changes, mostly to make the book less academic, as well as significantly shorter. Grudgingly, Beattie had agreed to make the changes, and had turned in a second version, around half the original size. Now they wanted to change the title.

No, Beattie said. He would never agree to *Bound in Terror*.

The editor checked around, and finally called back. Beattie recalled the conversation:

"Well, here's the situation, Robert," the editor told him. "I hate to say this, but you either go with this title, or there's no deal."

"Okay," Beattie said. "There's no deal."

The editor couldn't believe what he was hearing.

"Are you serious?"

"Yeah," Beattie said. "Just send it back. I'll tell everyone I'm talking to another publisher. Because I signed a contract for *Secrets Long Hidden*, and that's it."

"Why?"

"Because I've made these promises. I've told you, *"Bound in Terror"* describes exactly what happened to Vicki Wegerle. Exactly what happened to Nancy Fox, and if I am too close to these families, I am. And I'm not going to do it. And the subtitle *"The Hunt for the World's Most Elusive Serial Killer"*—I told the cops that I wasn't going to do anything to glorify the killer. The hunt for the BTK strangler is what the book's about, it's what the cops did, investigative reporters, the private investigators. No. It's no deal."

The editor wanted Beattie to call the victims' families as well as the ReTIRED COPS, and ask them if they'd rather not have a book published at all, or one published with the *Bound in Terror* title.

Beattie refused.

"I don't need to call anybody," Beattie said. "Because I've already made my promises."

By then his wife, Mary Ann, was in the room, listening to Beattie's side of the conversation. "She knows this whole story, better than anybody," Beattie said, "and to be worthy of my wife's respect, I couldn't possibly do this. So I said, 'It's been nice talking with you,' and I hung up."

So all of a sudden, after two years' work, after all his efforts to goad the killer into revealing himself, there was going to be no book. Or at least, not a book published by some outfit in New York that, as far as Beattie was concerned, wanted him to renege on his promises. He and Mary Ann would publish the book themselves if it came down to that, even if it only sold a thousand copies, and only in Wichita.

The following week, the editor called back with a compromise: would Beattie accept as a title "*Nightmare in Wichita: The Hunt for the BTK Strangler*"?

"Done," Beattie agreed.

Now, on March 1, Beattie had to rush to finish the last chapter, an epilogue, really, reflecting the formal charging of Dennis Rader. He had a little over two days to do it. But in the middle of this, suddenly his editor was no longer on the project. A new editor took over who was unfamiliar with the submitted texts.

"I went to 10:56 A.M. on Friday morning," Beattie recalled. "I hit the SEND key. Later that day, they sent me the [copy-edited] book, and they'd used the wrong manuscript." Beattie was told that the revised manuscript could not be found. Eventually it turned up. Over the weekend, the publisher's editors worked feverishly to edit both versions into one. In this process, the editors lopped off approximately 200 single-spaced pages—including some of Beattie's most interesting bits of reporting on the mystery that had terrified his city for more than three decades. But in the end, despite its troubled birth, *Nightmare in Wichita* would become a national best-seller.

37:

"Yours, Truly Guiltily" at Last

While all this was going on, the national news media had made tracks for Michigan, where Dennis Rader's grown daughter was living. Someone had published or broadcast a report, entirely erroneous, that Rader's daughter had turned him in to the police. In the absence of reliable court records that explained exactly how the arrest had happened—Judge Waller had sealed the affidavit in support of the arrest warrant—there was nothing in the official record to correct these tales.

As all this unfolded, the police chief in Farmington, Michigan, told reporters that the FBI had notified him on the previous Friday that its agents were at the Rader daughter's apartment in his town for the purpose of interviewing her, and taking a sample of her DNA. Because the arrest warrant had been sealed, none of the news media at that point knew that an earlier sample of Rader's daughter's DNA had already been obtained from medical sources in Kansas. Both DNA samples were obtained by court order.

It simply wasn't true that Rader's daughter had been suspicious of her father. In fact, the news of the arrest had hit her very hard.

In Wichita, a police captain now tried to clarify this. Any reports that Rader's daughter had turned him in to police were simply wrong, and unfair to her, said Captain Randy Landen.

"Whoever reported that, that's inaccurate," he said. Nevertheless, by Monday February 28, Rader's daughter was besieged by news reporters. She called the Farmington police to ask them to chase away the reporters; camera crews were encamped outside her apartment. Some waited right outside her front door to ambush her. The whole situation was very ugly—it certainly wasn't the daughter's fault that all this had happened. The media—at least the TV people—didn't care. All they wanted was a picture, and if Dennis Rader's daughter took a swing at them in a fit of emotion, that was all the better, the way they saw it.

A few days later, Pastor Clark tried to get some of the media to back off. He confirmed that the FBI had obtained a sample of the daughter's DNA.

"She gave the DNA for the purpose of clearing her dad," Clark told *The New York Times*. He'd been visiting Mrs. Rader when the daughter called, very upset. "She was caught in the middle of all this chaos."

The Sedgwick County district attorney, Nola Foulston, once again tried to make the situation clear.

"The DNA that was taken from the daughter in Michigan was taken after the arrest of Mr. Rader," Foulston told the *Eagle*, "and did not affect the original arrest of Mr. Rader."

Or even effect it, despite all the wild stories.

Sedgwick County Public Defender Steve Osburn took over the defense of Dennis Rader as soon as Rader's initial appearance before Judge Waller was over on the morning of March 1, and after only a few minutes, Osburn knew he had his hands full. How in the world was he going to defend a man charged with ten murders, five of which were more than thirty years old? Especially when that same man almost immediately told him that he'd already confessed to the crimes?

Even if the public and the news media didn't have access to the arrest and search warrants sealed by Judge Waller, Osburn did. And the picture they painted of his client was, to a lawyer, quite intimidating. The police had DNA. They had a computer disk sent by Rader in direct response to a police invitation to incriminate himself. They had page after page of material that the client himself had created, implicating himself in the murders—the client had even told the police where to find it. They had hundreds, if not thousands, of graphic examples of his client's obsession with bondage of women and children.

And they had the client's detailed, almost cheerful confession—thirty-two hours of it, all caught on videotape.

There was only one conclusion that Osburn could reach: Dennis Rader was on his way to prison for the rest of his life. The train was already so far down the tracks it could never be stopped. All he could do, and the other members of his staff could do, was make sure that the authorities cut no corners with respect to Dennis Rader's rights—not that they needed to.

The only good thing about the case that Osburn could see was that Rader would not be subject to the death penalty—the murders had all occurred when Kansas had no constitutionally approved death penalty statute. In fact, all but one case—that of Dee Davis—had occurred when the Kansas murder statute provided for a fairly short term of imprisonment for murder: 15 years to life. If the sentences on the first nine cases were run concurrently—fat chance, Osburn knew—conceivably Dennis Rader could be out on parole by the age of 70, with time off for good behavior. No wonder some people thought the laws bent over backward to benefit criminals.

Except for the Dee Davis case—*that* murder had occurred after the Kansas legislature had rebelled at the easy punishment for murder. The Davis murder had taken place under another statute, which mandated that, if a murder was sufficiently cruel—*aggravated* was the legal term—the sentence would be 40 years in prison without parole. The Hard Forty, it was called in Kansas. Clearly, Dennis Rader would be eligible for the Hard Forty. There was a faint chance that if he could prove that Rader hadn't killed Dee Davis, the lower prison terms on the others might apply. Not that any judge would be foolish enough to sentence BTK to concurrent terms and give him the chance to get out of prison after only a decade behind bars. Besides, it was clear that Dennis Rader *had* killed Dee Davis—he'd avidly admitted it.

Well, what were the other options? Osburn knew he probably couldn't attack the facts of the case. The evidence, especially with the confession, seemed overwhelming. Maybe, he thought, he could do something with a mental disease or defect defense. Clearly, Dennis Rader had to be a very disturbed individual. Hadn't Hannon and LaMunyon always said they were trying to find a very sick person? Maybe he could call the former police chiefs to the witness stand and get them to say that BTK was sick, since they'd already said so many times before.

The first thing to do, Osburn knew, was to get some professional forensic psychologists in to see what made Dennis Rader tick. He asked Judge Waller to sign an order permitting the defense to hire some mental experts, one of whom would eventually turn out to be Dr. Robert Mendoza, from Cambridge Forensic Consultants in

Massachusetts. Waller approved the money. But first, Osburn had to get a grip on all the investigative paper that the prosecution had spawned. Only then could he be sure of what to do. It was a daunting prospect.

By May, a substantial part of the investigative material had been turned over to the defense by the prosecution, but Osburn and his side were still working through it, trying to decide the most appropriate defense strategy. Nevertheless, it was time for Rader to enter a formal plea to the charges.

In discussions before this, Rader had wanted to simply plead guilty at his arraignment, scheduled to take place May 3. Why prolong things? He was guilty. He was BTK. They knew it, he knew it, everybody knew it. He wanted the whole world to know it—that was one reason he'd committed the murders to begin with. Why drag things out?

"We had to very forcefully counsel him," Osburn said later. "We told him, 'We haven't gone over all the ramifications of entering a plea yet. You can't possibly make a knowing plea until we've done that. Give us a chance.' "

In the two months he'd been in jail, a subtle change had come over Rader. It was no longer necessary for him to pretend, to maintain his cover, his "legend." For the first time in his life, the effort to play a role could be dispensed with. Like a snake shedding its skin, the "social Dennis" began to crack and peel. He was what he was—a nasty, perverted man who had taken pleasure in terrorizing helpless people. He had no interest in denying it. Why not, like Harvey Glatman, revel in it?

Rader's attorneys were taken aback by this. They were emotionally, even intellectually, unprepared for the sordidness of their client, and his Jekyll and Hyde personality. And yet, from time to time, they could see fragments of the "social Dennis" float back to the surface, flotsam and jetsam left over from a lifetime of conditioning. At times, Rader could seem perfectly reasonable, polite, even kind—it was hard to see him as someone who'd broken into people's houses, tied them up, terrorized them and then strangled them to death, let alone as someone so caught up in bondage fantasies that he'd regularly hung himself wearing women's clothing and a mask so he could take pictures of himself pretending to be a victim.

But at other times, Rader could seem as willful as a 3-year-old, Osburn recalled. He wanted publicity—that was all he wanted, and the more publicity, the better. In the end, Osburn said later, prosecutor Foulston would give Dennis Rader exactly what he wanted, more publicity than he'd ever dreamed of.

Insisting they still had to evaluate the evidence against him, Osburn and his colleagues managed to convince Rader to enter a plea of not guilty to the ten murder charges on May 3. Rader wasn't happy with this, but eventually went along with it. From Rader's point of view, once he thought it through, the not guilty plea insured that public interest in his depredations would only be heightened, giving him a chance to equal or surpass the notoriety of his idol—Harvey Glatman.

By late May, the defense had thoroughly if fruitlessly explored the possibility of the mental defense. According to some published reports, no fewer than five different experts examined Rader's mental condition. The assessments were kept secret, but by June 2005, one point was clear to Osburn and the others: Rader had known exactly what he was doing when he'd committed murder, known that it was wrong, and done it anyway. A mental disease or defect defense was out of the question. The only choice left was whether to go to trial and hope to contradict unassailable evidence, or plead guilty, just as Rader had wanted to do from the start.

On June 27, 2005, Dennis Rader appeared in court for the first day of his scheduled trial and pleaded guilty to ten counts of first-degree murder. The proceeding was televised live across the nation. Traffic downtown came to a near standstill as virtually everyone in Wichita found their way to television sets to see what would happen.

Calmly, as if he were giving a report to his commanding officer, Rader explained exactly what he had done to the Oteros, to the Brights, to Shirley Vian, Nancy Fox, Marine Hedge, Vicki Wegerle and Dee Davis—the trolling, the stalking, the planning, the breaking and entering, the terrorizing, the strangling.

"If I'd brought my stuff, Kevin would be dead today," Rader told Waller. "I'm not bragging or anything. It's just a matter of fact."

Over the years, Rader said, he'd stalked scores, maybe even hundreds of potential victims.

"I had a lot of them," he said. "If one didn't work out, I'd find another."

"So, all of these incidents, these ten counts, occurred because you wanted to satisfy sexual fantasies. Is that correct?" Waller asked.

"Yes," Rader said. "Um-hum."

The matter-of-fact dispassion of Rader's factual recitation left people in and out of the courtroom stunned. It was as if the understanding that his victims had been real people, not mere cardboard cut-outs existing simply for him, was beyond his comprehension. And others noted that this was BTK's biggest moment: he was in the spotlight at last, after all the years, and his carefully constructed shell of church congregation president and Scout leader could at last be cast aside. The real Rader was out of the closet, to everyone's shock or fear. At last Dennis Rader was someone *important*, as he had always longed to be.

"It's all about him," former chief LaMunyon observed. And former KAKE news director Ron Loewen, paying particularly close attention to Rader's demeanor, realized that this was BTK's penultimate fantasy: to be on national television, the baddest of the bad. Loewen wasn't surprised that Rader was so precise, so detailed in his description of his depredations.

"This wasn't someone who was stumbling, who was nervous," he said. "This was showtime for him. He couldn't ask for a better stage."

But Rader would soon have yet more stages, still more chances to out-Glatman Glatman.

Only hours after he'd entered his plea, Rader was interviewed once more by the defense psychologist, Robert Mendoza. This interview was taped by a videographer retained by Mendoza. Rader signed a release, permitting Mendoza to use the tape in future academic settings.

Mendoza asked Rader how he was feeling, now that he'd entered his guilty plea.

"I really feel pretty good," Rader said. "It's kind of like a big burden that was lifted off my shoulders. On the other hand, I feel like I'm a star right now."

The "burden" was less the guilt than it was the strain of maintaining his "social obligations," it seemed clear. Pleading guilty had cleared away the last of the no-longer-needed carapace. Rader told Mendoza he had no feeling at all for those he had murdered—to him they were simply objects, raw materials for his fantasies.

Mendoza asked Rader to try to explain how he had come to be the way he was.

"I started working out this fantasy in my mind," Rader said. "And once the potential [victim]—that person become[s] a fantasy, I could just loop it over. I could lay [sic] in bed at night and think about this person, the events and how it's gonna happen. And it would become real, almost like a picture show. You know, I wanted to go ahead and produce it and direct it and go through with it. No matter what the costs were, the consequences. It was gonna happen one way or another. Maybe not that day, but it was gonna happen."

This was exactly what Beattie had predicted: the narcissism of the killer had become so compulsive that he'd rather die than not go through with his desire. Knowing that the desire was wrong, he'd kept it hidden inside of himself, compartmentalizing his life, so that no one would ever guess, building up his outside persona, lacquering it in place day by day, year by year, until it was hard, rigid, almost impenetrable—so super-conforming, so regulated that the outside man was universally seen as incurably anal-retentive. But the more he'd bottled the poison up inside, the more powerful, the more toxic it became, until it finally and fatally vented—at least ten times over the years.

In this talk with Mendoza, Rader revealed several details about his past that seemed significant. He recalled having been sexually aroused at an early age when his mother spanked him. "Sparky" came to life when someone controlled him, and the association grew powerful over the years: if he became aroused when controlled by others, wouldn't others become aroused when controlled by him? Control and sex became so fused in his secret mind as to become inseparable.

Rader told Mendoza that he'd first noticed the Otero family shortly after they had moved in, in perhaps November 1974. He'd previously had a job working at Cessna—this was the first anyone had heard of that—and had lost it.

"That was demoralizing to me," Rader told Mendoza. This, too, was part of the profile—unemployed, underemployed, a deep-seated lack of self-esteem overcompensated for by the fantasy of having control, by the overweening narcissism.

The victims weren't really picked for the way they looked, or for their potential as sexual objects, Rader told Mendoza, and then validated Hazelwood's prediction:

"I don't think it was actually the person I was after, I think it was the dream. I know it's not really nice to say about a person, but they were basically an object. That's all they were. I had more satisfaction building up to it and afterwards than I did the actual killing of the person."

Eventually, Rader came to the kicker—why he had decided to resurface after so many years. It was Beattie, Rader said. He simply couldn't let Beattie tell "his" story.

"I was going to tell the story in my terms and not his terms," Rader told Mendoza. "They [the police, the news media and Beattie] already had the killings, so that's factual. But they didn't know how I worked and moved around the projects, the haunts, how I picked my victims. They didn't know how that worked. I could just really stir up the hornet nest up with the media by just showing them pictures and puzzles and playing a game with them."

And in the end, that was the only real point of connection between the hidden Dennis Rader—"Factor X" as he called the poison inside him—and the outside, the "social obligation" Dennis Rader. It was the only way the inside moral cretin could get the outside man to cooperate—to make it all a game, some sort of juvenile prank.

"Doll-o-Grams," indeed.

38:

"That Is Dennis Rader"

BTK KILLER CONFESSES, the *Eagle* headlined the following day. SILENT CITY LISTENS AS RADER DETAILS MURDERS SPURRED BY SEXUAL FANTASIES.

Eagle reporter Ron Sylvester captured the meaning of the moment and the mood of the city perfectly.

"Dennis Rader dropped his mask Monday," Sylvester wrote. "With no apology or visible remorse, the former church and Boy Scout leader pleaded guilty as Wichita's notorious BTK serial killer. Then he gave an extraordinarily detailed recollection of how he selected, stalked and strangled 10 people."

Osburn said the decision to plead guilty was made by Rader on his own. He said he hoped that the city could rest easier knowing that BTK was going to prison for the rest of his life.

"He has left no doubt that the BTK killer has been caught," Osburn said.

But while Osburn hoped that his most infamous client would be shuffled off to prison with a minimum of fuss after formal sentencing, District Attorney Foulston had other ideas. She wanted to drive a stake through the beast's heart, at least legally speaking, by presenting evidence of aggravation at Rader's sentencing, to make sure Rader got the "Hard Forty." This would require a full-dress hearing, with witnesses, who would be called to lay out in graphic detail all of Rader's perversities.

"When a community is deprived of information about what happened, it never rests," Foulston said. Getting the details out to the public, trying to answer questions about what happened, was vital to the administration of justice.

"I'm sure if it was up to the defense, they would rather skip the sentencing entirely and just get an e-mail from the judge," Foulston told the *Eagle*. "I think all defendants would rather it just go away and quietly slither out of town and off to the penitentiary. But that's not going to happen."

Foulston was right—Osburn thought an extended hearing, replete with crime-scene photographs, videos and horrid details, was not only unnecessary from a legal standpoint, but calculated by the district attorney to improve her chances in the next election. It was grandstanding, Osburn said. His side had offered to stipulate that aggravation existed—to accept the "Hard Forty" sentence—but Foulston's office had rejected the offer.

"I think personally hearing Mr. Rader stand up and say, 'I did it,' and give some very graphic details as to why people were selected and how he went about it—if that doesn't give closure, I certainly don't know what the state can add to that," Osburn said. Rader's plea statement was enough to satisfy the law, Osburn said, and having a lurid sentencing hearing was just overkill.

Osburn's main problem with the prosecution of Dennis Rader had nothing to do with the evidence against his client, or even Rader's weird desire to embrace the notoriety of being named the murderer. Osburn's problem—or at least, the thing that stuck sideways in his throat—was how the politicians had clamored to get in front of the cameras, now that BTK had been brought to book. Osburn in particular objected to District Attorney Foulston. It had bothered him when Foulston had insisted on serving Rader personally, while in court in March, with her decision to ask for the Hard Forty. All that did was get Foulston on the evening news, in dramatic *accusatory* fashion. It wasn't really necessary, although it was what one might expect from a politician who wanted to be identified with ending the worst murder case in Wichita's history.

But more substantively, Osburn objected to the district attorney's insistence that this full-scale evidentiary hearing was necessary to demonstrate the aggravation required for the Hard Forty. Rader was willing to stipulate—to agree to accept the Hard Forty—without any hearing, but Foulston had insisted that the public needed to know what had really happened, which meant all the gory, perverse details would come pouring out to the public. Osburn suspected that what was really in Foulston's mind was the opportunity to get massive amounts of publicity as she described, in detail, all of Rader's depredations and predilections. Such a hearing, Osburn knew, would probably be broadcast, maybe even nationally, which would hardly hurt Nola Foulston's political ambitions.

He could object, Osburn knew, but it would only make his public defender's office look bad. Dennis Rader was, at least is this sense, a sitting duck—but who would care? There was no real percentage in complaining about it for Osburn, his office or—and this was the most important—any of his future clients, if the public began to perceive the public defender's office as legalistic obstructionists. So Foulston had Osburn over a barrel, and there wasn't any real way to stop the district attorney from stripping a pound or two of flesh off Dennis Rader in some sort of show proceeding, the principal benefit of which would accrue to the future political desires of Nola Foulston. All Osburn could do was take it. As for Rader—chances were, this was something that he would really enjoy.

The district attorney's office was within its authority to reject the offered stipulation, though, and Judge Waller scheduled three days for a formal sentencing hearing for mid-August 2005. Rader was now in yet another race for publicity, this one with Foulston herself. By insisting on a hearing, Osburn thought, Foulston was giving Rader exactly what he most desired.

"We cannot let this just close the book and walk away. That would be so unfair to our victims and their families and to the community and the public that we serve." It wasn't just about the killer and his victims, or even his victims' survivors, but about the whole community, Foulston said.

In the wake of BTK's plea, Beattie received congratulations and appreciation from people all over town. There was no doubt, former chief LaMunyon said, that Beattie's decision to write a book about the case had caused Rader to resume contact after all the years, the development that had led directly to BTK's capture. Rader simply couldn't stand it that Beattie might get more attention than the long-sought killer. Others noted that the search of Rader's "motherlode" at the Park City City Hall had turned up a copy of the March 2004 issue of *ReTIRED COPPER*, the newsletter that had featured the item about Beattie's book—that meant that Rader had read it just before resuming his communications in March 2004. And in a jailhouse interview with KAKE reporter Larry Hatteberg, Rader had said simply, if revealingly: "I'll bet Beattie's gloating now."

As for Beattie himself, he now had a chance to tell the whole story—he'd calculated from the start to get BTK's goat, to stimulate him to communicate again, he told the *Eagle*. It was all because of the killer's intense narcissism, so obvious from the years of communications, beginning with the library letter of 1974. It was clear that BTK simply couldn't abide anyone taking attention away from him, even the three half-wits the police had first arrested in the autumn of that year.

"The ancient Greeks taught that the gods punished hubris," Beattie told the paper. "I thought that if BTK continued to communicate, he would eventually be caught."

On August 17, 2005, the Sedgwick County District Attorney's Office began presenting the aggravation evidence against Dennis Rader. This proceeding, too, was broadcast on national television, by Court TV. For weeks before the hearing, news media people from across the country had been making their reservations for Wichita, to be there for the denouement of the long-running case. Regardless of Foulston's intent—whether legal or political—Rader knew that once more he would be the star of the show. Even better, from Rader's point of view, the tape of his final interview with Dr. Mendoza had somehow been furnished to NBC's *Dateline*, which broadcast portions of it to the nation the week before the sentencing was to take place. He was the star, of course.

Foulston's plan was to call as witnesses each detective who had been assigned to investigate the long-dormant BTK cases once Rader had resurfaced the previous year. That way, she and her associates could explain to the public exactly what BTK had done during every crime, and what Dennis Rader had later said about it. To bolster this testimony, the district attorney's office had prepared a lengthy PowerPoint demonstration, illustrated with highly disturbing crime-scene and autopsy photographs, pictures of things seized during the searches, and excerpts from the statements Rader had made to the detectives during his interrogations. Members of the victims' families were given reserved seats in Judge Waller's courtroom, and were warned that the presentation contained a large number of unpleasant details. Among those in attendance were the surviving Oteros—Charlie, Danny and Carmen. Also there were Steve Relford and Kevin Bright, along with Dee Davis' son and members of the Fox, Hedge and Wegerle families.

Rader sat quietly at the counsel table as each detective took the stand, recounting the vile crimes, and what Rader had said about them.

Assistant District Attorney Kevin O'Connor led off with the Otero case. He asked Ray Lundin, an agent of the Kansas Bureau of Investigation, if he'd interviewed Rader about the Otero murders.

He had, Lundin said.

"Okay. And how—What did he refer to this family that he murdered? How did he refer to them?"

"That was his 'PJ Little-Mex' or 'Project Little-Mex.' "

"And these 'projects,' what does the *projects* mean? What did that mean to Rader?"

"These were his undertakings that he—the things that he was working on. They were people. They were, you know, potential victims of his that he would work on. Some of them he ended up killing, and some of them he didn't, but—"

"And he had—he literally had hundreds of *projects*, is that correct?"

"Yes, that's correct."

"And he kept detailed records about his little projects, didn't he?"

"Yes, he did."

"And these projects again—these projects that Rader

called 'projects,' were actually people, living, breathing human beings?"

"Yes, they were."

Lundin recounted Rader's description of how he'd killed the four Oteros.

"And did he tell you what Josie was doing as she watched what he was doing to her family?" O'Connor asked.

"She was, you know, screaming for her mother," Lundin said that Rader had told him. "And, as you can only imagine, and I remember how he kind of callously said, you know, 'She was over there yelling . . . "Momma, Momma, Momma,"' something like that, and—"

"And during the interview, he actually mimicked a little girl yelling, 'Mommy, Mommy, Mommy,' is that correct?"

Yes, Lundin said, that's what Rader had done.

O'Connor called another KBI agent, Larry Thomas, who had also re-investigated the Otero ease, once BTK had resurfaced. The assistant DA wanted to get some additional testimony on the callousness of Rader's behavior, necessary to demonstrate the aggravation.

"And, again, there's been some testimony that—when he talked about what Josie would say, would he mimic a little girl?"

"Yes, he would—he actually would change his voice to mimic the voice, and, also, use some animation of his body to show the positions of the bodies."

"And so, when he'd describe it, he'd actually get up and demonstrate it, right?"

"Yes, that's correct."

"And during the course of this interview, did it appear to you that he seemed to be extremely proud of what he had done?"

"Yes, it was very matter-of-fact, and used the animation, and, also, drawing pictures to help illustrate the details."

"Now, there are some photographs here that are going to depict Josie down in the basement. This is a crime-scene photograph of Josie as she appeared down in the basement?"

"Yes, it is."

"Okay. And she is—she has a gag over her mouth, is that correct?"

"Yes, she does."

"And her lips were swollen in that?"

"Yes."

"And her tongue was—what about her tongue?"

"Her tongue was protruding aside of the gag."

"Now, did you specifically ask Rader why he took Josie to the basement?"

"We asked—during the course of his explanation of this particular crime scene—why he chose the basement."

"And there is a quote behind you from Rader about his fascination with bondage in a basement, is that correct?"

"Yes, that is his statement."

"Okay. And he indicated to you it's the best place to hang somebody, because it's solid?"

"Yes."

"And it's like a dungeon?"

"Correct."

"And he indicated to you that at his parents' house, his folks' home, as he calls it, he would do—he would do this when they weren't around?"

"Correct."

"Okay. He'd find— There was a sewer pipe down in his basement that was similar to the one in the Oteros'?"

"Yes."

"Now, did you find anything in his stash—or what he

would call his motherlode—that supported this statement here, that he actually hung himself in his parents' basement?"

"Yes. There were photographs."

"Now, this is a photograph here to my left. It is a Polaroid photograph, the one I have the cursor on; is that right?"

"That's correct."

"And this was located in Rader's stash?"

"Yes."

"All right. And who is this person here that's wearing women's pantyhose, has binding over him, has a gag over him, and is wearing a women's bra? Who is that?"

"That's Dennis Rader."

39:

"My Mask"

The sentencing hearing continued for two days, illustrated by similarly graphic photographs. Whenever a particularly gruesome picture was about to be shown, O'Connor or Foulston would warn the Court TV camera operator, and the lens would switch away, either to a prerecorded image or, more often, to Rader himself. He continued to sit quietly at the counsel table, dressed in a suit and tie, neatly groomed, looking as if he'd just come from the local Kiwanis Club meeting. It was impossible to believe, simply looking at the stolid middle-class image of the man, sitting placidly at the counsel table, that he had done these things.

Eventually, after going through the horrors of the Bright house, the Vian atrocity, the degradation of Nancy Fox, followed by the Hedge, Wegerle and Davis murders, the testimony turned to the fetid undersoul of Dennis Rader himself. The photographs of Marine Hedge in the church basement were awful; as they came on the PowerPoint screen, Pastor Clark, who had been sitting in the rear of the courtroom, had to get up and leave; sometimes even the strongest Christian spirit needs a break.

Foulston finished up the Dee Davis murder by asking Sedgwick County Detective Sam Houston about the plastic mask that had been found with her remains. She gave him the mask to hold; Houston held it up for the court to see.

"This is a plastic mask that's been painted."

"And is that one of those very thin type of plastic masks?"

"Yes, it is. It's a thin—thin plastic with this cord on it. It appears to be like a, like a venetian blind cord."

"All right. And has that been painted over, the original mask itself?"

"That's correct. The mask itself has been painted a flesh-tone color, red lips have been added to it, with black parting the lips. There has been black that's been added to the nostrils to make it more life-like, and also eyebrows and eyelashes have been added to this."

"And eyebrows?"

"Yes, ma'am."

"And that would have been the mask that was found next to Dolores Davis as she lay in repose under the bridge when she was found by law enforcement officers?"

"That is correct."

"And this is also the mask that Dennis Rader [said] he placed on Dolores Davis to make her look pretty or more feminine, is that correct?"

"That's correct."

"And when you discussed this with Dennis Rader, what else was there, about that mask? What was he doing with that mask?"

"I asked him, 'Did she wear the mask?' and he said, 'Yeah,' and he stated—he said, 'That's my mask.' And I said, '*Your* mask?' And he said, 'Yeah, that's my mask, I wear that mask, too.' And he stated that—I guess I had a strange look on my face—and he said, 'Well, I— I pose myself in bondage pictures with this mask, and you'll find those in my stash."

"So he would use that personally as his own mask?"

"Yes."

"And then use it for his bondage escapades, is that right?"

"That's correct."

"And then he utilized it to pretty up the deceased, Dolores Davis?"

"He stated that he put it on her to—to take his pictures, to pretty her up, to make her more feminine-looking."

"Did he indicate whether he had more than one mask?"

"He said he had a couple. He said that he— he bought this up in—in Hays, Kansas, when he was up there working and trolling."

"Okay. And so that's one of a collection of masks that he might have had?"

"That's correct."

Foulston turned to Osburn and asked him if he wanted to inspect the horrid mask.

"No," Osburn said shortly.

"When you had worked with the other officers in doing the search warrants, did you locate photographs or other items indicating that Mr. Rader indeed did use masks for bondage purposes?"

"Yes, he did. Yes."

"Okay. Now again, Mr. Rader had indicated that he had placed the mask on Mrs. Davis and that he had photographed her, is that right?"

"That is correct."

After showing some graphic photographs of how Dee Davis' remains had been found, Foulston returned to Rader's fantasy world.

"Again, you said that Mr. Rader was wearing the mask and that— Now, he uses the words here, those are 'me assimilated.' Do you know what he meant by that?"

"I believe he meant *simulating* bondage."

"Simulating?"

"I believe it meant *simulating*, but he stated 'assimilated.' "

"And again, his discussion about the dressing up in

women's clothes and doing his sexual things and wearing those masks, is that right?"

"Yes."

"Again, this is a close-up photograph of that mask, is that correct?"

"That is correct."

"And here we have some other photographs of masks. Can you explain what these are?"

"These masks are basically the same style of mask, except they're marked different. They have these areas here on the cheeks, would be like rouge or something like that, to bring that out. This appears to me to be another mask up here. This is another mask in this picture here, with the chains, the—the rope, the bindings."

"Where did these photographs come from?"

"Those came out of his collection that was found during the search warrants."

"There's some information that he gave with regard to that. Would you explain?"

"He stated that he painted the flesh color, put some nice lips on it, a little bit of a smile, like a pretty girl. He told me that he—he would wear the mask to do his sexual fantasy stuff, his self-bondage. He'd put—put the mask on and wear that. He would also take pictures of it so—looking more female, and that he looked like he was in distress, like he was—he was a victim, or that he was posing as one of his own victims."

"And this photograph, can you tell me what this is?"

"This is a picture that was found in his—in the search warrant of Mr. Rader, where he's tied himself to a chair, wearing a wig and wearing one of these masks."

"And do you know where this photograph might have been taken?"

"This could have been at a motel, this could have been at his mother and father's house."

"So he also did this at his parents' house?"

"That's correct."

"In the basement?"

"That's correct."

By the morning of the second day, Foulston closed her evidence presentation by calling Ken Landwehr to the stand. She asked Landwehr if he had the impression that Rader thought of himself as one of them, that is, a cop. Landwehr said he thought that's what Rader believed—it made him more eager to talk, Landwehr agreed.

"Mr. Rader's not a law enforcement officer, he's a dog-catcher, is that right?" Foulston asked.

"Yes, ma'am."

"And you weren't there to be friends with him, were you?"

"No, ma'am."

"In your discussions with Mr. Rader, did he discuss with you his independent, individual personalities?"

"Yes."

"What did he tell you?"

"He said he had a compartmentalized situation where he was—he had social contacts, and that's what he would call his family and the people at church. And then he had [his] business, and of being under 'Factor X,' to be the serial killer."

"And that one was— Were they exclusive from each other or were they built into one package?"

"They were all him."

Foulston asked Landwehr about the motherlode. A photo of the infamous filing cabinet appeared on the screen.

"Yes," Landwehr said. "These items were kept at his office that he said that he kept locked."

"All right. And then when you open the drawer you see a number of items and—and this is called what?"

"This is what he referred to as his motherlode."

"All right. And these are all individually labeled books or binders and files that would be related to what?"

"Some were related to sexual fantasies, some were communications, some were different ads that he had cut out and things that he had."

"So he had that right at his fingertips in the office?"

"Yes. He was in the process— He told me that he was going to put all of these on a disk, so he would get rid of the originals; but he was going to put these on a computer system of some sort while scanning them so he would have them."

"Okay. And he also kept collections of things at his home, is that right?"

"Yes, ma'am."

"It's a pretty small home, is that right?"

"Yes. I'd say right around nine hundred square feet, probably."

"And within this home he had what he called hidey holes?"

"Yes. He did have one particular hidey hole that he hid things."

"Now, the exhibit box that I put back next to you, that's the same box that was in his closet with his uniforms, is that right?"

"Yes. This is in his southwest bedroom, the master bedroom of the residence, and that is where he would— That is where that was, this item was found."

"Okay. Let's take a look a little bit inside that box, if you will."

Landwehr opened the box.

"I've pulled out a stack of three-by-five cards," Foulston said, "and put a rubber band around this group. And

I've got a smaller group here. Okay, now, tell me what these are."

"These are what Mr. Rader referred to as his slick ads. These were things he would cut out of magazines and out of mailings, basically, whether it be a Penney's ad, a Kohl's ad, any type of ad that would have either children, women, sometimes young boys, that he would cut out and then he would place them by tape, or glue them onto a three-by-five index card such as this, and he would make his notations on the back of these for his sexual fantasy of what he would do to each of these."

"Now, these are just normal advertisements? These are just normal advertisements that one might find in a Sears catalog, is that right?"

"Yes, ma'am."

"There's— In most of these, now there's some that have a little bit more pornographic tone to them. But generally, [they're] just an advertisement for a bathing suit or a bra from a catalog, is that correct?"

"Most of these are, but then there will be some cutouts that I would say would probably come from something like *Playboy*, *Penthouse*, something like that as well."

"All right. But he could take an ordinary picture and make it into an extraordinary sexual fantasy, is that correct?"

"That's what he said he could do, yes."

"But that's by his making?"

"That is correct."

"Something ordinary he could make extraordinary?"

"In his opinion, yes."

On the back of each card, Rader had devised a template of sorts, basically a series of boxes. Into each one he'd written some inscrutable abbreviations. The abbreviations matched a list of fantasies Rader had neatly written down on a separate piece of paper. Foulston fished out one of the cards, and asked Landwehr to describe it.

"This, can you describe the photo? Hold it up so it can be seen. And that displays a little girl, maybe four years old, on the front?"

"Four to six, I would say, in a swimming suit, something that you would maybe see in a Kmart ad or something like that."

"All right. So he's taken that swimsuit model, of a little child, and made that into a sexual fantasy card?"

"Yes."

"All right. And then here's an adult one we'll give you, and this is a bra advertisement. And hold that one up. And what does it say on that one?"

" 'Boobies on red—' "

" 'Boobies'?"

" 'Boobies on red.' I can't read any more."

"Okay."

"And 'sexual fantasy' on this one, on a red sheet, hands bound, legs spread."

"Then at the bottom?"

"It says on the bottom, 'CN, bra woman, BRN,' probably for brown, 'Kmart four-seventeen of '03.' "

"So that indicates where he cut it from, his sexual fantasy, and her arms are behind her back—"

"Yes."

"And so he's clipped it and then he's designed a sexual fantasy to go with that?"

"Yes, ma'am."

"And these are what he calls his slick ads?"

"Those are a few of his slick ads."

"Oh. There are more of these?"

"He had hundreds, if not thousands, of those, I believe."

"All right. And these are on kind of like playing cards almost, aren't they?"

"They're five-by-three index cards, something you'd put a recipe on or something like that."

"Okay. So you can— They're portable?"

"Yes."

"Carry them with you?"

"Yes."

"Okay. And they have— Are there any males in these?"

"I know that there are a few cut-outs that he did on his communications that he sent to us of young boys, but no adult males."

"Now, what do you call— What do you call a person who has a sexual interest in little girls?"

"A pedophile."

40:

Into the Abyss

After Foulston had finished putting on all her evidence, Waller turned to Osburn for the defense.

"Does the defendant desire to put on any evidence?"

"We do not, Your Honor," Osburn said. What was there to say? That Dennis Rader was a devout church member, that he was a loving husband, a father of two, who'd just happened to have murdered ten people because he was sick? Sick he may have been, but it simply wasn't any mitigation for the atrocious deeds he had committed. So Osburn kept silent.

After a short break, the court agreed to hear from the victims' survivors.

Charlie Otero went first.

It had been a hard thirty years for Charlie Otero since the day his mother, father, sister and brother had been murdered. He'd had trouble of his own, eventually winding up in prison in New Mexico. Who knew what might have been if half his family hadn't been wiped out? In coming to the sentencing hearing, it was the first time he had seen his brother Danny and sister Carmen in years—it was the most bittersweet of reunions. Now the day of reckoning for the sick, selfish man who had caused so much wreckage in people's lives was finally at hand.

"My name is Charlie Otero," he said. "I am not here to recount the personal loss I have felt for over thirty years, but to speak for all the members of my family, living and dead. Not only my siblings and I, but the entire families of the Oteros and the Burgoses [Julie Otero's maiden name] suffered from the actions of one Dennis Rader. I would like at this time to state that the criminal actions of Dennis Rader caused irreparable damage to the very fabric of my blood family: sons, daughters, uncles and cousins, a father and mothers, aunts and grandmothers. All lost the precious moments my family's very existence would have brought them during their lifetimes. Their lost lives are missed yet to this day.

"Dennis Rader did not ruin my life, though. He caused me to challenge my faith, change my future forever, and separated me from the rest of my loved ones for over thirty years. Yet I have never allowed his actions to send me to the dark side. A son's love for his mother would not allow Dennis Rader to tarnish her memory. The lessons I learned from my father and mother transcend the evil doings of Dennis Rader. No action or sentence bestowed upon Dennis Rader will begin to compare with the reckoning he will endure when his time for judgment comes before the Lord. I truly believe the Lord will pass judgment and sentence as is befitting Dennis Rader's actions and beliefs. No amount of posturing or deception will save him from the eternity he has created for himself with his time here on earth. I only hope that the sentence passed on to him by the judicial system of the State of Kansas denies him the opportunity to spend his remaining days with anyone or anything besides himself, for that is more than he deserves.

"Despite Dennis Rader's efforts to destroy my family, we survive, stronger and closer now, more than ever. Our love for each other was forged with pain and loss. Yes, it took years of straying down different paths, but in the end we all, Danny, Carmen and I, have found our ways back to each other with a unity and love to be proud of. As far as I'm concerned, when it is all done, Dennis Rader has failed in his effort to kill the Oteros. Thank you."

Next was Carmen. She directed her statement directly to Dennis Rader.

"I'm Carmen Julie Otero Montoya," she said, giving her married name. "Although we have never met, you have seen my face before. It is the same face you murdered over thirty years ago. The face of my mother, Julie Otero. I will not address you as Mr. Rader, because *Mister* is a word of respect. As in, 'Mister, can you help me?'; not 'Mister, are you going to kill me?' BTK is how you want to be known and I will not give you that satisfaction. Rader is an appropriate name for you, as one who invades, a surprise attack. That is nothing to be proud of. Rader, when you took away my mother, you took someone who meant a lot to a lot of people.

"My mother loved life, her friends, a good laugh, dancing with my dad, and she loved to help people. But most of all, she loved and lived for us, her family. She showed me how to love, to be a good person, to accept others as they are and, most of all, to face your fears. I'm sure you saw that in her face as she fought to live. My mother against your gun. You are such a coward. Since they were children, my father lived—*loved* my mother more than any kind of love you could ever comprehend. He adored her. To this day, I love to hear stories of how they were. My father was a hard-working man, and we always felt secure. He made sure we had what we needed, but at the same time we understood there was always someone else more in need.

"My dad loved to see us having a good time, and he never passed on it—passed on a dance with my mom even in the commissary. He loved trips to the beach and to the country. We always went with friends and family.

Those good times were very important to him. The thing that everyone remembers of my father is that he demanded respect, but that he gave it in return. Everyone knew you didn't mess with Joe's family. I'm sure you could feel his love for his family as you took away his last breath. You are such a coward.

"My sister Josie, you should not have the privilege of even saying her name. Such a sweet girl. All she ever wanted was to be happy and successful in school. She had dreams. She was my shadow and at the same time her own person. When we moved to Wichita I told her that I hated it because it was so cold, and people were so different. She told me, 'You'll get used to it, give it a chance.' That was part of Josie's beauty. She always tried to see the bright side of everything. It's amazing to me that you could be so cruel to a sweet, beautiful child.

"His name was Joey, *not* junior, but I guess it really doesn't matter to you. You took away the most loveable, fun, outgoing, friendly and adorable little brother anyone could ever imagine. He tried so hard to keep up with Charlie and Danny. Joey was a magnet. He attracted people of all ages. He could have done something big with his life, but you took care of that, didn't you? A man with a gun against a little boy. You are definitely a coward.

"Rader, you not only affected my life, but you took away the joy of the ultimate grandparents, aunt and uncle relationship my children deserve. My children, my grandchildren, my nieces and nephews will be told of their family with love. You see, in my world, family is everything, not your 'social obligations.'

"Just recently I realized that I could not remember my mother's voice. It was a painful discovery, but as I put my thoughts on paper, it comes to me: I am my mother's voice, and I know we've been heard."

Kevin Bright came next. He'd long before recovered

from his wounds, although he still had troubles with his body's ability to regulate temperatures, and sometimes with eating. He often thought of his sister, Kevin said, and was especially proud that she had fought back so hard against Rader.

"I would like to say that . . . the pain and suffering he's caused our family, and the loss of such a beautiful young lady of twenty-one, over thirty-one years ago—I think about her and what she'd be doing nowadays, if she could have had a life. Her—her execution by that monster was— He got to go on and live *his* life, thirty-one years now, raising a family, children and career and everything; and, he snuffed out ten people's lives, people who had done nothing [to him]."

Kevin said he blamed the early death of his mother, from cancer, on Rader—the depression she'd felt on losing her daughter had taken a terrible toll on her.

"I'd like the Court to give him the maximum sentence he could get," Kevin said, "but also, [I'd ask] that he'd be isolated. I don't know if this is possible, but I'd like to see him serve the rest of his— I know the death penalty is not an option. But my sister and the other victims, they received their death penalty by his hands, and I would like to see him spend the rest of his life— I hope he lives forty more years, but I want him to be, you know, aware. Right now he's not shown any remorse, no remorse, no compassion, no— He had no mercy, and I think that's what he ought to receive." Kevin said that he hoped that the prison would deny Rader, as much of a normal life as possible—no books, no magazines, no newspapers, none of the small pleasures of life. He went on, the one adult who had survived an attack by BTK.

"And I just— Charlie [Otero] was saying he's being judged here now, but eternity, when he stands before the Lord for eternity, for his judgment, if he's still in his sins that he's committed here, he will spend it by himself in darkness. And you know, that's—that's what I'd like to tell him. Thank you for letting me speak."

After Kevin came Steve Relford. Like Charlie Otero, Steve had had a tough life since the murder of his mother, including drug problems, and a prison sentence of his own.

"My name's Steve Relford. Shirley Vian is my mother. I haven't prepared for this statement but, you know, I'd just like for him to suffer for the rest of his life and, you know, I don't— That's all."

Steve sat down. It was clear he wanted to say more, but thought better of it, given the setting.

Steve was followed by Beverly Plapp, Nancy Fox's sister.

"I cannot begin to explain to you, there are not words to make you understand what losing Nancy has meant to me and my family," she said. "I lost a friend, a confidante. My children will never have an aunt, and I'll never have another sister. Nancy's death is like a deep wound that will never, ever heal. As far as I'm concerned, Dennis Rader does not deserve to live. I want him to suffer as much as he made his victims suffer. But then, when I think about that, and his sick, perverted way, he'd probably find that as some kind of pleasure or reward. This man needs to be thrown in a deep, dark hole and left to rot. He should never, ever see the light of day. And I have some afterlife scenarios for him: on the day he dies, Nancy and all of his victims will be waiting with God and watching him as he burns in hell."

Stephanie Wegerle followed.

"I'm speaking to you today on behalf of myself and my brother, Brandon. It's been almost nineteen years now, that my brother and I had the most important woman in our lives taken from us. My brother and I had to go through so many important moments in our lives without her. Every day is a struggle to get through without her. It's not fair that we had so little time with her. I only had ten years with her. Brandon only had two.

"Anyone who knew my mom knew how much she loved her family. She loved her children, her husband, her parents and her sister. And she loved her in-laws like they were her own parents, brothers and sisters. She adored her nieces and nephews. Even our friends were considered family to her. There's nothing she wouldn't do for any one of us. We didn't have enough time with her. It's not fair that her three grandbabies will never get to know her. She doesn't get to see me with her grandchildren, and she doesn't get to see her baby Brandon with his first child . . . It's not fair that my four-year-old son has to ask why his [grandma] can't come home. He draws her pictures. We should be able to take these to her, but they just sit on the fridge. Even at four he knows it's not right, that she should be here with us. And what did my baby do to deserve feeling this way? What did any of us do to deserve this?

"Don't let this monster have any comforts as he lives out his remaining years in prison. He isn't worthy."

Jeff Davis, son of Dee Davis, came next. It was clear he had thought for a long time about what he wished to say.

"For the last five thousand, three hundred and twenty-six days I have wondered what it would be like to confront the walking cesspool that took my mother's precious life. Throughout that time, I always envisioned this day as being one for avenging the past. I could think of nothing but savoring the bittersweet taste of revenge as justice is served upon this social sewage here before us today. Now that it has arrived, surprisingly, I realize that this day is not just about avenging past crimes.

"Sitting here before us is a depraved predator, a rabid

animal that has murdered people, poisoned countless lives and terrorized this community for thirty years, all the while relishing every minute of it. As such, there can be no justice harsh enough or revenge bitter enough, in this world at least, to cause the pain and suffering which a societal malignancy like this has coming. Therefore, I have determined that for the sake of our innocent victims and their loving families and friends with us here today, for me this will be a day of celebration, not retribution."

Davis now ran through a long list of angry words he could have used to describe Rader, or how he thought of him.

"But I won't hurl these invectives at you or I won't rain these curses down upon you, because you're not smart enough to understand most of the words I would use anyway. And if you— Even if you could begin to fathom the depth of my hatred for you, I would still refuse to waste any breath on you, because that would once again allow you the satisfaction of being in the limelight, and that attention I refuse to allow you. As of today, you no longer exist.

"Today, the focus finally moves out from under the shadow of your depraved shadow of hell's darkness into the light of your victims and their families. Speaking for my mother, with us in spirit, for my own family, and I hope for the entire family of survivors here today, we dedicate this day to the memories of those who cannot be with us. Today we also celebrate with this community the relief in knowing that we will never again be terrorized by a monster's demented fantasies. Today, we will each silently remember a father, a brother, a wife, a mother, a sister, a daughter, a grandmother; all those who we loved so deeply and miss so dearly still. Today, we will quietly reminisce on all that they meant to us. We will smile at all the silly things they did that made us laugh, and we will renew our pride in who they were. Today, we will thank them for shaping our lives, for being there when we needed them, for setting the example of what we should be, for making us who we are, and for allowing us to be their living legacies."

Davis made the point that Rader had made a new family of sorts—those who had suffered at his hands, among them even Rader's own wife and children.

"From this point on, we declare our independence from the tyranny of your actions. While you begin your slow and painful descent into hell, we will choose to rise above our pain. While you sink into an emotional abyss of hopelessness and despair, we will channel our grief into positive endeavors, those life activities which would please the ones we have lost. While you agonize over the reality that your last victims were ironically your own family, we will embrace the new family we now have, with whom we will always share a common bond forged from the pain of adversity and loss. While your body wastes away in prison, we will renew ourselves by incorporating into our lives those characteristics modeled by our loved ones: humility, compassion, honor, integrity, kindness, selflessness and love; traits which your twisted, cancerous mind cannot comprehend, I realize. While your wretched soul awaits pronouncement of the one true justice, your damnation to hell for eternity, we will thank God for every day he gives us, realizing as only we can just how precious life really is.

"Finally, we want you to know that we who could so easily have succumbed to your quagmire of madness, will not give you that satisfaction. Your despicable actions will not defeat us. Our very lives will be testimony that good can triumph over even the most hideous form of evil and perversion. Just as your days are now over, ours are just beginning. In the final analysis you have to live with the cold reality that while all of us here will overcome your depravity, you have now lost everything and you will forever remain nothing. May that thought torment you for the rest of your tortured existence."

Now it was Dennis Rader's turn to speak. But as he rose for his final turn in the public spotlight, every member of every family in attendance—the Oteros, Kevin Bright, Steve Relford, the Fox family, the Wegerles, Jeff Davis and his daughter—every single one of them rose, turned their backs on him, and walked out of the courtroom.

And Beattie, watching all this unfold on television from within the chambers of Judge Richard Ballinger—Nancy Fox's friend who had helped make all this possible almost two years before—did the same thing.

Those who did listen to Rader, though, got the very essence of the man. Speaking for more than half an hour, he pedantically tried to correct the record—the smallest detail of what the police or prosecutors had described as his murderous actions did not escape his notice if it was slightly off. He tried to tell the stories of the victims, as if he were one of them. He tried to claim the mantle of a good man who had become a monster through no fault of his own. As if this was not enough, he then embarked on a long list of thanks—to his lawyers, the police, his wife, Pastor Clark, even his barber in the Sedgwick County jail. The longer he droned on, the more he gave out accolades, the more jaws dropped in the courtroom: it was as if Dennis Rader was giving an acceptance speech for a community award. He even said he hoped that some day his victims and their relatives could forgive him.

LaMunyon had been so right: to Dennis Rader, it *was* all about him. He seemed utterly incapable of absorbing or even perfunctorily acknowledging the human destruction his actions had caused, the chasms of hurt he had created in the hearts of so many.

Then, at the end, he turned to the seats in the rear of the courtroom vacated earlier by the victims' family members, who had now become a very special family of their own.

"Finally, my final apologize [sic] to the victims' families. There's no way that I can ever repay them. That's all, sir."

Foulston rose.

"This was a man who hid his life and hid his deeds in order to continue his ability to continue his sexual passions. This is a man who might say he's human and not a monster. This is a man who might stand up in court today and—and act like he has tears in his eyes or crocodile tears. But the fact is, when I saw him on *Dateline*, maybe I missed something, but this was an individual who loved the media attention, enjoyed being BTK, and said he was a star, and seemed to relish the fact that he had committed all these homicides.

"And today in court, when he faces sentencing, this is a completely wilted flower or crashed meteor. But something's different when he's facing the bottom line, than it was when he was being interviewed and talking very proudly about all the things he had done over those thirty years. So I think that we have a better idea of who this person is, and know that he's an individual that just hid . . . under the umbrella of being a husband, a Cub Scout leader, and held positions of respect and authority, as a pretty good guise, in order to be able to get away with what he was doing.

"And obviously even today we even get critiqued by someone who wants to be in control as to how our PowerPoint presentations are done, you know? And then we also get the Golden Globe awards, with Mr. Rader taking control of the courtroom, in order to give his final criminal justice awards of the week."

Dennis Rader, Foulston concluded, should not only get the Hard Forty, he should get the maximum of life in prison for all the other nine murder counts as well—sentences to be run consecutively. Not only that, she continued, Dennis Rader should be prevented from having any books, any newspapers, any magazines—any printed media at all, to prevent him from making any new amateur pornography in prison. He should be locked away forever, she said, until everyone could wipe his memory from their minds, as if he had never existed.

Waller mostly agreed. He told Rader to stand. And with that he sentenced the most despicable man in the history of Wichita to nine consecutive life sentences, to be topped by one more life sentence, the Hard Forty. That way, the earliest Dennis Rader could be eligible for parole would be in 175 years.

And even that was not enough, some thought.

41:

Narcissism and Sherlock Holmes

Narcissism is defined by the American Psychiatric Association's *Diagnostic and Statistical Manual of Mental Disorders* as "A pervasive pattern of grandiosity . . . need for admiration, and lack of empathy, beginning by early adulthood and present in a variety of contexts," and indicated by at least five of these nine criteria:

(1) has a grandiose sense of self-importance (e.g., exaggerates achievements and talents, expects to be recognized as superior without commensurate achievements)

(2) is preoccupied with fantasies of unlimited success, power, brilliance, beauty, or ideal love

(3) believes that he or she is "special" and unique and can only be understood by, or should associate with, other special or high-status people (or institutions)

(4) requires excessive admiration

(5) has a sense of entitlement, i.e., unreasonable expectations of especially favorable treatment or automatic compliance with his or her expectations

(6) is interpersonally exploitative, i.e., takes advantage of others to achieve his or her own ends

(7) lacks empathy: is unwilling to recognize or identify with the feelings and needs of others

(8) is often envious of others or believes that others are envious of him or her

(9) shows arrogant, haughty behaviors or attitudes

There can be little doubt that Dennis Rader exhibited most if not all of these nine criteria in his life. As a person with "narcissistic personality disorder," as the experts call it, Rader would be one of a very small group of people—the experts say that less than one percent of the population "suffer" from the disorder. Probably significantly more than half are men. The term "narcissism" comes from the Greek myth of Narcissus, who was said to have fallen in love with his own reflection in a pool of still water, and became so obsessed with admiring it that he starved to death. It was first noted by Sigmund Freud; variants were later observed by Freud's early disciple, Carl Jung, in the archetype of the "eternal youth," *puer aeternus*.

The origins of narcissistic personality disorder are not well-understood, although it is thought to originate somewhere between infancy to early adolescence. Some have suggested that it may be the result of childhood trauma, perhaps abuse, inflicted by parents, other authority figures, or even peers. Excessive narcissism, in behaviorist terms, can be seen as compensation for failures and abuse experienced in early life. When connected to a sexual compulsion, such as bondage and raptophilia—the need to rape—it can be deadly. Some studies have suggested that as many as half of all serial murderers and sexual predators may exhibit the characteristics of "narcissistic personality disorder."

Additionally, when coupled with learning disabilities, such as dyslexia, the disorder can be further exacerbated. It is potentially significant that of the two most notorious serial murderers brought to justice in the past few years—Dennis Rader, and before him, Gary Ridgway, the so-called Green River Killer—both appeared to be severely dyslexic, with concomitant failures in school, and social maladjustment.

The real question about "narcissistic personality disorder," as applied to Dennis Rader, however, is what it meant—and did *not* signify to those who spent so many years to identify him—to the police.

When Wichita police were told in late 1974, following the recovery of the "letter in the library," and again in early 1978 with the receipt of the Nancy Fox letter and poem, that BTK was a "narcissistic sexual sadist," it was information that to them held no real meaning. To detectives, it was simply a bunch of jargon—the sort of thing that shrinks might come up with to explain or even label the killer, but not information that was particularly useful. Yes, the killer was a sadist—that much was obvious from the bindings, and the description of the crimes by the survivors. That the crimes were sexual in nature was equally obvious.

"Narcissistic," to the police, meant that he only cared about himself. But many offenders are at least somewhat narcissistic, and the full import of the diagnosis wasn't fully appreciated then—there was no practical way to ferret out a male narcissist from the Wichita population as a whole, especially not when the narcissist was so obviously adept at concealing himself in plain sight. The idea of giving every man in Wichita a personality test to identify the 600 or so men with narcissistic personality disorder who, statistically speaking, might be expected to live there was absurd.

What was missing from the police investigation was any practical notion of how to apply the realization that the killer was a narcissist to the investigative process. Hearing from the experts about "narcissism" was, to the police, something like getting the opinion of Sigmund Freud. To them it was all very theoretical, when what was really needed was a dose of Sherlock Holmes—someone who could translate the theory of narcissism into effective police action, someone who could examine the record for inferences about the nature of the killer's real-world actions, and apply them to the theory. That was what what Dr. Harrell had tried to do, only to be rebuffed.

But by trying to keep BTK's communications secret, the police in effect cut themselves off from the only source they actually had for this sort of information—the public. Essentially, that was Beattie's contribution to the solution of the crimes—to take advantage of the killer's narcissism, to use the fact that the killer thought so much of himself as to be unable to bear the idea that someone else would get more publicity than he would from his crimes. Beattie pricked away at the narcissistic ego until the killer succumbed to his grandiose compulsions, exactly as Beattie had predicted he would. Beattie acted on his inference that the killer would feel compelled to "set the record straight," as he had with the first letter. In this, he had far greater insight into the nature of the killer than the police had during their thirty years of trying to understand him.

There were a number of other steps that the police

could have taken in the first year of the murders that they also overlooked.

First among these were the obvious characteristics of the "letter in the library," which was typewritten, badly spelled, and not photocopied. By the late 1970s, Wichita police were aware of predictions by the FBI's Robert Ressler, John Douglas and others that the killer was possibly a criminal justice student at Wichita State, as indeed Dennis Rader was at the time. Why the department never took the "letter in the library" to criminal justice instructors at Wichita State to see if they had similar examples of typing and writing has never been adequately explained. Conceivably, an instructor at the university might have recognized the apparent dyslexia contained in Dennis Rader's own university coursework, as well as the typewriter face: Had that happened, Rader might well have been investigated and identified before Nancy Fox and Shirley Vian were killed in the late 1970s, and Marine Hedge, Vicki Wegerle and Dee Davis were murdered in the 1980s.

The BTK case was, while not unique, highly unusual in that it featured written communications from the killer. As with the Zodiac in California, BTK got a peculiar charge out of issuing his communications, which was certainly an indication of extreme narcissism. These communications, as Beattie eventually demonstrated, were the killer's Achilles' heel. But rather than trying to make full use of them, the police in Wichita tried to suppress them—even, in some cases, dismiss them entirely.

As noted, by doing this, the Wichita police essentially deprived themselves of their best weapon against the killer—the public. By using the inferences they could have drawn from the idiosyncratic communications—the dyslexia, the incompetent grammar, the list-making, the sheer, preachy anal-retentiveness of them, along with the expressed admiration for other serial killers—the police might have fashioned a series of polarizing "character lenses," informational releases to the public that could have been useful for prioritizing tips, at least when applied back-to-back-to-back, much as a series of lenses screens out unwanted images.

If a tipped suspect, for example, exhibited one of the character traits that could have been inferred from the 1970s communications, but not others, he could likely be eliminated. But if that suspect had *all* of the inferred characteristics when all the inferences were applied, he could be moved to the top of the list for intensive investigation. Applying these character lenses to the tips would have resulted in a far more manageable investigative universe.

But by withholding the inferences listed earlier in this book, or, perhaps, by not even realizing them to begin with, the police limited themselves disastrously when it came to help from their best ally, the eyes and ears of the public.

In the wake of his sentencing, Dennis Rader was whisked off to El Dorado Correctional Facility in Kansas, there to spend the rest of his days. No one who saw Dennis Rader during his interrogations by the police, or during his "Academy Award" speech at his sentencing, can possibly believe that he will ever have any remorse for his deadly predations. But Wichitans, at last, have seen the true face of the pathetic, execrable Wizard; the curtain was torn away, to reveal nothing more than a disgusting caricature of a human being.

And on the day that Rader went away, the sun finally came out in the Peerless Princess of the Plains, and all was at last the way it should be.

Until the next time.

Author's Note and Acknowledgments

I came to Wichita, Kansas, in August 2005, in time to see the sentencing hearing for Dennis Rader, the confessed "BTK" murderer of that city. By that time, it was all over but the grumping—the grumping by many Wichitans who were by then thoroughly sick of Dennis Rader, and especially those who were talking about him, which meant mostly the national news media like me.

Parachuting in to write about something that took more than three decades to unfold is an inherently dangerous thing to do, at least for anyone who prizes accuracy in recounting events. The inescapable fact was, the people of Wichita had lived with the monster BTK for thirty years—they knew better than anyone else what he had done, and what it meant to them. So, too, did their own local news media, principally the city's daily newspaper, *The Wichita Eagle*, and the city's several television stations, most prominent among them KAKE-TV. What chance did I have to understand anything that they hadn't realized years before?

Yet, surprisingly, I discovered there was an important part of the story that hadn't received much attention—the background of Wichita lawyer Robert Beattie's deliberate attempt to cajole the long-sought killer into revealing himself. When the hearings were over, I contacted Beattie, who graciously consented to be interviewed. Over the next two months, Beattie provided a wealth of background to the events he had watched unfold over his entire life. Provided via many emails and numerous telephone conversations, that this book exists is primarily due to Robert Beattie's desire that the complete story be told. If I've failed to address important parts of that story—and I hope I have not—it was certainly not through Bob Beattie's inadvertence.

This book was primarily assembled from analysis of several comprehensive legal documents—the Sedgwick County District Attorney's Statement of Evidence, an 88-page compendium of the basic facts of the case, including Dennis Rader's arrest and confession; as well as the transcripts of testimony taken at Rader's sentencing hearing. A secondary source, the extensive coverage of *The Wichita Eagle*—superb following the arrest of Dennis Rader—was also extremely helpful in sorting out the course of what took place. So, too, was Beattie's bestselling book, *Nightmare in Wichita.*

As always, there were numerous individuals who assisted in the preparation of this book, by agreeing to numerous interviews. Besides Bob Beattie, the author wishes to thank Hurst Laviana of the *Eagle*; Robert Ressler and Roy Hazelwood, both formerly of the FBI; Kevin O'Connor of the Sedgwick County District Attorney's Office; Steve Osburn, of the Sedgwick County Public Defender's Office; former Wichita Police Officers Charles Liles and Roger Stewart; Cathy Henkel of *The Seattle Times*; and the staffs of the Sedgwick County District Court, the Sedgwick County Historical Museum, the Wichita Public Library, and the staff of the Sedgwick County Recorder's Office. Special thanks are also due to D. T., who provided an invaluable recollection of what it was like to live in the shadow of the monster.

Carlton Smith

South Pasadena, California

2005